The High Fells
of
LAKELAND

By the same author

NON-FICTION

Portrait of the River Derwent
The Young Mountaineer
Climber's Guide to Pontesford Rocks
The English Outcrops
Matterhorn Man
Tiger in the Snow
Because it is There
The Book of Rock Climbing
North Face
Otztal Alps

FICTION

The Devil's Mill
Whistling Clough

The High Fells of
LAKELAND

WALT UNSWORTH

Illustrated

ROBERT HALE · LONDON

ISBN 0 7091 3505 X

Robert Hale & Company
63 Old Brompton Road
London S.W.7

Printed in Great Britain by
Ebenezer Baylis and Son Limited
The Trinity Press, Worcester, and London

To Duncan
in memory of the 'back o' Skidda''

Contents

Illustrations

All photographs except those provided
by the author are by Geoffrey Berry

MAPS

Acknowledgements

My thanks are due to the many specialist writers on Lake District lore and landscape whom I have consulted in the preparation of this book, and especially to the following for allowing me to quote passages from their work:

Rock Climbing in Britain by J. E. B. Wright (copyright c. 1958 Nicholas Kaye Ltd) by permission of Kaye and Ward Ltd.

Entity by Colin Mortlock, by permission of Mr Mortlock and the Climbers' Club Journal.

Fell Days by Graham Sutton, published by Museum Press, by permission of Pitman Publishing Ltd.

Miss Harriet Martineau's guide-book, written in the middle of the last century, has been used extensively to point up differences between then and now: I recommend this book to anyone interested in the Lakes at the height of the Romantic period.

A book like this is enhanced by its illustrations and I would like to thank Bill Comstive for his excellent cover picture and Brian Evans for his painstaking compilation of the maps. For the bulk of the illustrations, however, I must thank Geoffrey Berry of Kendal, whose fine photographs are well known to Lakeland goers. The remaining pictures are my own.

Last, but not least, my thanks are due to my wife for all her hard work on the final draft of the manuscript.

Walt Unsworth
Worsley, 1972

Introduction

WHEN John Ruskin, that nineteenth-century arbiter of all that was good in Art and Nature, declared that no landscape was perfect unless it had a mountain in it, he was merely voicing a generally accepted public opinion of his time. Perhaps today we are a little more sophisticated in our tastes, less dogmatic in our opinions as to what constitutes beauty, but even so Ruskin's dogma would find a large and ready following. Ask any child to paint an imaginary picture of a pretty landscape and there is almost certain to be a hill in it somewhere.

Love of mountains is a luxury which only a high civilization can afford. A Tuareg from the Sahara would find the vast undulating wheat lands of central France much more beautiful than the vale of Chamonix: only to us, who can buy as much bread as we want, ready wrapped from the corner store, could the situation be reversed. That it is reversed—that most of us find mountains attractive and beautiful, is an unquestionable fact. How else does one account for the perennial popularity of countries such as Switzerland and Austria? How else account for the fact that all our National Parks embrace mountain or moorland?

This appreciation of mountains really is a most astonishing revolution. For thousands of years mankind regarded mountains as evil places, the home of dragons and demons. They were looked on with fear and apprehension and named with terrifying names. Even when fear was absent, they called forth contempt as being unproductive and useless to Man.

The *volte-face* has been sudden and complete. Two hundred years have been sufficient to convert us from mountain haters to mountain lovers. The Romantic school of poetry and painting have been given much of the credit for this conversion, but in fact they were merely reflecting a logical stage in civilization. Until the primary necessities of food and shelter were easily obtainable, Man had no time for the appreciation of less material things. The Industrial Revolution, despite its several evils, was at least as much

13

responsible for awakening an awareness to natural beauty as any other factor.

Still, we can call it Romanticism for the sake of convenience: it rose in a crescendo during the nineteenth century. Mountains became fashionable as they had never been before and have never been since. Who today would think of building a Bel Alp or Riffel Alp, those amazing hotel complexes which arose in Switzerland during the Victorian era? Even amongst our own hills, all the really grand hotels are of Victorian origin.

For the Romantics mountains were an aesthetic pleasure, a beautiful backcloth to be looked at and admired, but never touched. It was all in the mind. True, there were a few hardy souls who, right from the start, actually climbed the mountains, but they were very much a minority and regarded as cranks or dare-devils. When the cult began to grow it infuriated Ruskin. "You are turning the mountains into greased poles!" he moaned, like some latter-day Canute.

The tide swept over him. Mountains became more than objects of admiration, they became playgrounds and with the increase of leisure time and money amongst the great mass of the population, what began as a trickle has now become a flood. There are still many who prefer to just stand and stare—perhaps the majority— but the interaction between man and mountain is increasing at all levels throughout the civilized world.

We have come a long way in our appreciation of mountains during the last two centuries, but one tends to forget that the mountains themselves have not changed significantly. Their awesome aspect which so terrified our ancestors can still be very real, as anyone who has been benighted or witnessed an avalanche or even been lost in the mist for an hour or two can testify. The happiness they give to thousands is tragically to be weighed against the misery and pain they cause to others. "The mountains give, and the mountains take," said Don Whillans, one of our foremost mountaineers, and he speaks from long practical experience. It is not all pure joy.

As far as Britain is concerned, the fells of the Lake District have always been prominent at every stage of this developing love of mountains. At the height of the Romantic period, as the home of Wordsworth and his fellow Lake poets, it was for a time pre-eminent. The combination of hill and water is such that no Romantic could resist it, and the fact that it was encompassed in a relatively small area must have made it appear like a jewel to the Victorians.

Fell-walking was at first confined to a few adventurous souls (including the poet Coleridge, who descended Broad Stand on Scafell in 1802) but the numbers quickly grew as the appeal of mountain adventure spread. Napes Needle on Great Gable was climbed by Haskett Smith in 1886 and is frequently, though somewhat erroneously, taken as being the start of rock-climbing in Britain. In the field of mass movements, the Lake District saw the first Youth Hostel to be established in Britain and the first Outward Bound School, and on a somewhat different plane it was here that Canon Rawnsley began the preservation movement that was to become the National Trust.

Even from these outline facts it is easy to see that the Lake District has always been in the forefront of mountain developments and I think one is entitled to ask, why? Why not Snowdonia, or the High Peak, or the Highlands of Scotland? Why is it that experienced travellers return again and again to this small north-west corner of England?

Compactness has already been mentioned and plays no small part in the reason for the district's unique appeal, but it is far from being the whole story. If we try to analyse it with what old Khayyam called "reason absolute" we discover an alarming breakdown in logic. No reason is perfectly tenable: it is arguable that there is nowhere in the Lake District as pretty as Dovedale in Derbyshire, no crag to compare with Clogwyn du'r Arddu in Wales, no ridge that is anything like a match for the Cuillins of Skye, no valley as grand as that of Glencoe. But taken as a *whole*— that is quite a different matter; and in the Lake District the whole is much more than a sum of the parts.

There is an undeniable charisma about the whole district which cannot be explained in rational terms. Perhaps we ought not to seek explanations, but be content to form part of a cult which this charisma has engendered over the past two centuries.

The general topography of the Lakeland fells is not difficult to understand because it follows a radial pattern like the spokes of a wheel. True, some of the spokes are a little bent and you need considerable imagination to accommodate Skiddaw and the Eastern fells in the general pattern, but it serves as a basis for understanding.

The centre or hub of the wheel lies well to the west of the area at Esk Hause and if we start in the south and east, the radial spurs, taken clockwise, are: Bowfell–Crinkle Crags–Coniston Old Man range (a very bent spur, this, and severely cut by the Wrynose Pass) the Harter Fell–Ulpha Fell range; Scafell and the Screes; Gable–Kirk Fell–Pillar–Haycock; the High Stile–Red Pike range; The Dale Head–Robinson range, with its complicated outliers beyond the Newlands Hause, spreading in all directions and ending with Grisedale Pike; the short, crag-infested spur which leads to Cat Bells; the even shorter and more craggy spur of Glaramara; and finally, the long tortuous ridge which begins dramatically with the Langdale Pikes then bifurcates, with one branch running above Langdale to Loughrigg and the other streaming north over High White Stones, Ullscarf and High Seat. These form the true wheel, but beyond the basic pattern lies Skiddaw and Blencathra in the north, and the whole complex of the Eastern fells including such notable summits as Helvellyn, Fairfield and High Street. With a little imagination even these latter can be made to fit the general pattern, if one regards them as broken spokes which have been pushed to one side: certainly there is a large gap where they might have been fitted had Nature been more methodical, a gap now occupied by the low wooded fells around Hawkshead and the lakes of Windermere, Esthwaite Water and Coniston. This wedge-shaped gap, incidentally, which reaches a northern apex at Ambleside, is the only large area of comparatively low-lying country in the whole district; the only penetration of what would otherwise be a 360°-circle of high fells.

The wheel-like structure of the high fells has had a profound influence on communications. The central hub is totally immune to motor roads and in the western fells there are only four passes which attack the great ridges in frontal assault: Wrynose, Hardknott, Honister and Newlands—though there are a few more that manage a short, sharp ascent over the tail-ends of various ranges. In the east, before we reach Shap, only the Kirkstone Pass is motorable; though it is an easier and better road than any of those in the west.

From this it can be seen that travelling by car between the valleys is no easy matter. To give just one example: from Seathwaite in Borrowdale it is barely a five-mile walk over Sty Head to Wasdale Head, but the same journey by car is ten times that distance.

Though all the major valleys are served by surfaced roads nowadays (even if they do end at the valley head) these roads are twisting and narrow, and in the case of the lesser known valleys, very narrow indeed. Travel is never easy: it takes longer to reach Wasdale from Kendal than it does to reach Kendal from Manchester.

Indeed, there are only three truly arterial roads in the entire district: that from Windermere to Keswick via Ambleside, the great access route from the south; the Penrith to Cockermouth road, the widening of which for heavy lorries is at present threatened, and the Kirkstone Pass road from Penrith to Windermere. Of these, the Windermere to Keswick road has always borne the brunt of the traffic, particularly heavy during summer week-ends, though the recent extension of the M6 to Penrith is already causing a change in pattern with many more motorists now using the northern approaches.

Inconvenient though the road system may be for the local inhabitants, I doubt if any of them would want it any other way. There can be little doubt that it is the poor communications which have preserved the district from commercial exploitation, and helped it to retain so much of its own character.

The railways, of course, made even less of an impact on the district than did modern roads – except in so far as they served to bring tourists to the fringes, and created the village of Windermere out of nothing. Until a few years ago one could enter the district by four popular stations, but the rails to Coniston and Lakeside have been torn up and the stations converted to other uses: only Keswick and Windermere remain, and the former is now scheduled for closure.

Over a hundred years ago, when the railway first came to Windermere, Harriet Martineau applauded the good it could do for the district but was well aware of its physical limitations. What she wrote at that time might also be applied to modern roads:

> The railways skirt the lake district, but do not, and cannot, penetrate it: for the obvious reason that railways cannot traverse or pierce granite mountains or span broad lakes. If the time should ever come when iron roads will intersect the mountainous parts of Westmorland and Cumberland, that time is not yet; nor is in view—loud as have been the lamentations of some residents, as if it were to happen tomorrow. No one who has ascended Dunmail Raise, or visited the head of Coniston Lake or gone by Kirkstone to Patterdale, will for a moment imagine that any conceivable railway will carry strangers over those passes, for generations to come. It is a great thing that steam can convey travellers round the outskirts of the district, and up to its openings. This is now effectually done; and it is all that will be done by the steam locomotive during the lifetime of anybody yet born.

Substitute Sty Head for Kirkstone or Stake for Dunmail Raise, and you will see what I mean about roads.

Not only has the communications affected the development of the Lake District from the point of view of the inhabitants, it also affects the way in which the visitor conducts his holiday. It is not, for example, like Snowdonia, where one can stay at any of half a dozen centres and still be within reach of most of the mountains. There it is not uncommon for a climber to stay at Capel Curig but climb at Llanberis, or to walk Snowdon one day and the Carnedds the next—this is quite alien to the Lake District way of things.

In the Lakes if a climber stays in Borrowdale he is very unlikely to spend his time climbing on Dow Crag at Coniston—getting there would take up half his day, and similarly a walker based on Coniston is hardly likely to attempt the traverse of Blencathra. Centres, as such, have a distinctly limiting effect in the Lake District and are really only valid for a week-end visit. For any period longer than this the cramping effect of most centres becomes apparent—for walkers, at least—and there is an urgent desire to move on.

And this is only right, because of all the mountain areas in Britain, the Lakes is the one area that one should move *through*, and on foot. It was designed by God as the perfect walking country, moving from valley to valley, staying perhaps a day here and a day there to sample more closely the particular delights of some small corner, but essentially moving on, bit by bit, in an exciting journey of discovery. As an introduction to the district there is no finer way, and I would go so far as to say that anyone who has not walked the Lakes in this fashion does not know what the district is all about.

For rock-climbers, of course, it is a little different: no one would suggest that a climber should porter all his complicated tackle from crag to crag, day after day, but a fortnight's holiday could more profitably be spent between three centres such as Langdale, Borrowdale and Wasdale, than in a minute examination of any one of them singly. In any case, one would have to be a particularly young and unromantic climber of the hardest sort not to fall for the charm of the high fells and take time off from rock-climbing to experience the wider pleasures of the district by walking some of the ridges.

For walkers and climbers alike—the people who are really concerned with the high fells—the great tourist centres of Keswick, Ambleside and Windermere are simply jumping-off places and play very little part in their explorations of the district. It is the valley heads that matter—the Dungeon Ghyll Hotels, Wasdale Head, Seathwaite, places of that ilk—and the small hamlets that command the approaches to the fells such as Elterwater, Coniston or Buttermere. These are the places to aim for when considering a tour of the high fells, and all of them contain hotels, farmhouses and Youth Hostels where a night's lodging and good food may be obtained.

Nowadays, one can be certain of faring better than the unfortunate party of Victorian undergraduates who arrived at Wasdale Head to find the hotel full. The local parson helped them out by lodging them in his own house and when the Sunday sermon came to be delivered the undergraduates thought that the text was most appropriate: I was a stranger and ye took me in. It was only when the parson presented them with a stiff bill at the end of the week that they fully grasped the sermon's meaning! For as long as I can remember, and probably well before that, it has been virtually impossible to obtain accommodation in the popular centres during the peak periods of the year without prior bookings. It is a fine romantic idea to wander at will over the fells and descend to some remote valley at eventide seeking a bed for the night; but alas, the chances are you wouldn't find one. At Easter or Whitsun, the chance of obtaining casual accommodation at the Dungeon Ghyll Hotels or the Wastwater Hotel, say, is about one in a million. It is very sad, in a way, as is anything which restricts the absolute freedom of the hills, but the pressures are such nowadays that there are often ten people competing for every available bed-space. Only those hardy souls who are prepared to bivouac can sample the real freedom of the hill-wanderer today, for not even the camper is immune from the pressures of our modern leisure society; today he is limited and controlled in all the valleys by enormous sheep-pens called camp sites. That it must be so, I totally accept, for I can remember Langdale in the days just before they restricted camping, when every Easter saw the head of the valley looking as though it was occupied by the tented hordes of Ghengis Khan. It is still sad, though, that we have to restrict our freedom.

A foreigner is once reported as saying, "In England they don't have a climate—they just have weather." And one can see his point, of course, especially so far as the mountains are concerned. Put simply: it rains more than usual.

This is not a peculiarity of the Lake District, as some people seem to think, but is a common factor in all mountain areas, resulting from natural physical laws. It is something that any fell-walker simply has to put up with—though he can choose a time of the year when prolonged rain is less likely. There are those who claim that no such a period exists, like the unlucky man weather-bound for days on end at Seathwaite:

"Does it never do anything but rain here?" he demanded of the farmer.

The farmer thought for a moment. "Aye," he said at last. "Sometimes it snaws."

But we must not take the joke too seriously, for often there are prolonged periods of fine weather when the fell tops stand sharp against a blue sky and the view from the summits stretches from Morecambe Bay to the distant Pennines. June and September are favoured months for good weather, in my experience, though May and October run them close. Winter, too, can be a good time, surprisingly enough, especially February—and at that time of the year the fells often have a powdering of snow which gives them an Alpine quality. In fact, the finest day I ever remember in Lakeland was a February day spent on Glaramara.

It is all rather hit and miss, though, this weather lore. I have spent Easters in the Lake District when it hardly stopped snowing and other Easters when we climbed shirt-sleeves fashion on the high crags, and sun-bathed on the tops. You never can tell, and it is sound strategy to hope for the best and prepare for the worst.

Sometimes one hears fellwalkers mumbling about how they enjoyed walking over Bowfell in the pouring rain or struggling dangerously over Scafell in the mist, just as some alpinists claim to have enjoyed bivouacking on Mont Blanc. It is a load of hogwash: nobody *enjoys* these things; though they may have to endure them for the sake of further enjoyment later. But there are few things more annoying than to postpone an expedition because of the weather only to find that about noon the clouds part and the day becomes fine. It is a matter of judgement, really, but where the matter is in doubt the response should always be *go*. You will never learn about the fells if you only see them in fair disguise.

There are dangers, of course—considerable dangers if you are unwise or unwary. You must have the proper gear and you should know how to use it, and there are several good books on the subject readily obtainable. If you have never walked in the fells before then it is obviously prudent to try something fairly short and simple first, and to choose good weather to do it in. If you have never climbed rocks, then for God's sake don't try it until you have had some proper instruction—the mountain rescue teams have quite enough work on their hands!

In the following pages I have taken the cartwheel pattern of the fells and treated them spoke by spoke in clockwise sequences. It is not a guide-book (Wainwright has seen those off!) but purely descriptive and reminiscent. It will, I hope, evoke pleasant memories for those who have already walked and climbed in the high fells, and stir the imagination and ambitions of those who hope to do so one day.

I

The Coniston Fells

It has always seemed to me that the beautiful fells which rise in such perfect grouping above the village of Coniston encapsulate all that is best in Lakeland. Here is the district in miniature: riches compressed into small compass.

Consider for a moment what it has to offer: fine peaks connected by high ridges, tarns of a grandeur unrivalled in the western fells, and in Dow one of the finest climbing crags in the district. Around its periphery are wooded valleys and gills to rival anything in Borrowdale, and at the head of Church Beck, the best-remembered traces of that mining activity for which Lakeland was once famous. A man could walk these Coniston fells and come away with a truly representational picture of the Lake District—which cannot be said of many fells, and certainly none in such a well-defined and limited area.

As a group it turns its best face towards the east, where a series of high corries carve out hollows from the main watershed. Fortunately this is the way of approach—these fells are extroverts, hiding none of their lights under bushels. They are of instant appeal, therefore, even when seen from a distance. On the west and northern flanks, their secret sides, they are dull and uninspiring—all the goods are in the shop window.

Even from a distance the Coniston fells are appealing and they are best seen from the shores of Coniston Water, somewhere north of Blawith, say, or from the Blawith Fells. From these vantage points one can look directly into the deep recesses, all blues and mauves. Dow Crag appears in profile, sombrely dark in the afternoon, tinted with shafts of sunlight in the morning, and the peaks, because they are observed end on, as it were, group together in pleasing symmetry.

Nearer at hand one becomes conscious of the powerful in-breeding between fell and village. There really cannot be any other centre for an exploration of these fells but Coniston itself, the two are so close, physically and historically, as to be quite inseparable. Coniston serves only the Coniston fells (there are no other high fells within easy access) and the fells in their turn owe their allegiance completely to the village. Such an interdependence between community and mountain is rare indeed for a village the size of Coniston.

I suppose Coniston *is* a village, though some might call it a town by local standards, and there is no doubt that Victorian industry has given it a veneer of township. But it is not another Keswick or Ambleside: torn between the two conflicting interests of tourism and industry Coniston never quite made either.

It is hard to say why this should be, for Coniston was popular enough in Victorian times and enjoyed the advantage of being one of the few places in Lakeland connected to the outside world by railway. The railway has gone, and road access is awkward and narrow, and yet the village is unquestionably the finest centre for the gentler kind of walking in the whole of the Lakes. Glen Mary, Tilberthwaite Gill and Tarn Hows are worth anybody's time and energy to see and it could be argued that there is more *prettiness* within easy walking distance of Coniston than there is even in Borrowdale, that mecca of the romantic.

But the village itself is not pretty, and the railway which brought in the tourists also carried out the copper and slate for which the locality was world famous. Tourism and industry always make unhappy bedfellows because the latter invariably stunts the growth of the former, and yet, such is the irony of life, that industry which is defunct becomes itself an object of tourist curiosity. This is happening at Coniston: there can be few people now who look upon the old copper mines as a blot on the landscape, for age has mellowed them into archaeological relics of our heritage, just as surely as it did with the abbeys and castles of earlier times.

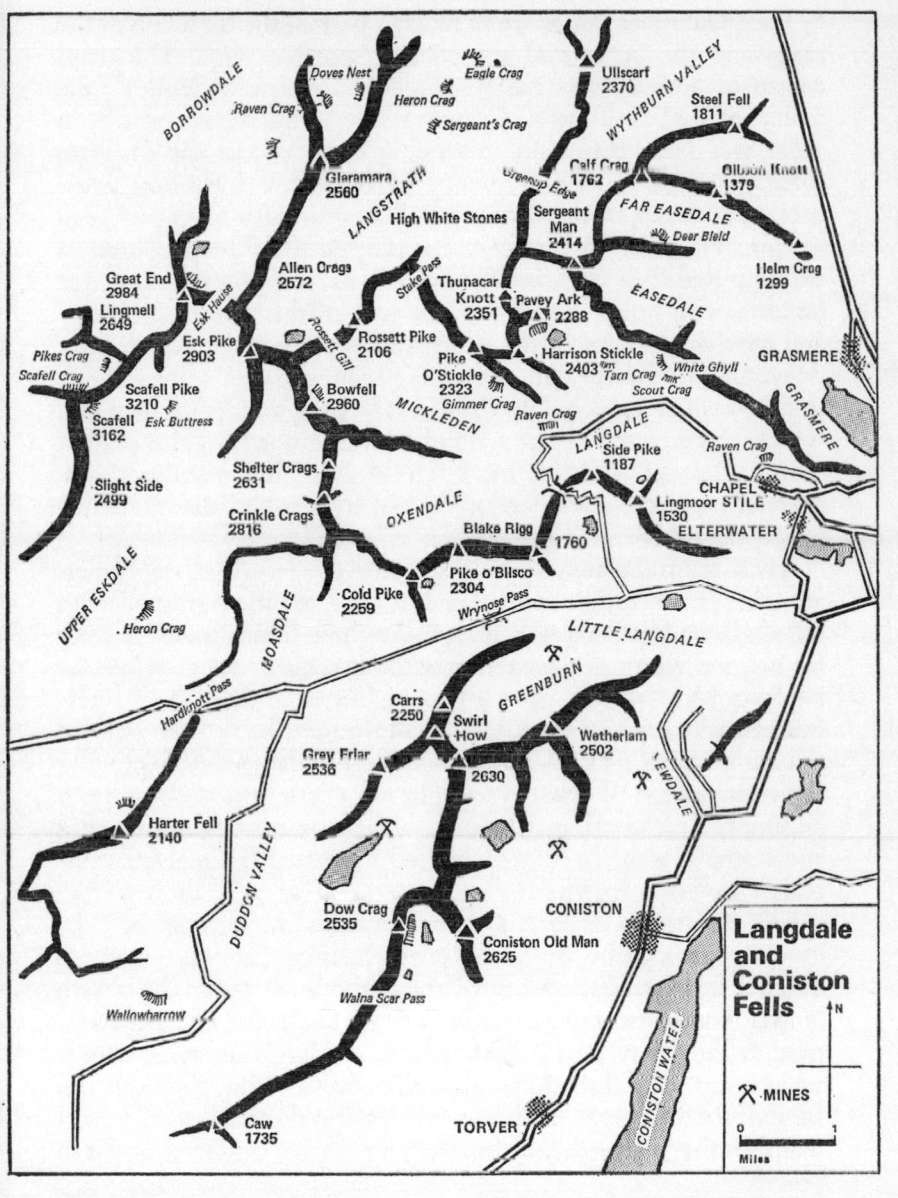

Langdale and Coniston Fells

BORROWDALE

Doves Nest
Raven Crag
Eagle Crag
Heron Crag
Sergeant's Crag
Ullscarf 2370
WYTHBURN VALLEY
Steel Fell 1811
Gibson Knott 1379

Glaramara 2560
LANGSTRATH
High White Stones
Calf Crag 1762
Greenup Edge
Sergeant Man 2414
FAR EASEDALE
Deer Bield
Helm Crag 1299
EASEDALE

Great End 2984
Lingmell 2649
Allen Crags 2572
Esk Hause
Stake Pass
Thunacar Knott 2351
Pavey Ark 2288
GRASMERE
GRASMERE

Pikes Crag
Scafell Crag
Esk Pike 2903
Rossett Gill
Rossett Pike 2106
Pike O'Stickle 2323
Harrison Stickle 2403
White Ghyll
Tarn Crag
Scout Crag

Scafell Pike 3210
Scafell 3162
Esk Buttress
Bowfell 2960
MICKLEDEN
Gimmer Crag
Raven Crag
LANGDALE
Side Pike 1187
Raven Crag
CHAPEL STILE
Lingmoor 1530
ELTERWATER

Slight Side 2499
Shelter Crags 2631
OXENDALE
Blake Rigg
1760

Crinkle Crags 2816
Cold Pike 2259
Pike o'Blisco 2304
Wrynose Pass

UPPER ESKDALE
Heron Crag
MOASDALE
LITTLE LANGDALE
GREENBURN

Hardknott Pass
Carrs 2250
Swirl How
2630
Wetherlam 2502
LEWDALE

Harter Fell 2140
Grey Friar 2536
DUDDON VALLEY

Dow Crag 2535
Coniston Old Man 2625
CONISTON
CONISTON WATER

Wallowbarrow
Walna Scar Pass

Caw 1735
TORVER

**Langdale
and
Coniston
Fells**

N

⚒ MINES

0   1
Miles

The old copper mines are as much a part of the high fells as the crags and the becks and are equally worth a visit. The main centre of activity was the so-called 'Coppermines Valley'; the valley of Red Dell Beck. Coppermines Youth Hostel stands in what was once the main processing area, where the ore was sorted, and there is still plenty of evidence, including some miners' cottages, of the thriving little community that once lived in this high place in the fells. For the industrial archaeologist a walk up Red Dell Beck is a field day in more senses than one, for he can spend hours identifying the uses of the various buildings and seeking the sites of the numerous water-wheels which once drove the machinery. (In 1850 there were thirteen water-wheels in this small area, including the Great Wheel, 30 feet in diameter, which was situated about a hundred yards north of the present Youth Hostel.) Most of us, however, will just wander about, wondering at the hardiness of the old miners and the incredible efforts they made to win their ore.

Away from the actual processing sites the efforts of the miners are even more readily appreciated, for the fellside is littered with old shafts and mill-races, which make these fells somewhat risky for anyone who wanders about without taking care of where he is going. Most of them are easily seen, but all of them are dangerous places to try and explore. The old miners had some tricks of the trade which make derelict mines highly dangerous, including the construction of what we might call 'false bottoms', without getting too technical, in which an apparently sound floor of mud and stones is actually only supported by rotten timbers and conceals a yawning chasm.

The mill-races, or leats as they are called in mining, act like moats guarding the upper fellsides—Kennel Crag is almost a moated fortress. The earliest of these, the one nearest the Youth Hostel, was constructed in 1824 and the latest in 1852. Breached though they may be in a few places, sending out water spouts which turn the fellside into quagmire round about, they can still be awkward to cross, and it says a lot for the quality of workmanship that they are still functioning so well after almost 150 years!

Copper was mined at Coniston from 1599, and possibly earlier.

At the height of production in the middle of the last century, not less than 600 people were employed in and around the Coppermines Valley. Most of the present remains date from post 1830.

Until the railway opened in 1859 the copper was transported to Greenodd, then a thriving little port, and shipped from there to St Helens in Lancashire where it was turned into copper sheet for sheathing the bottoms of wooden sailing vessels.

But the decline was rapid. The end of wooden ships, the exploitation of overseas copper beds on a vast scale, and the increasingly difficult task of pumping water from the deep levels (some of which were a thousand feet below ground) all combined to make the Coniston workings uneconomic. By 1889 the labour force was reduced to a few dozen and the mines closed at the turn of the century, though there have been spasmodic attempts to work some of them since.

The walk up to the old mines is a good introduction to the Coniston fells because it leads right into the heart of the group; to the secret corries and half-hidden crags which are all too often missed by walkers who think only in terms of the high ridges. And it is a fascinating area; a great broken bowl whose rim is the ridge line sweeping round from Wetherlam to the Old Man.

If you go up beyond the mines to Levers Water, crossing the old leats in what is a boggy and sometimes exciting expedition, you come to a fine high level tarn of unusual size, hard pressed by the main ridge. It is a wild place, and the stone of Simon's Nick looks as though it has been cleft by the sword of some evil giant in days gone by. In mist, the sense of desolation is almost overpowering and the feeling of apprehension only too real, for all this area is littered with deep unfenced mine shafts.

From the tarn it is possible to climb up Cove Beck to Levers Hause and descend from there into the Duddon Valley: a route I frequently took in my younger days because it was the steepest and most direct way from one place to the other. In those days, if a route was not steep, it was hardly worth considering, and I seem to have spent half my young life crawling about on the steeper slopes of the Coniston fells.

Once, I remember, I climbed straight up the steep slopes above Low Water, laden as usual with a heavy ex-army rucksack and I nearly frightened myself to death in the process. The day was baking hot, the scree shimmered in the heat and the slope became steeper and steeper, my pack heavier and heavier until I was convinced that I would collapse from exhaustion and roll all the way back to the tarn. I probably would, too, for the downwards view was aerial to say the least, and I reckon that this fellside must be one of the steepest in the district. In fact, given a hard winter it would probably make admirable snow climbing, similar to that of Y Garn in Wales.

But steepness was not the only problem we came across in the Coniston fells during our youthful wanderings. On one occasion, indelibly printed in my memory, three of us came down from the Tilberthwaite fells below Wetherlam in atrocious weather, the rain beating in great swathes across the fellside, gusted by the wind. Our precise location was in some doubt (it still is) but I recall the horror of the mists parting to reveal a wide barrier of thick yellow gorse separating us from the valley. Such was our condition, however, that we decided to push straight through the gorse as being the quickest way down. What a nightmare of a decision that proved to be! The gorse scratched and clawed at our capes (no compact weatherproof clothing in those days) as we stumbled over roots and hidden rocks, and to add to our discomfort, the rain returned with greater force than ever.

It was a trap from which we thought we would never escape. At one stage, totally exhausted, we found a great rock rising out of the gorse and we scrambled on to it for momentary relief. Cut and bruised we just lay on the rock gasping, caring nothing about the rain lashing over us.

Of course we eventually got down and even walked all the way back to the Youth Hostel in Elterwater, I believe, but I do not remember ever again having such an agonizing time on any mountain as I did that day on the Coniston fells. Not that it dimmed my enthusiasm one bit, or that of my companions. It was just one more mountain experience—the hard way!

There is so much of interest about the lower slopes of the Coniston fells, so many secret ways, that days could be spent exploring them without even venturing on to the high tops. The whole of Yewdale is such a place, for here can be found some of the great quarries of the district, numerous old mine shafts and a gorge without equal.

The Lake District has been fortunate in its quarries, taken by and large. Some of the tips may be unsightly but there is nothing to compare with the obliterating scale of the quarries in Snowdonia and the Peak District; nothing to equal the bowel-ripping devastation of the landscape such as you see at Llanberis or Eldon Hill.

In the fullness of time the quarries, like the mines, become naturalized and romanticized, objects of admiration rather than the reverse. And why not? Like Everest, they are there, part and parcel of the high fells, an integral piece of the mountain scene. They reveal to us the bare bones of our mountains and they often do it in a manner which is dramatic, even awe-inspiring.

If you go and look at the Yewdale quarries—Black Hole, Hodge Close, Moss Rigg, or others of lesser ilk, you cannot fail to be impressed by the grandeur of their grey walls. Disapproval gives way to admiration—if only admiration for the men who worked in such places.

So too with the mine shafts and adits which lie all over the Yewdale fells like permanent man traps. Who would work in such wild surroundings at such a dangerous job? What sort of men is it that can stand such a life? Even the late Professor Joad, who once declared that a walk he had taken was spoiled by the sight of a single telegraph pole, would have felt some spark of admiration for the quarrymen and miners of these wild fells. We are brought face to face with the truth that ugliness is a relative word and that what we once considered ugly can become acceptable, even noble, when all the connotations are known to us.

The quarry chasms of Yewdale are more than matched by Tilberthwaite Gill, a gorge of great natural beauty, and certainly the best of its kind in the Lake District. From the road, the gorge is hidden, but it soon reveals itself as a deep slash in the fellside running up towards Wetherlam. Here are rocks and trees and water in savage juxtaposition; the very essence of classical romantic landscape. How Ludwig of Bavaria would have loved this place!

For the hardy, inquisitive explorer, though, the gill is not what it used to be, a real adventure. The path used by today's walkers traverses the fellside high above the gill itself and though it does allow occasional glimpses into the depths they are too rare to give a proper impression of the place. The Victorians, with their eye for a good thing, converted the gorge into an exciting ramble by linking dizzy footpaths by frail wooden bridges which crossed the rushing stream right in the heart of the gorge. There is no doubt but that it was the proper way to see the gorge, and even during the last war it was still possible for an athletic scrambler to use what remained of the old tracks and decayed bridges. What a unique way into the fells it was!

Now the way seems impassible unless you are prepared to do some wading and moderate rock climbing.

These recesses of the Coniston fells are so often ignored by the ardent fell-walker, who, intent on the heights and peak bagging, strides past them with only a casual glance. Yet Coniston (like Borrowdale) is a place to be explored if its true worth is ever to be apparent.

There is one corrie, however, known alike to explorer, walker and climber, and that is the hollow of Goat's Water, cradled in a perfect hanging valley formed by the steep western slopes of the Old Man and the precipitous face of Dow Crag. As a setting for a tarn, nothing could be more grimly majestic. Though it may not be awe inspiring in the manner of Blea Water, Bowscale or Scales Tarn, where the rock and scree funnels down to the water's edge like huge natural tun-dishes, Goat's Water is full of a stark realism that brooks no challenge. When first you see Dow Crag rising from the screes above the tarn you have the feeling that this is what mountains are all about. There is nothing romantic here: though only a mile or two away from the lush beauty of Yewdale, Goat's Water is a continent away in conception. It is the very core of mountain realism.

The best way to see it is by the Walna Scar Road from Coniston or Torver, from which a well-marked track leads up into the heart of the corrie. Beyond a rocky step in this path the tarn bursts into view with a suddenness that is startling, its dark waters overshadowed by the immense bulk of Dow Crag. Other approaches are too high to be aesthetically satisfying and, in fact, the tarn and crag look their worst when seen from the Old Man, thus bearing out once again Ruskin's dictum that a high vantage point is seldom a good one.

At the beginning of the tarn, a little way up on the right, is a distinctive rock outcrop whose little slabs have seen the first faltering steps of many rock-climbing beginners. It is a good vantage point from which to contemplate the tarn and the crag and it will commend itself also to the keen photographer. The latter must be prepared for less than satisfactory results, though, unless he is equipped with a good wide-angle lens, for Dow Crag is long and it is difficult to get it all into one picture.

There are paths on both sides of the tarn and on a first visit it is difficult to know which to choose. The best view is obtained by keeping the tarn between yourself and Dow Crag, but the great bastions of rock belonging to the latter are in themselves a powerful inducement to take the path on that side. In either event both ways lead to Goat's Hause, from whence it is a fairly easy stroll to the top of the Old Man (2,635 feet), the highest of the Coniston fells. As a way up this popular fell, this approach is almost perfect for it follows a classic line and is infinitely preferable to the tourist route.

But meanwhile the tarn and crag brood in their majesty. They have, as can well be imagined, long been popular tourist sights, though there seems to have been some confusion over their names until recently. The crag is spelt 'Dow' on Ordnance Survey maps and most visitors have no hesitation in making it rhyme with 'wow', but George Abraham, a Keswick man who was one of the great pioneers of climbing on the crag, spelt it 'Doe' in his guide-book of 1906. Collingwood, the Lakeland historian, explained that it was written 'Dow' and pronounced 'Doe', and just to confuse the issue further, in her guide-book of 1855, Harriet Martineau called it "Dhu Crag"!

The last name would make sense, of course, because *dhu* is Gaelic for black, though why the crag should have a Gaelic name is not clear, and in any case, sense is the last thing one expects in the names of Lakeland fells. One of the great charms of the area is the aptness yet irrational nature of the names for the fells. Looking at the map it seems as though some topographical Edward Lear has been let loose among them. Who, for example, was Sergeant Man? Did Noah create Pavey Ark? What happened to the dollies on Dollywaggon Pike? And, prince of all names, what irreverent dalesman named a fell Great Cockup? The mind boggles at some of the Lakeland names.

Dow Crag is not the only name in dispute hereabouts. The tarn itself—Goat's Water—proves to be Gait's Water in the original version, and this name was used in guide-books as recently as 1937.

No matter what name you give to Dow Crag, there is no dispute over the fact that it is one of the three greatest crags in Lakeland, to be compared only with Scafell and Pillar. Other crags have their moments: the sheer savagery of Dove Crag, the great shambling bulk of Rainsborrow, the immediacy of Gimmer or Castle Rock, but only Scafell, Pillar and Dow approach perfection in form and function. In Snowdonia, things are somewhat different—but perhaps this is no place to stir up the age-old rivalry between Wales and the Lakes!

Dow Crag is big and bold and well worth a close inspection even if you are not a climber. From across the tarn (which gives the most comprehensive view) you can see the five buttresses which are logically, if somewhat prosaically, labelled A to E, from left to right. Between the buttresses are the deep, savage-looking gullies—perhaps the most impressive set of gullies to be found on any crag in the district. There is a gully at each end of the crag too, beyond which the rocks continue in a more broken fashion, quite useless for climbing but steep enough to be dangerous.

From the lower end of the tarn a track can be seen trickling its way up the enormous scree blocks to the foot of the rocks. Not so long ago this track was almost indistinguishable amongst the weathered stones but such has been the increase in usage during the last decade or so that it now stands out like a pilgrim's highway and can be seen from miles away. It leads to a strange little boulder cave, which has sheltered many a climber from the worst of a storm, and from there to the toe of C Buttress.

On close acquaintance the rocks seem well broken-up, lying back at an easy angle and liberally sprinkled with ledges; easy enough to tempt the foolhardy wanderer into trying to climb

Coniston Water and Wetherlam

them. In truth, as a climb C Buttress is not hard—but it is a lot harder than it looks, and it is not the place for a happy scramble, armed with only a pair of boots and a box of sandwiches. C Buttress, in fact, is an ideal climb for a novice to follow an experienced leader, because it is fairly long and full of variety without ever becoming desperate.

Writing as one who for years has advocated that a climbing career should begin on the little outcrops of the Pennines, this recommendation of C Buttress may seem illogical, for there are few routes less like an outcrop climb than this. The point is, that though a novice will learn more about the techniques of climbing from a gritstone outcrop in a day than he would from a week in Wales or the Lakes, he needs to counterbalance his techniques with the 'feel' of a big climb. He also needs to learn rope handling, especially if he has done most of his outcrop climbs on a top-rope. This is where routes like C Buttress come in: there is a sense of height and total involvement such as the outcrops seldom give. The technique needed to climb it is unlikely to bother anyone who has had preliminary training on gritstone, because even the elementary gritstone climbs are technically harder than C Buttress, and so the novice can concentrate on the sheer enjoyment of a big climb.

There is something much harder just round the corner on the right of the buttress: a tall slit of a chimney, blocked by chockstones, and known as *Intermediate Gully*. I did this climb some years ago with Ed Adamson, a small but wiry climber who thrutched his way up and over the chockstones like a ferret, whilst I, being much taller, wriggled, squirmed and performed all sorts of contortions. Imagine, if you can, trying to climb a very narrow stairway from which someone has removed the stairs and has further tried to impede progress by blocking the way with an interminable series of stone bolsters. The effort required involves almost total exhaustion and we both emerged at the top gasping like netted salmon. It is unquestionably the most tiring climb of its kind I have ever encountered.

Intermediate Gully was first climbed by Edward and John Hopkinson in 1895. They were two members of a remarkable family of five Manchester brothers, all of whom were brilliant in

3

The summit of Harter Fell with Bowfell and Crinkle Crags in the distance
Stickle Tarn, Langdale

their chosen professions, and all good climbers. If they had a fault it was that of modesty, for they seldom told anybody about their exploits and as a result have never been given their proper place in climbing history. They even discovered the vast crags on the north face of Ben Nevis and failed to mention them until Professor Collie rediscovered them some years later.

On the same day that Edward and John were struggling with *Intermediate Gully*, Charles, another of the brothers, was climbing a route in Easter Gully now known as *Hopkinson's Crack*. Both of these climbs are graded 'severe' in modern guide-books and are far below the highest standards of present-day climbing, but both were considerable achievements at the time they were done.

It was, of course, early days for the sport and climbers tended to look for natural lines of ascent such as the gullies and chimneys provided. Dow was an obvious crag for such an outlook, and in fact, Edward Hopkinson had visited the crag as early as 1888 to take part in the first ascent of *Great Gully*, a huge bowl-shaped depression near the left-hand end of the rocks which funnelled down into an impossible narrow gully. It was the first and most obvious route on the crag, though the ubiquitous Haskett Smith had done a couple of easy scrambles a year or two previous.

For the ascent of *Great Gully* there gathered the best climbers of the day: Haskett Smith himself, Edward Hopkinson, Cecil Slingsby, the Masons, and a young man whom Slingsby had introduced to rock climbing, Geoffrey Hastings, destined to become a companion of the immortal Mummery. In the event, young Hastings led the climb, though he avoided the first and infinitely the hardest pitch. The Hopkinsons came back in force the following year to put this right.

There is little doubt that had they recorded all their various ascents or had they climbed for longer, the Hopkinson brothers would have earned themselves a larger niche in climbing history. Their standards were far in advance of most of the pioneers; at least equal in skill to the great O. G. Jones or Fred Botterill. But Fate intervened: in 1898 the eldest brother, John, and two of his children, were killed whilst climbing in the Alps. Such was the nature of their relationship (their motto was "Who can separate us?") that out of respect for John, the remaining brothers never climbed again.

A crag like Dow attracted all the early climbers as a matter of course: seeming to stimulate them into some of their best efforts. Jones came, led *Central Chimney* and his eponymous route in Easter Gully; the Broadricks came and made their finest routes, as did the Abrahams and the Woodhouses. Strange how family parties played such a large part in the early development of this crag.

Since those promising days, much harder climbs have been made on these bold buttresses, including one of the longest and most difficult girdle traverses in the country. Some of the climbs are classics, in particular the three eliminates, and especially *Eliminate A* which threads its tenuous way up the bold front of A Buttress. Nevertheless, there was a period after the last war, when developments were taking place on Scafell's East Buttress and the Eastern Fells, during which Dow suffered a lapse in popularity amongst the best climbers. Unfashionable for some years, its fortunes have revived more recently with new fierce routes on A Buttress such as *Balrog*, that are well up to the modern hard standards of achievement elsewhere.

It has always seemed to me that Dow's chief attraction is the quality of its climbs in the 'severe' grade, because they are nearly always up to standard, and there is such a variety of them. I can think of no other large crag that quite matches Dow in this respect.

The huge buttresses and gullies of Dow are not really the places for anyone but climbers, though there is no reason why walkers should not traverse below the rocks and admire the natural architecture. There is also the so-called Easy Terrace crossing the top of Lower B Buttress and then continuing over C and D into Easter Gully, but one is loth to recommend it to anyone without climbing experience. It is in some ways similar to Jack's Rake on Pavey Ark, but a bit more difficult and a lot more exposed, and the descent into Easter Gully rather nasty.

A pity really, because Easter Gully is itself well worth seeing: a rock cauldron of magnificent proportions, from the floor of which the walls shoot up in a most impressive manner. But alas, even this is denied the pedestrian, for in the lower twenty feet or so the gully is guarded by a prodigious chockstone, the ascent of which would prove trying to anyone not accustomed to rock climbing—especially bearing in mind that one has to climb *down* again!

The Goats Water approach to the summit of Coniston Old Man may well have been the route that Harriet Martineau had in mind when she wrote her guide-book of 1855. After advising the traveller to follow the Walna Scar Road until Dow Crag appeared in sight she adds in a delightfully vague way "the travellers must turn to the right, and get up the steep mountain side to the top, as best he may". Not for our Victorian forefathers the step-by-step instructions of our modern guide-book writers!

Harriet always went for the easy way, if there was one, so one can only suppose that the quarry tracks which form the present tourist route had not been made in her time. Nowadays, this track makes one of the easiest ascents of any major fell in the district: a fact confirmed by the presence of numerous tourists at the summit any fine summer's week-end. Only Helvellyn and Skiddaw can rival the Old Man in public popularity, and they are much higher fells. In fact, at 2,635 feet, the Old Man is only in the middle league when it comes to height, and only five feet higher than the adjacent summit of Swirl How, but it happens to be the highest summit within the county boundaries of Lancashire and that alone would ensure its popularity.*

There are other things going for the Old Man, too. Take its name. What advertising executive could have thought of a more catchy title for a fell? There are three places I know where this evocative 'Old Man' ploy is used (there are probably more): Coniston, the Old Man of Hoy, and Helsby Old Man in Cheshire. All are popular with tourists.

More tangible than this, however, is the view from the summit, which on a clear day is one of the best in the district. Near at hand is Dow Crag and Goat's Water, but looking south the fells are seen to fall away in wooded knolls which lead the eye out to the

---

* If the proposed boundary revisions go through, Lancashire will lose her share of Lakeland, including Coniston Old Man.

broad sweep of Morecambe Bay with its sands and blue sea. I find such counterpointing necessary for a high viewpoint: it is essential to look away from the mountains and see the whole sweep of Mother Earth. In the heart of the fells this is rarely possible, and summit views tend to disappoint—always, but always, the best views are from a medium height. I have been, at one time or another, on most of the highest summits of the Alps and quite frankly the views are—extensive, nothing more.

Coniston Old Man deserves better than the ascent by its quarry track, but the track does have its uses. For one thing it is so broad and well marked that you could not get lost on it even if you tried, and for the most part it is very safe. No doubt this has contributed considerably to saving the lives of dozens of day trippers caught out on the fell in a storm or mist, and for the fell-walker it does give a rapid way down into Coniston, especially if he is sharp-eyed enough to quit the track before its final downwards curve and follow the much pleasanter path to Church Beck and the village.

Though the Old Man takes precedence by its height and name over the other fells of the Coniston group, there are few fell-walkers who would deny that the finest peak is Wetherlam (2,502 feet). Wetherlam has shape and *élan*: it looks every inch a mountain, which is more than some of its bigger brethren do. Personally, I would go further in its praise and claim that it is not only one of the most attractive mountains in the Coniston group, but one of the best in the whole of Lakeland.

Seen from the boggy reaches of Greenburn, rising out of Little Langdale, this opinion may well appear totally unjustified, for Wetherlam, like the rest of the Coniston fells, puts all her goods in the shop window, and that faces south-east, towards the village —though it could be argued that from further down Little Langdale the view of the mountain rising above the foreground of Low Fell and Birk Fell makes a composite whole.

The real fell-walker, however, always prefers the finely curving ridge route, especially if it leads directly to his summit and on Wetherlam, the Ladstones ridge provides just such a way to the top. It begins above the Dell Copper works, shaly and quite steep, then rises gracefully to the summit, with splendid views of

Red Dell Valley and the curious outcrop of Kennel Crag. In winter the ridge has an alpine air about it—for all the world like one of the easier ridges of the Tyrol, for example.

The descent can be made by the Black Sails ridge to the foot of Lever's Water, which makes a pleasant and satisfying traverse of the fell, but most walkers would want to complete the day by walking the whole ridge round to the Old Man of Coniston. And why not? Down to Swirl Hause and then up the rocky steps of the Prison Band to the summit of Swirl How (2,630 feet); the hub of the whole system and the second highest of the Coniston fells. From here the two Carrs (2,575 feet), usually looking black and formidable and much more ferocious than they really are, are easily attainable, as is Grey Friar (2,536 feet), that fine sentinel overlooking the Duddon.

Grey Friar and Carrs, however, lie off the main walk and their inclusion does mean some retracing of steps—but the distance is short and the going easy, and in any case this is the only really justifiable way of reaching these summits because neither make satisfactory ascents in themselves because they are too short for that.

From Swirl How the main ridge travels south over the shoulders of Great How and Little How Crags in a gentle descent to Levers Hause, then rises over the swelling crest of Brim Fell (2,611 feet) to the summit of the Old Man. As a ridge it is broad but distinct with broken crags overlooking the eastern bowl of Coniston and steep turf curving down to Seathwaite. When mist shreds over the crags, the ridges assume a fearsome aspect but the going is always gentle, on fine springy turf. In good weather it is more of a stroll than a walk—perhaps the easiest high-level ridge in the western fells.

Circumstances alter cases, as they say. I once walked the whole of this route in an afternoon of fine spring sunshine and was back in the village for tea time, so rapid is the going once the Prison Band has been climbed, yet on another occasion, doing the route in reverse, I was caught by such a thick mist that I lost my bearings completely on Swirl How, failed to strike the Prison Band and ended by descending over the Carrs to Wet Side Edge and Little Langdale. As I was staying in Coniston it meant a long walk back round by Yewdale in the pouring rain—a salutary lesson in using the compass instead of relying on pure arrogance!

From Coniston the fells seem so high and impenetrable that it looks as though any easy access to the west is out of the question. Yet this is not so: the Walna Scar Road traverses the foot of the Old Man in a gentle ascent, climbs up to the ridge line just below Brown Pike and then dips swiftly into the Duddon Valley.

It is one of those old pack-horse trails which can be traced in several parts of Lakeland; a natural line of communication between one valley and the next. Who made it is anyone's guess: but it is still serviceable and, compared with some other popular walking routes, relatively unaffected by erosion. Whoever it was, they made a good job of it.

As a way westwards from Coniston it can hardly be bettered, giving superb views, first of Morecambe Bay and later, down into the wooded recesses of the Duddon.

The Duddon (or Dunnerdale, as some prefer to call it) is one of the prettiest valleys in the Lakes, and the Walna Scar Road, descending into Seathwaite, enters into the very heart of it. Here is the Wallowbarrow Gorge, one of the secrets of Lakeland, and Wallowbarrow Crag, a climber's playground of fairly recent discovery.

Beyond, the fells rise again in great amorphous swellings; the Ulpha and Birker Fells, traversed by a narrow motor road from Ulpha, which begins and ends in some of the steepest gradients to be found in the district. The road penetrates what would otherwise be unknown country, as bleak as anything behind Skiddaw or over in the east, and gives access to Devoke Water, a large lost tarn nestling in the heights above nowhere. From the road, the fells away to the north and east pile up in knobby, craggy splendour.

The lonely road bisects this vast area and in doing so robs it of its only attraction, that of solitude, for the summits themselves are of no account and the walking is dreary. There is only the scenery: the intimate views of Devoke Water or the distant panorama of the central fells, and though this latter is truly superb, it is a sad fact that it can be equally well observed from the comfort of a motor-car.

Yet it is a strange irony that these undistinguished uplands should have as their highest point and northern apex a mountain that some regard as the most beautiful in all Lakeland: Harter Fell. What a superb little mountain it is! Whether you see it rising above the dark fir forests of upper Duddon or better, look at the many faces it presents to Eskdale, Harter Fell cannot fail to stir the imagination.

No fell was ever designed for climbing more than this one: it is irresistible to anyone who feels the attraction of mountains.

The easiest way up is by the spur which descends to the summit of Hardknott Pass, but it is an inconvenient starting point and probably most walkers climb it by the Grassguards track which starts at the stepping-stones across the Duddon then makes its way by the edge of the forest to the open fellside above. Few people seem to tackle it from Eskdale, for this too is often inconvenient as a starting point and the fell is very steep on this side, the summit seemingly guarded by unclimbable crags, yet this can be the best way of all, for you face the full challenge of the fell, and provided you use common sense, the major obstacles are easily circumnavigated or overcome.

From the summit of the fell there is a majestic view into the recesses of upper Eskdale. The curling beck, backed by the crags and rugged outline of the Scafells, looks like the very heart of solitude, and contrasts sharply with the wide and pleasant grasslands of the lower valley.

The whole of Harter Fell seems littered with crags, though the Ordnance Survey are for once reticent about showing them on the map. As boys, we scrambled about on the rough rocks long before we ever knew the use of a rope or had even heard of belays. We frightened ourselves on the bigger slabs of Demming Crag, and probably other young scramblers did the same. It was quite a few years before 'proper' climbers came along and turned our scrambling place into a respectable, guide-book annotated, climbing ground.

I never visit the Duddon Valley or Harter Fell without remembering how, as a youth, I learned a very expensive lesson in the care of equipment. John Barford had not then published his splendid little Penguin paperback, *Climbing in Britain*, which was to bring to the mass of people the accumulated wisdom of the hills and so most of us went by trial and error. This was a case of error.

A group of us had crossed the Coniston Fells in mist and heavy rain, to arrive wet and miserable at the Youth Hostel at Troutal. The farm (for such it was) was welcoming and cosy, with a huge kitchen fire before which a multitude of garments and boots were steaming themselves dry. It did not take long before we too had changed to dry clothes and put our own wet gear alongside the rest.

It was my first real pair of boots, bought with hard-earned pocket money and just broken in. They dried beautifully before the fire, and then proceeded to bake in their own juices and the impregnated dubbin with which it was then the fashion to lard them. By the following morning they had baked rock-hard: a perfect pair of unbendable, inflexible, immutable boots. Their hardness was inconceivable: it was as if they had been petrified in some quick-acting limestone well of the Peak District.

I sobbed a silent sob, chucked the boots into the dustbin, and climbed Harter Fell in plimsolls, just that little bit wiser.

2

The Langdale Fells

ONE Easter, a few years ago, I sat on the broad grassy platform above the first pitch of Middlefell Buttress looking down into the head of Langdale. It was an amazing scene: it looked for all the world as though the valley had been occupied by the tented hordes of Ghengis Khan. There were tents everywhere; green tents, white tents, orange tents, blue tents, tents to accommodate the solo walker and tents big enough for a battalion of Boy Scouts.

It was a remarkable testimony to the popularity of this valley, visual proof that Langdale is one of the great meccas of the British mountain scene.

Nowadays, camping in Langdale is strictly controlled, with all the tents neatly coralled into the compound of the official camp site, and although regimentation of any kind is anathema to most climbers, I doubt whether it has had any effect on the popularity of the valley.

The chief reason for this, apart from its own considerable attractions, is that Langdale is the most quickly accessible of all the arteries leading into the central core of the western fells—and especially for visitors from the crowded towns of Lancashire and Yorkshire. With the opening of the northern extensions of the M6 motorway this situation may change and more visitors may be diverted to Borrowdale or Patterdale, but I rather doubt it. Langdale has become too well-established a centre to be more than marginally influenced by such developments.

A tradition has been built up, and in the mountaineering world tradition is a powerful thing, even among the young climbers who sometimes like to pretend that it does not exist. Langdale was the first Lakeland valley to provide rock-climbing at a high standard and low level thereby cutting out the necessity for long fell walks such as were demanded by the traditional crags of the pioneers—Gimmer was a symbol of the emergence of rock-climbing as a separate sport in its own right, devoid of Alpine overtones. After Gimmer came Raven Crag, White Gyll and the two little Scout Crags, all at a low level and adding variety to the higher and more traditional fare of Pavey Ark and Bowfell. So Langdale became a major rock-climbing centre—it had always been a centre for fell walking anyway.

The Dungeon Ghyll Hotels, Old and New, became famous partly because they were at the centre of things and partly because of the personalities of their owners: Bowman, Cross, Gurney—these are names known to years of Langdale *habitués*. Club huts were established, and there are now probably more climbing huts in Greater Langdale than in any comparable area in Britain; indeed, about half a mile lower down the valley than the New Hotel, there is a veritable hamlet of them, where the Raw Head, Robertson Lamb, and Bishop Scale huts group together by the roadside.

Then too, there was for a few years the famous barn at Wall End farm, known to the *cognoscenti* as Ike's Barn, which sheltered many of the new breed of climbers who were putting up some remarkable climbs: hardy individualists, whose dress and manner often shocked the conservative element, but whose influence was for the ultimate benefit of the sport. Ike's Barn was not for the fastidious (a friend of mine once preferred to sleep in his car!) and it is difficult to realize that many of those who stayed there, and who got up to all sorts of wild pranks, are now the respected Presidents and Secretaries of famous climbing clubs.

So you see what I mean when I say Langdale has a tradition, and it will take more than a new motorway to break it.

It always seems to me that Langdale is a place for mountain realists, unlike Borrowdale which is for romantics. Romance has no place here, for though the fells are picturesquely grouped at the head of the valley, they intrude in a stark and bold fashion that makes no concessions to a sensitive soul. Perhaps that is why, unlike Wasdale, Buttermere or Borrowdale, Langdale has never been the setting for a Lakeland novel.

The grouping of the fells is all-important in Langdale, with the prominent heads of the Langdale Pikes dominating everything. The picture of them as seen from the old road between Chapel Stile and Raw Head has probably figured on as many postcards as the celebrated view of Friar's Crag at Keswick, but this does not make it any the less startling or attractive when seen in the flesh. It really is quite remarkable how this group of peaks pop up through breaks in the landscape in all directions and are immediately recognizable, even from a distance. The visitors who sail on the Windermere ferries, and who never put a foot on the fells, recognize the Langdale Pikes, if they recognize nothing else. Surprisingly, they are not very high fells these Pikes—Harrison Stickle, the highest, is only 2,403 feet, and the nearby Allen Crags is well over a hundred feet higher—yet who would recognize Allen Crags on a postcard? Not one person in a hundred: it takes more than height to make a real mountain.

The Pikes look good from almost any angle or distance, but my own personal preference is to see them from Side Pike, bathed in the glow of a morning sun. Then you can pick out every facet of their rocks and every twist of their two great becks. Gimmer reflects like a straw-coloured mirror and Pavey shows the true immensity of its great, ledge-strewn face.

If the Pikes tend to dominate the Langdale scene, other fells also have their visual attraction. Chief of these is the fine valley head culminating in Bowfell, one of the truly great mountains of the Lake District, though Bowfell is one of those mountains which looks even finer the closer you approach it. Lingmoor too, is not without its quieter appeal and has its own little Side Pike to give it an unusual aspect.

Strangely enough, the valley as seen from the summits of the surrounding fells is seldom exciting. There is nothing of the vignette quality that Wasdale possesses, the prettiness of Borrowdale or Duddon or the superb grandeur of upper Eskdale. It seems to run away and diffuse towards Windermere without shape or substance, and is a photographer's nightmare as far as composition goes. The only view which approaches the highest quality is that from Rossett Pike, which, incidentally, gives another fine look at Gimmer.

There can be no doubt in anybody's mind as to which is the most popular walk in the fells around Langdale, for the deeply scarred track ascending behind the New Dungeon Ghyll Hotel to Stickle Tarn, tells its own story. For the day tripper it has the convenience of starting immediately from the car park, and it is short enough to be accomplished without fatigue in a brief afternoon, even by those whose fitness might otherwise be suspect. A good walker will make the ascent to the tarn in about forty-five minutes and it is my boast that, suspecting the hotel bar was about to close, I once made the descent in twelve minutes exactly.

It is a walk for all the world and his wife, and it begins to look like it—the usual track going up the left side of the gill is threaded to ribbons like a war-tattered banner, and cut to the bone by a million scrambling boots. Here is human erosion at its worst, more savage than the erosion caused by nature. It is a problem not confined to the Mill Gill path (though it is the worst example) but one which exists throughout the Lakes and other areas too. How are we to preserve these tracks from the wear caused by tramping feet? There have probably been ten times more ascents made of Mill Gill since the war than there were in the previous two thousand years, so the problem is new and as yet nobody has faced up to it. It may be already too late.

Worn and hackneyed though the Stickle Tarn ascent may be, it still remains one of the best of the short walks that the Lakes has to offer.

The sad part about it, so far as Mill Gill is concerned, is that there is no need to use the worn path at all. A perfectly good track goes up the other side of the beck (and if followed in its entirety, is much more exciting than the usual one) or it is possible to follow a less distinct and somewhat steeper path up to Tarn Crag and reach the tarn easily from there.

From the tarn you can carry on to the tops of the Pikes, but the majority of trippers are content to sit on the low stone wall of the little dam that once provided power for the gunpowder works in Elterwater and look across the placid waters of the tarn at the rearing buttresses of Pavey Ark.

What a finely situated crag this is, rising so boldly over the waters of the tarn. It is, as its name suggests, like a great arc of rock, very steep and lined with gullies and cracks. In its upper part, above a curious sloping break known as Jack's Rake, it seems liberally coated with grass and yet loses nothing of its steepness. It seems near enough to almost reach out and touch but this is an optical illusion brought about by the sheer height of the rocks, which tower for some six hundred feet.

Pavey Ark is such a dominating crag that it demands to be climbed by anyone who is a real fell-walker. There is an easy way up on the left where the path can be seen snaking round by the col between the crag and Harrison Stickle, or a more adventurous, little-used way up on the right by means of a short scree gully and a long grassy rake which is quite invisible until you come upon it.

I once had a curious experience here. I was taking some youngsters up the scree gully when one of them slipped and lay prostrate on the stones exclaiming in genuine fear that he was falling off the mountain. His companions stood around, hands in pockets thinking it was a joke and telling him in no uncertain terms to get up and get moving, but he remained adamantly clutching the scree and it took us some minutes of coaxing to get him to his feet again, when he was finally persuaded to make a shaky re-start. His confidence soon returned and he never again had any fear of mountain slopes, but the moral is this—do not assume that everyone is accustomed to mountains: some people have a mortal fear of even the simplest of slopes. On another occasion a friend of mine had a terrible time persuading a new companion to descend the *path* down Aaron Slack, above Sty Head: the man had this irrational fear that he would fall off the mountain.

Combining the two routes previously mentioned makes an interesting traverse of Pavey Ark, providing the weather is clear. If it is bad though, this fell is a good place to stay away from because unless you happen to know it intimately it can be confusing and dangerous.

The most exciting way to the top of Pavey Ark, however, is to scramble up that curious feature known as Jack's Rake; a ledge-cum-groove which slopes up from right to left across the impressive face of the great crag. Its line across the face can be traced easily from the tarn and once it has been embarked upon there is no difficulty in following the correct way—there is no choice in the matter!

It begins above the scree at the foot of the crag near the conspicuous gash of Rake End Chimney and rises at first quite steeply in a groove eroded into the rocks. In wet weather this part is distinctly unpleasant because the groove acts as a drainage channel for the upper crags, but the wetness does not materially affect the difficulty of the ascent. It is high quality scrambling in impressive rock scenery, but curiously unexposed because of its grooved formation—the left-hand wall of the groove (ascending) screens the precipitous downwards view. Higher up it becomes more open, but the way is broader, the going easier and the crossing of the head of Great Gully is the last difficulty of note, after which it is scrambling over easy slabs to the summit.

Jack's Rake has become the Hörnli Ridge of the Lake District, the one challenge that every fell-walker feels obliged to accept sooner or later, and just as the famous Matterhorn ascent has been subjected to all sorts of gimmicks and stunts, so too has the rake, though to a lesser degree. People take dogs up it, climb it by night, and do other equally preposterous things just to show how clever they are. How then does it rate in difficulty? Well, like the Hörnli Ridge of the Matterhorn, it is fairly easy if you are experienced in climbing—but not as easy as some would have you think.

Comparing it with other well-known scrambles that fell-walkers find themselves on from time to time, I would say that Jack's Rake is more ambitious an undertaking that Striding Edge, Sharp Edge or Crib Goch in Wales but not as difficult as the similar but less well-known terrace of Dow Crag (see Chapter 1) and nowhere near as difficult as A'Chir in Arran or a dozen similar scrambles in Skye. In conditions of ice and snow it makes a splendid climb—but only for a competent roped climbing party!

It is surprising how many tourists believe that Mill Gill is Dungeon Ghyll: on account of the hotels, one supposes. Actually Dungeon Ghyll is a much more spectacular rift, but curiously well hidden from general view. As a way up Harrison Stickle from the valley it is without compare, and the challenge lies in seeing for how long you can stick with the gill before being forced out on to the open fellside. From the top of the Stickle it is then easy going to the top of Pavey Ark, and if this is followed by a *descent* of Jack's Rake (if you know the way) the walk is one of the most exciting in Langdale.

Stickle Pike, the remaining member of the famous trio of summits, is for some reason the furthest away from Stickle Tarn. It is a curious peak, shaped like a beehive, with a distinctive top that is reached by a scramble, something after the fashion of Causey Pike away to the north. Its frontal aspect facing into Mickleden (the upper northern branch of Langdale) looks fiercely steep, as indeed it is, and it is seldom if ever climbed this way, but from the back this impressive fell turns out to be nothing more than a pimple on a rolling moor, easy of access. Nevertheless the final little scramble gives piquancy to the ascent, and there is always the remote chance of finding an ancient stone axe on the way down, for the scree gully on the eastern side of the peak is the home of the celebrated stone axe factory.

It was a vein of particularly hard rock that led to the establishment of the prehistoric axe factory and the manufacture of stone tools seems to have taken place in several sites on the moor behind Pike o'Stickle, but so far the great scree shoot down besides the peak has yielded the best finds. The factory is a comparatively recent discovery, and one wonders how many fell-walkers have descended this gully unaware of its importance to the ancient world. That is was important is shown by the fact that axes of the Langdale stone have been identified in several parts of Europe, indicating a thriving export industry.

A friend of mine treasures an axe he found there some years ago, but a stone axe is so much like the common scree to the untrained eye that you need to know exactly what to look for. I have never found one (perhaps because I have never searched diligently enough) but there is no reason why one should not, even in such a well-known site. Last year I was walking along a flinty path in Buckinghamshire near a large village, and explaining to my two rather cynical children how one often came across stone

The Langdale Pikes from Lingmoor with Lingmoor Tarn
Pavey Ark, Great Langdale

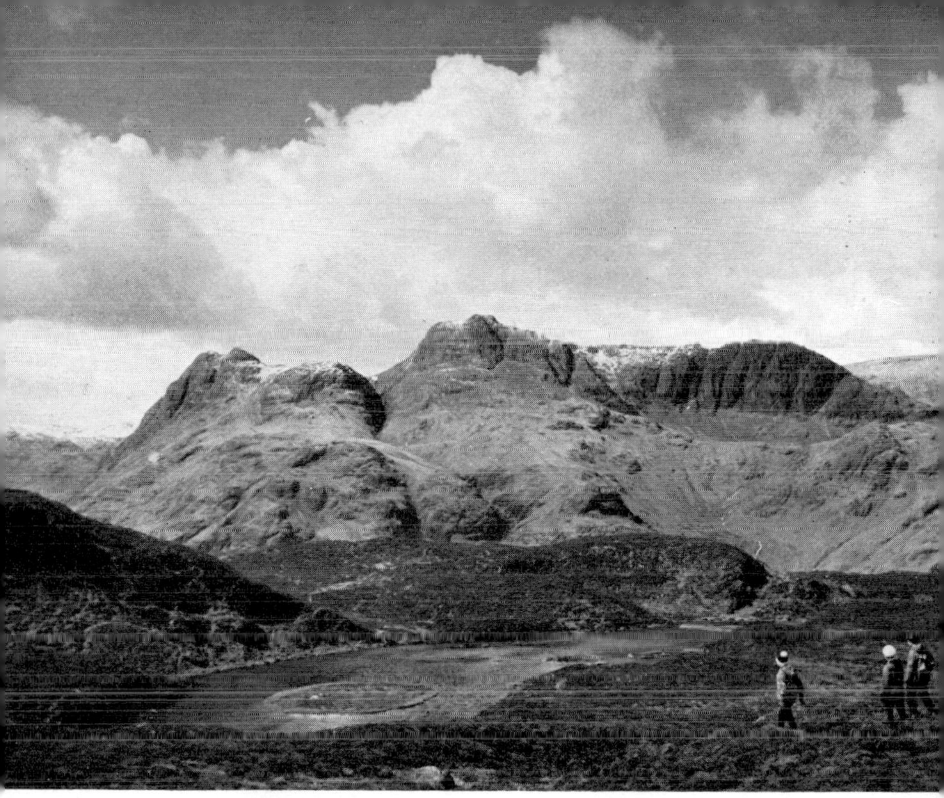

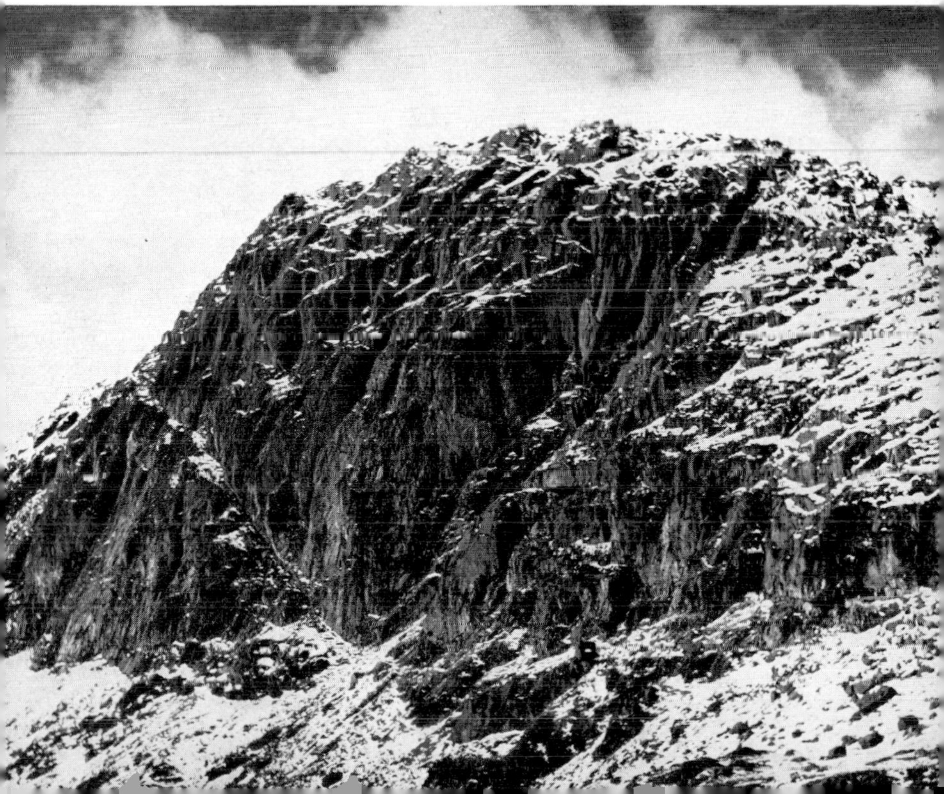

implements by chance when, stooping to illustrate my point, I picked up a perfect arrow-head. The kids thought I was a magician (I was a bit stunned myself!) and though we spent the next half hour combing that path we came across nothing else of value. If it can happen in a populous part of Bucks, it can certainly happen in Langdale! One word of warning though. Do not let your acquisitive instincts get the better of your mountain judgement. The gully is quite steep and there have been several careless accidents in it.

Pike o'Stickle is hardly worth an ascent of its own, being too short a day for the amount of climbing involved. Nor does it really fit in with Harrison Stickle and Pavey Ark: they make uncomfortable bedfellows, because climbing Pike o'Stickle means missing the best parts of the route I mentioned earlier.

The relatively low level of the Langdale crags can make descents from the Pikes awkward, and in mist highly dangerous. Apart from the axe factory gully (and that is steep enough to require special care) it is really not very safe to try descending directly into Langdale from the Pikes unless you are thoroughly familiar with the area.

The fact is that this side of Langdale, all the way from Chapel Stile to the Stake Pass, is much steeper than most people imagine and there are crags and outcrops scattered about the fellsides in profusion. Some of these rocks are of considerable height and over the years have become popular with rock climbers. In more remote circumstances they would no doubt be ignored, as minor outcrops, but since most of them are only a few minutes' walk from the nearest parking place, they are always well frequented.

Most popular of all are the rocks above the Old Dungeon Ghyll Hotel: Middlefell Buttress and the Raven Buttresses. In terms of beer and shelter they must be the most accessible crags in Britain, for they are only a few minutes' steep walk up the scree from the back bar of the hotel.

It is probably for this reason that Middlefell Buttress has seen the start of so many climbing careers. Not only is it very accessible, it is also reasonably long and easy. Along with its Welsh counterpart—the Milestone Buttress of Tryfan—Middlefell is one

4

Climbers on Gimmer Crag

of those climbs which every climber has done at an early stage in
his career—or perhaps I should say that it was, for fashions change
and many beginners these days seem to go straight from the gritstone outcrops to the 'severe' and 'very severe' of the larger hills.
A pity really, because in doing so they miss much of the charm
that was once such a feature of climbing, but which nowadays is
increasingly lost in the competitive attitude of the sport.

Not that Middlefell is a particularly attractive climb. Apart
from the various ways up the first pitch, the rest is more or less
simple stepping up—the descent down the neighbouring gully
can be much more hair-raising, especially if some climbing oaf is
coming down behind you, kicking stones. But the buttress gives
a novice plenty of scope to learn how to handle the rope, and the
stances and belays are classical in size. Surprisingly enough it was
not climbed at all until 1911 and then by a very strong party of
gritstoners: Laycock, Herford and Thomson.

The adjacent Raven Crag is much steeper and an altogether
different proposition. Here the climbs are short exercises of three
or four pitches, mostly around the 'severe' grade, quite fine and
exposed. My own particular favourite is *Centipede*, a climb I have
always thought of as compressing a good deal of interest into a
relatively short space, though in fact it happens to be one of the
longest climbs on the crag.

Lower down the valley, on the Red Bank road from Chapel
Stile, is a similar sort of crag, though rather more compact and
not nearly as frequented. This is Raven Crag, Walthwaite, which
boasts only a handful of routes, but has one superb climb known
as *Route II*—a must for anyone who can tackle fairly hardish
'severes'. All the climbs here are stiff for their grade, and the
exposure is quite remarkable for a crag so small. It has been called
'the hard man's Scout Crag'.

Two other small crags which have achieved some note on these
slopes of the valley are Tarn Crag and Scout Crag, whose climbs
are in the easiest grades, a fact which has made them into rock-
climbing nurseries for beginners. Tarn Crag is high-up on the
flanks of Mill Gill, and though it looks rather impressive from
a distance (most crags do), closer acquaintance is disappointing.
It must be one of the least distinguished crags in Lakeland, but

for beginners it does make a convenient change from Scout Crag, and is never crowded.

Scout Crag, on the other hand, is one of those places where there always seems to be somebody climbing, no matter what the season or weather. It lies a little to the right of the entrance to White Ghyll and actually consists of two crags, one well above the other on the fellside, known as Lower and Upper Scout. There is also, lower still, a famous split boulder whose strenuous crack was at one time regarded as something of a test piece.

I wish I had a pound note for every novice I have taken on Scout Crag—I would be a tolerably wealthy man! Many is the time I have sworn never to go near the place again, and yet, another beginner comes along and I think where to go—and then suggest Scout Crag. It is not that I have not tried other places: I have—and generally found them wanting. If you start on something too hard, you frighten the poor beginner to death, and if you start on something too easy, he becomes bored. In either case, he is unlikely to be attracted to climbing as a sport. You must try to show him what it is all about, without taking him beyond his powers.

No crag I know can do this like Scout. The climbs are only two or three pitches, but they are steep and exposed (surprisingly so for their grade), the belays are good but the stances are reasonably small. The holds, which the novice grasps at hopefully, are positive and uncomplicated—but they have a charming habit of turning small just when exposure is greatest and need most desperate. All good stuff for the beginner.

Immediately to the left of Upper Scout is the deep gorge of White Ghyll which has impressive crags of a much more serious nature than any so far mentioned: along with Pavey Ark and Gimmer, White Ghyll is one of the trio of great crags which this side of Langdale has to offer. It is a major rock face in Langdale climbing; steep and intimidating.

It is worth a stroll up the narrow Ghyll, even if you are not a rock-climber, just to look at the powerful architecture of the crag. It begins with strange fluted towers, after which more broken rock gives way to a sloping break (another rake, but not for walkers) and finally the boldly thrusting upper buttresses. All this is mostly for the 'v.s.' man, but there are some good 'severes', too, for the less ambitious climber. The earliest of these lie on the bubbly slabs at the top of the Ghyll; uncomplicated slab routes, open and pleasant. Somewhat harder, but well worth doing, are the *Chimney Route* and *Hollin Groove*, whilst the easiest of the more technical routes are *Slip Not* and *White Ghyll Wall*.

The *Chimney* is probably the classic line, and has the distinction of not being a chimney climb at all in the generally accepted sense. It looks forbidding and strenuous, like one of those gritstone grooves on the edges of Derbyshire, only bigger by far. In fact, it turns out to be an exercise in delicacy more than anything else. Nevertheless, looking up at it, one wonders how the late Robin Smith, that superlative Scots climber, managed to survive a fall from the crux when he was once attempting to climb it solo.

White Ghyll has always seemed a cold and cheerless place to me (perhaps because I once had a new anorak stolen there!) but nobody could call Gimmer cheerless. Gimmer comprises sunny open slabs and walls where the routes are laced so closely that it is hard to distinguish one from the next on a guide-book picture, though they are easy enough to distinguish once on the crag. Like White Ghyll, it has little to offer the novice, though unlike White Ghyll it does have a fine collection of open 'severe' routes for the average climber.

There is no denying the unique compactness of Gimmer as a climbing crag: it's all there in a single glorious pillar, like a jewel with many facets, each of which glitters in turn. No other major Lakeland rock is so concentrated, or for that matter, so clean. In some ways it is too good, almost artificial in concept like some enormous climbing wall, for the dross has been sifted away to nothing, the rock refined to incredible purity.

The lines are good, almost without exception, from introductory tit-bits like *Asterisk* to the long, rambling *Bracket and Slab*, or the classic *Crack*; perhaps the finest ordinary 'v.s.' route in the valley.

One climb, of course, has dominated the story of Gimmer in post-war years, and that is Arthur Dolphin's famous *Kipling Groove*, so called because it was considered "ruddy 'ard". It was far ahead of its time, and like another route that was ahead of its time, the *Central Buttress* of Scafell, it has the distinction of being known simply by its initials—*KG*. Not that the two climbs should be compared any further: they are different concepts entirely. The *CB*, too, stood pre-eminent amongst British climbs for fifteen years or more, and amongst Lakeland climbs for longer still, whereas such is the rapid advance of modern climbing that Dolphin's route was quickly overtaken in severity. Nowadays it is not even the hardest on Gimmer—though it remains one of the best and most popular.

One of the older classic problem pitches on Gimmer is *Amen Corner*, a feature of *B route*. It is an awkward little step: a square platform with walls about fifteen feet high and ever so slightly impending so that you tend to be pushed the wrong way by the rock. To me it recalls one of those days when nothing went right. We had bombed up to the Lakes in Ed Adamson's Mini, and I was driving the last lap, up the Lythe Valley road to Bowness. The road has been improved in recent years, but in those days it was narrow and twisting all the way. Suddenly, the inevitable happened—I zigged when I should have zagged, and with a horrible bang, ran smack into a road sign. "Dangerous Bend" it said.

A sorrowful examination revealed a flattened road sign (by incredible good fortune it had been loosely set up) and one very dented bumper, which later cost me a fiver. However, the car was otherwise undamaged and we continued to Langdale and Gimmer.

Already our spirits were pretty low and the grey skies of Langdale did nothing to raise them. As we reached the crag, the rain began to descend in torrents. Normally, not being particularly hard men, as the saying goes, we would have packed up and returned to the ODG bar, but Gimmer was Gimmer, and we knew it would go even in the rain. We did *Joas*, which gave us no trouble, then we decided to do *B Route*, to take us to the top of the crag.

Amen Corner was slippery and vile. Neither Ed nor I could make any impression on it. Finally Ed, making a desperate last effort, was almost up when his feet shot from the greasy rock. He landed on the platform feet first and was about to shoot off into space when I fielded him.

He had sprained his ankle, and there was nothing else for it but to retreat down the climb—fortunately not a difficult job—with Ed on a short, very tight rope and me coming behind, holding him, and the rain bombarding us like wet glass marbles. It was definitely not our day!

As Don Whillans once said, in one of his frequent flashes of native inspiration, the mountains give and the mountains take. These same Langdale fells that took away the last dregs of pleasure on that wet day at Gimmer, have given me much more than they have ever taken. I mention one occasion because it involved Ed Adamson again, and it gave us both one of the most enjoyable days we have spent in the fells.

This time the sun was shining, but there was a cool breeze, and we had hit upon the notion of combining walks and climbs in a complete mountain ascent. We began at Lower Scout, for openers, then went to the upper crag and climbed *Route One*, from the top of which we contoured round the fellside into White Ghyll. Up the bed of the ghyll we scrambled to the slabs and then up the slabs themselves to the head of the ghyll.

Our next objective was Pavey Ark, about half a mile distant, but we covered the boggy ground in no time and set about the *Crescent Slabs* which took us in three or four glorious open pitches to Jack's Rake, quite near the start of a climb called *Cook's Tour*. Up *Cook's Tour* and so to the top of the crag, and the fell.

In total distance I doubt if we had covered more than a mile and a half, but we had risen 2,000 feet, well over half of it by rock climbing. None of the routes were hard, but there was a special sense of well being, as we moved from climb to climb, slowly nearing our goal.

That the goal was Pavey Ark is, I think, very fitting. No matter how you look at these fells, whether as a walker or rock climber (or indeed, simply as a tourist out for the view) you are inevitably turned back to Pavey. Pavey Ark is the hub and crux of it all.

There will be rock-climbers who disagree with me about this (though the walkers will not). They will point to Gimmer or White Ghyll and say that one or other of those excellent crags is

far superior to the tottering 'choss' above Sprinkling Tarn. I disagree. Pavey has character. There are climbs on it as hard as
anything on Gimmer or White Ghyll—*Astra* for example—but
the crag has vast areas of grass and lichen and bracken and goodness knows what else, all thrown together in a glorious heap.
There is no polished jewel here: no glittering facets cut ready to
wear. Rather is it like a diamond mine—the jewels are there but
you have got to dig them out.

There have been some very strange names given to rock climbs
by the climbers who first put them up, and non-climbing readers,
having come across a few already in this book, might be forgiven
for wondering whether there is any sense in them. Usually there
is, and Langdale is especially rich in climbs of this kind.

The pun, the allusion (the more obscure the better) and the
sequence are all great favourites, and I am not alone in regretting
the ultra-modern tendency to bestow names that are completely
irrational and often ugly. There's a climb on a gritstone crag
called, believe it or not, *Mohammet the Mad Monk of Moorhouse*,
though nobody seems to know why. We have not sunk to such
a low state yet in the Lakes, and I hope we never shall.

In the early days names were simple—*North Climb*, *South Gully*,
Jones's Climb and so on with occasionally more flowery names
such as *Easter Gully*, *Innominate Crack* (a contradiction in terms,
of course) or *Moss Ghyll*, but as time went on the sheer number of
climbs, especially when so many were close together, demanded
a widening of the imagination.

The literal and mathematically minded went in for the no-
nonsense stuff of *Route A, B, C, D* etc. (Gimmer) or *1* and *2*
(Scout Crag) with the more learned brethren resorting to Greek—
Alpha, Beta, Gamma etc (Gable), and had they had it all their own
way our climbing guide-books would be as dull as a telephone
directory.

Fortunately humour and wit were at hand, as they usually are
when climbers are around. Take Gimmer, with the well-known
Kipling Groove already mentioned—surely a more doubtful,
harder route starting from the same point could only be called *If*?
Or what about the *double entendre* of *Whit's End*, the simple

humour of *Joas* (Just One Awful Sweat) or, when the original name was refused publication in less permissive days, *Asterisk*?

A play on personal names sometimes gives a route: *Lyon's Crawl*, and the very aptly named *Cook's Tour*. Taking the mickey (in the gentlest possible way, of course) is not unknown. When a new climb was made on Scout Crag between Routes 1 and 2, what else could it be called but *Route 1·5*?

The happiest hunting ground for names in Langdale eventually proved to be White Ghyll. Climbers can never resist a sequence, and once some of the earlier routes—the Chimney, the Wall and so on—had been disposed of, the eye of Jim Birkett fell upon a climb called *The Gordian Knot*, which in turn, so it is said, had been inspired by a local feature of rock called Swine Knot. Birkett was just beginning to probe the harder lines of the crag and soon we had *Slip Knot, Haste Knot, Granny Knot, Why Knot, Perhaps Not* and finally *Do Not*. Other climbers, other names, but now and again another Not has been added to the Ghyll—*Question Not, Not Again*, and Joe Brown's contribution, *Laugh Not*.

Taken out of context few of these names make sense, but once you understand what lies behind the thinking, they become natural. It is usually the case with rock climbs.

The other side of the valley has some quiet walking country over Lingmoor and into Little Langdale, but nothing to compare with the fells so far described. A motor road crosses by Blea Tarn, steep and narrow, giving superb views of one of the district's loveliest tarns, and the ancient white farmhouse well known as Wordsworth's 'Solitary'. Side Pike is the best ascent here (it has some amusing rock climbs too—not all that easy) and the view across the valley is magnificent. I remember one evening, after a day of incessant rain when we had done nothing, we came out of the Old Dungeon Ghyll bar to find the clouds gone and the moon out in full glow. In sheer exuberance we walked up the pass and ascended Side Pike, to look down on Langdale bathed in soft ghostly luminescence.

Beyond Blea Tarn, however, the fells mass to gather themselves into some sort of order before rising to the Pike o'Blisco (2,304 feet), the last member of the Langdale Pike tribe. This is a fine fell, one that is well worth the effort of the ascent, rocky and of the sort of shape a child would draw as a mountain if asked to do so.

The trouble with Pike o'Blisco is that because of the deep col wherein lies Red Tarn, it is separated quite sharply from the rest of the magnificent fells making up the head of Langdale. It falls between two stools: it is not in itself sufficient to make a satisfactory expedition, yet the col (about 600 feet of descent) is enough to make more ambitious fell-walkers approach the ridge from Oxendale by the well-known Brown Gill, thereby omitting Pike o'Blisco. I feel that it is a mistake, interesting though Oxendale may be. The head of the valley ought to be traversed from Blea Tarn right round to Dungeon Ghyll or the job is only half done.

It is really quite surprising how few of the major valley heads can be traversed in a satisfactory ridge walk. Some are bisected by motor roads, but the majority are interrupted by breaks or *longueurs* which ruin the conception of an integrated traverse—Wasdale and Ennerdale are both invalidated on this account, for example. It is generally the smaller side valleys in the Lakes which provide the best ridge walks of this kind—the head of Newlands, or Coledale, for instance.

In my opinion there are only four major valley heads which offer a genuine 'horshoe' ridge walk. These are Troutbeck, Kentmere, Langdale and Eskdale. Of course, the longest and hardest is the Eskdale Ring, which sweeps around the magnificently wild corries at the head of that valley and includes the Scafells, whilst the prettiest is the delightful Kentmere Horseshoe (see Chapter 9). Troutbeck is short and rather boring, but Langdale, though it has more *longueurs* than the others, includes a greater variety of peaks than any.

As a walk it suffers from the fact that it can be quite easily quit at several points by well-known tracks, and so it tends to be done in bits, but it is really not too much for a competent fell-walker to complete on a fine day, and the satisfaction of the whole is always more than the sum of its parts.

After Red Tarn is begins modestly enough with an ascent of the spiky summit of Cold Pike (2,259 feet) though this too is generally

omitted for a long ascending traverse to the start of the famous
Crinkle Crags (highest 'crinkle' 2,816 feet) one of the best mountain ridges in Britain. It is a switchback course up and down the
rocky lumps which gives the fell its apt name—five 'crinkles' in
all, and an exciting walk with views down Oxendale and the wild
valley head of Eskdale, for Crinkle Crags and Bowfell also form
part of the Eskdale Ring walk.

The going is rough but not unduly so and there is only the well-
known 'bad step' on the way up to the highest top that needs to
cause anything more than momentary reflection. The step can be
avoided by various detours, but it is not really so bad that a bit of
determined scrambling will not overcome it. In winter, of course,
the situation may be very different—I once did the traverse solo
under conditions of snow and ice when I prudently circumvented
the ice-draped 'bad step'—but then, the whole traverse under
such conditions is a much more serious affair.

Beyond Crinkle Crags and Shelter Crags comes the grassy col
of the Three Tarns where the track up the Band meets the main
ridge and crosses into Lingcove Bêck for Eskdale, the easiest pass
between the two valleys of Eskdale and Langdale for anyone on
foot. It is an eerie place, the Three Tarns (I always seem to count
four tarns—or is it five?) a kind of dead haven between the rocks
of Crinkle Crags and Bowfell. In mist it has a loneliness comparable
only with Sprinkling Tarn near Great End: a sort of lost loneliness, compounded of small waters lapping sadly against barren
shores.

Bowfell (2,960 feet) comes next, a mountain of crags, though
on the ridge walk these are not in evidence (or should not be, if
you are on the right route!) Bowfell is one of those fells whose
summit is a mere high point and whose real glory lies in its penultimate slopes, which have nothing to do with the walk in hand.
What is more important to the walker in this respect is the tricky
nature of the descent towards Angle Tarn and the top of Rossett
Gill—the only really safe plan is to make to Ore Gap, though
there are various almost indistinguishable tracks picking their
ways down through steep scree and minor crags.

At the top of Rossett Gill, as at the Band, the route crosses a
major track and an early descent can be made into Langdale. But

who would want to descend Rossett Gill from choice? Better to continue and climb Rossett Pike (2,106 feet), one of the most unjustly neglected peaks of the Lake District, and the one giving by far the best views of Upper Langdale. In winter this is a superb mountain, and some of the gullies on the Mickenden face give splendid snow routes, suitable for beginners to practise the art of step cutting, or simply as an interesting way up a grand fell.

Unfortunately the ridge beyond Rossett Pike is the last of the great ridge line that one has followed round the valley head. Beyond it the ridge flattens out into Martcrag Moor; a mile of tedious bog where the Stake Pass crosses from Langdale to Langstrath for Borrowdale. It really is a *longueur*, but the shapely Pike of Stickle seems temptingly close and helps a weary walker towards his final goal, until at last the long easy track down to the New Dungeon Ghyll Hotel forms a fitting end to a magnificent walk.

All the way along the Crinkles—Bowfell portion of the walk there are fine views to the Scafells, over Lingcove Beck and the wild head of Upper Eskdale, and as I mentioned earlier, these fells form part of the Eskdale Ring which begins and ends at Brotherilkeld Farm. But unless you were doing the Ring, the approach from this side is less preferable to that from Langdale. It is neither as varied nor as beautiful and the walk over the moors above Moasdale tends to be boring and boggy. Moasdale must rate as one of the least attractive valleys in the district. If Eskdale has to be the starting point it is much better to climb direct to Crinkle Crags by Lingcove Beck and Adam-a-Cove, and descend from Bowfell by Ore Gap and Lingcove Beck—a splendidly wild circuit.

Though the valley head walk is the supreme joy of Langdale for the hardy fell-walker it is not the only one. A shorter route, but one which ranks amongst the best in the district, is the Climbers' Traverse which contours round below the crags of Bowfell. Done in its entirety, this walk also serves as an introduction to two of the best loved—most hated tracks in the Lakes: the Band and Rossett Gill.

The Band is a long tongue of fellside descending into Langdale from the Bowfell ridge, and dividing the upper part of the valley into two branches, called Mickleden and Oxendale. At the foot of the Band lies the strangely named farmhouse of Stool End and the path goes through the farmyard and then more or less up the crest of the spur. At first it is steep and gravelly, but once the initial slopes are over, it eases considerably to pass through a brackish area of peat before finally sloping off up the shoulder of Bowfell to Three Tarns. It is an easy standard walk, and it is certainly the quickest, safest way off the high ridges in bad weather, but it is because of this—because it is so seminal to Langdale walking and is so often done, that it sometimes raises antipathy. "Not the Band *again*!" goes up the cry.

The Climbers' Traverse leaves the main path after it flattens out. In fine weather there is no difficulty in finding the way, but in mist it can be very tricky indeed, as more than one poor crags-man has discovered to his chagrin. The track ascends towards the fell top and then turns sharply right to traverse the steep fellside below an impressive series of crags. Seldom is a walker permitted to encroach so magnificently on the preserves of the rock climber, for the path literally touches the buttresses in places, and what with the steepness of the fellside below, he gains some idea of the true savagery of the mountain world.

For the most part the going is easy, if airy, with one or two rock steps to add piquancy to the route. However, there is at least one place where it is possible to make a mistake and follow a track which leads to a nasty little outcrop traverse guaranteed to give a walker rapid palpitations. The place is obvious if you have the misfortune to reach it, and the advice is equally obvious —go back and choose the alternative path. The fact that easy ground is so temptingly close is no excuse for acrobatics in such a place.

There are some curious rock formations on this route: the huge easily-angled Flat Crag, like a minor Idwal Slabs, the fluted savagery of North Buttress, and the very bold classical outline of Bowfell Buttress. From the walkers' viewpoint it is all very impressive—more so than Dow Crag, which has a similar traverse, and rivalling Scafell, Gable or Pillar.

Cambridge Crag is a landmark for a different reason. Here a spring gushes from the rock with crystal clear water of undeniable purity. It is, quite naturally, a favourite 'brewing-up' place for climbers and walkers, though I wish they would have the decency to take away their rubbish and not leave it to foul the path.

The highlight of the traverse comes at its very end, as though the whole thing had been superbly stage-managed. Bowfell Buttress rises like an enormous rock beehive, breathtaking in its sheer majesty.

It is an obvious challenge to rock climbers but it seems to have been ignored until 1902 when a large party, including L. J. Oppenheimer, made the first ascent of the now famous ordinary route. They called it, quite simply, *Bowfell Buttress*, perhaps under the impression that having made a direct ascent, there would be nothing else worth doing. They were wrong, of course, for in the years since then another ten routes have been added to their original line.

Nevertheless, Oppenheimer and his companions chose that route well. They unerringly picked the plum; the original *Bowfell Buttress Route* is quite definitely 'the route of the crag', as climbers say when they mean it is the best and most natural line.

It is nowhere hard—'v. diff.' at the most—but the combination of slabs and cracks are such as to be almost aesthetically perfect. Jerry Wright, who as a Lakeland professional guide made two hundred ascents of this climb, wrote:

> Once upon a wet and cloudy morning two experts, following the advice that it was a good climb for such a day began the ascent in improving weather conditions. They were so absorbed by its interest that they took little notice of the rising clouds and the sun breaking through. They were still there under brilliant blue skies in the late evening having gone up and down the route four times; they came away reluctantly after, as they put it, "two thousand feet of perfect rock climbing!"

Well, that was a few years ago: the modern expert is so taken with technicalities that it is doubtful whether any young 'hard man' would spend the day there—more likely he would be tempted by the extreme climbing of the *Sword of Damocles* on the North Buttress—but the story illustrates the quality of the climb.

In the easier grades I can think of only two other routes to match this one in all-round quality: *Black Crag Buttress* (Troutdale Pinnacle) and the *New West* on Pillar.

The Buttress juts out from its parent fellside to which it is connected by a narrow rocky neck. There is a gully on each side, one, North Gully, is almost inaccessible except to a determined scrambler, but the other, a wide scree gully between the Buttress and Cambridge Crag, is the way up to the summit ridge from the end of the Climber's Traverse. It is not a pleasant scramble, distinctly steep near the top, but easy enough for any sure-footed walker. In winter, however, this gully becomes a notorious trap and has been the scene of at least one fatal accident.

John Stogden, an alpinist, came this way with two friends in the snowy winter of 1869.

A mass of black crag rose from the snow at the base of the couloir [he later wrote] which now rose steeply straight above us, with the summit of Bow on the left. The snow was at first in capital order, and the angle (by clinometer) 30°. As the angle gradually increased the snow got gradually harder, till on reaching about 45° it became necessary to cut steps. The slope got steeper and steeper, steps were always necessary, and at last having come up 350 feet or more, we found ourselves within a few feet of the top on a slope of 63°, with an overhanging cornice of ice above us, and the snow nearly up to our waists for a few feet below the top, which I could just reach with my ice axe. The next few minutes must have been pleasant to my friends below me, as the cornice was gradually tumbled upon their ears in a shower of icy fragments. Then I pulled myself up by my hands on to the level snow field above, and a short run up easy slopes brought us to the top.

Later on, that same day, the party tried glissading on Great End and after an accident to one of them, were lucky to escape alive to Wasdale Head.

From the top of the ridge the route descends to Angle Tarn, and from there a well-marked track leads to the gap at the top of Rossett Gill. It is worth while pausing in the gap to look around, not because the scenery is particularly beautiful (much of it is hidden by outcrops) but because this is one of the great gateways to the western fells; perhaps the greatest of them all. Thousands of walkers pass this way every year because it leads from Langdale to practically everywhere else of importance—Borrowdale, Wasdale, Eskdale, the Scafells, the Gables, you name it and it is almost certain to be reachable via Rossett Gill. Sometimes it is not the best or perhaps the most direct way, but familiarity and a good track can be powerful inducements.

In winter, the upper part of the gill can be hard snow demanding that steps be cut or kicked; in summer, under a hot sun the whole ascent becomes an interminable grind. Even more so than with the Band, Rossett Gill enjoys a love-hate relationship with fell-walkers and climbers. I think the main reason for this is that the steep twisting track often comes as the final descent after a long hard day. Too often the Gill plays the part of the straw that breaks the camel's back, and if it happens to be raining at the time, well, the combination is too much even for the strongest mentality to bear with equanimity.

But the gill is a hard grind, however you look at it. I remember how once, to save money on bus fares, I walked with my camping gear over from Old Dungeon Ghyll to Seathwaite in Borrowdale. It was Friday evening, summer-time, but with scarcely enough daylight left to make the journey in comfort and I knew I would need to hurry. I also knew Rossett Gill.

The gill almost brought me to my knees. It is definitely not a place to rush up with a heavy load. Salt sweat trickled into my eyes as I tried to focus on each landmark in turn, determined to reach it before collapsing; then the next, and the next—I reached the screes near the top before I gave the gill best and sagged down for a well-earned rest.

The rest of the journey over Esk Hause and down Grain's Gill into Borrowdale was child's play compared with Rossett. I didn't need another rest and managed to pitch my tent on Seathwaite's tiny camp site well before the sun finally set.

North of the Langdale Pikes a long, undulating ridge travels in a series of high fells towards Castlerigg and Keswick. Properly, these are part of the Borrowdale fells (see Chapter 6) but in the southernmost reaches, between Greenup Edge and Pavey Ark they throw down a series of small spurs and valleys towards

Grasmere, which are usually walked from that village, or from Langdale as the most convenient centres.

High White Stones (2,500 feet) and the attendant Sergeant Man (2,373 feet) are the highest tops in this fascinating region, but they are also the least interesting, and indeed one might go as far as to say that High White Stones, amongst the bigger fells, bids fair to rank as the least interesting of them all. Not so the lesser heights or the two valleys of Easedale and Far Easedale.

These are not fells for integrated walks but rather for unusual ascents and the variety of rock, heather and water. Easedale and Codale Tarns, and the waterfall of Sourmilk Gill have been tourist attractions for many years: it was the most sincere contact with wild nature that many Victorian tourists experienced—though there was a refreshment hut, whose ruins still remain near the head of the Gill, to give them sustenance.

Tarn Crag (1,861 feet) separates the two valleys and rises like a rocky sentinel over both, despite its relatively minor height. On the Far Easedale side, where the surroundings are harshly unrelieved by any tarns or tinges of romanticism, is the bold buttress of Deer Bield; a crag every bit as unusual as its name. It is the 'quare fellow' of Langdale rocks, rather remote from the centre of things, boldly impressive and with an overhanging central pillar that is almost detached from the fellside, leaving a prominent gash on either side. These clefts—the Crack and the Chimney —together with the buttress between them, are a trio of hard climbs that do justice to such a stern crag. They are among the best of their kind for the expert climber. Deer Bield is not a crag to court popularity, despite its famous climbs, nor yet one to inspire affection.

Easedale is undeniably attractive, even pretty in its way, but Far Easedale offers more entertaining walking. For years it has provided a popular route from Grasmere to Borrowdale, over Greenup and down past the curious Lining Crag to Stonethwaite. There are crags and outcrops all the way on both sides of the valley and I wonder that more climbing development has not taken place here, though the routes would probably be short. In winter, the scenery of snow-draped rocks is magnificent.

The northern rim of Far Easedale comprises a good but rather

Helm Crag, Grasmere, with snow-covered Steel Fell beyond

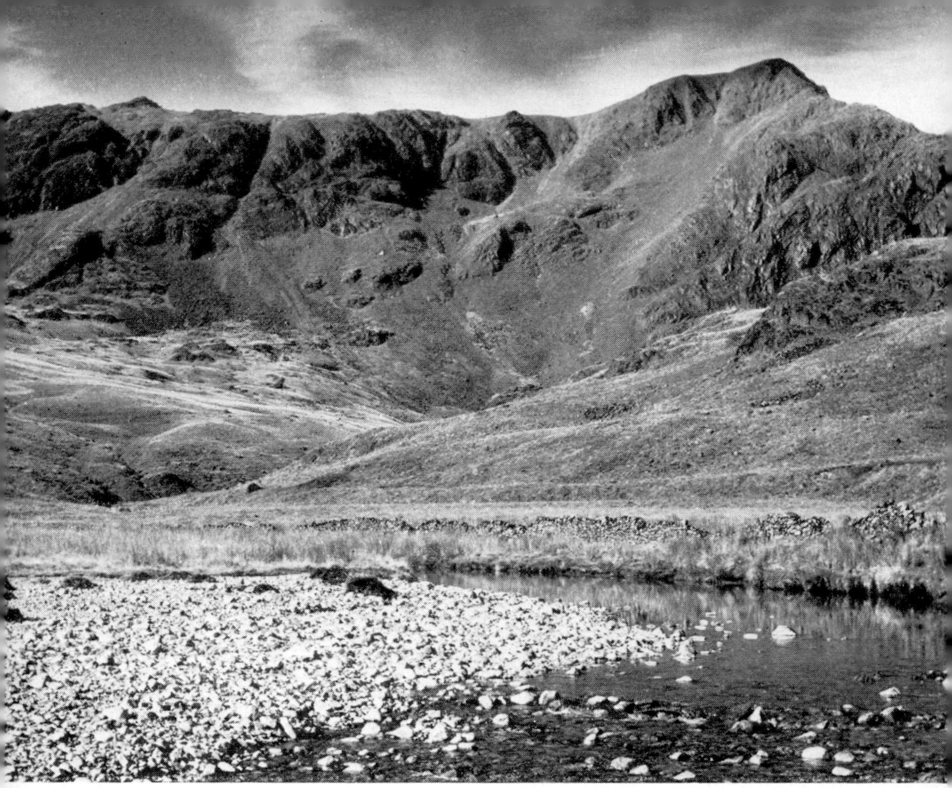

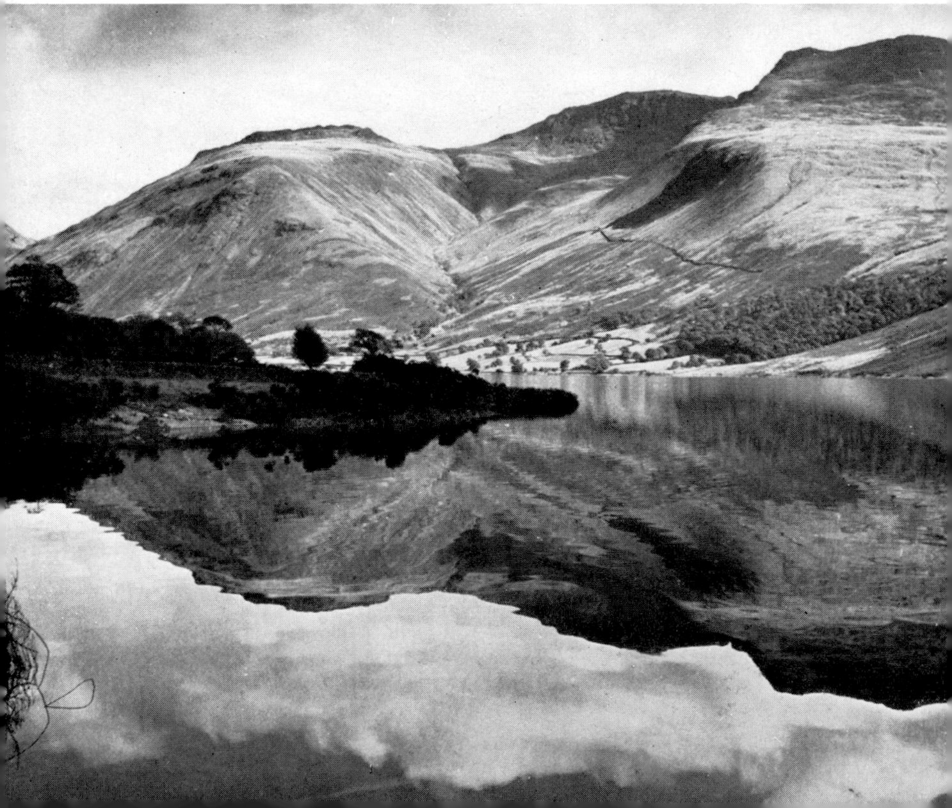

short ridge walk from Helm Crag (1,299 feet) over Gibson Knott (1,379 feet) to Calf Crag (1,762 feet), three summits which are satisfyingly rocky. Helm Crag is well known, of course, as the shapely terminal peak directly overlooking Grasmere, where the Victorian tourists gave names to the 'faces' made by the rocky profiles of the summit crags such as 'The Lion and The Lamb'; a fashion which has been inflicted on various crags in Britain, and which in my opinion is too twee for words.

The actual summit of Helm Crag is one of these blocks, a pointing finger of rock that is not too difficult to climb and is satisfactorily restricted on top, like a bigger version of Adam (or Eve) on Tryfan. Curiously enough, there are very few mountains south of the border which have such spiky summits.

The rest of the ridge is equally interesting, and those who like a scramble can make it almost as difficult as they wish by including sundry outcrops, though there is no need for this if you simply wish to amble along. From the final top, Calf Crag, you can look down into the utter desolation that is Wythburn Valley, a place to be avoided at all costs—it probably ranks as the boggiest valley in Lakeland.

5

The eastern precipices of Scafell from upper Eskdale
The Scafell Group reflected in the still surface of Wastwater:
(left) Lingmell, (centre) Scafell Pike, (right) Scafell

3

Scafell

THE summit is bare of everything that grows, except moss. Not a blade of grass is to be seen: and it follows that the herdsman and shepherd never have to come here after their charge. Blocks and inclined planes of slate rock, cushioned and draped with moss, compose the peak . . . the greatest mountain excursion in England.

The writer, Harriet Martineau; the place, Scafell Pike, and though Miss Martineau wrote her description in the middle of the last century it still captures the nature of England's highest summit. The two mountains which form the principal substance of this group of fells are indeed barren of everything that grows. They are rock wildernesses of broad summits, scratched by 'paths' worn by thousands of boots, and, in the case of Scafell Pike, adorned by a cairn of monumental proportions, which replaces the pole erected by the Ordnance Survey in Harriet's day.

Rocky grandeur is the keynote of the whole group. Trees play no part here, even in the attendant valley, and though there are tarns and waterfalls, and the sombre lake of Wastwater to vary the prospect, the overriding conception is that of rock. Within this group lies the grandest and most savage scenery you will see in the entire district; seldom rivalled, never excelled.

It is a group of integrated parts rather than an integrated whole. Even from a distance parts stand out and distract from the mass; features so prominent that they are subject to comment: the gap of Mickledore, Scafell Crag, Piers Gill—these have a trick of commanding attention. To enjoy the mass you must go to Bowfell or Crinkle Crags, from where the Scafells really look the part,

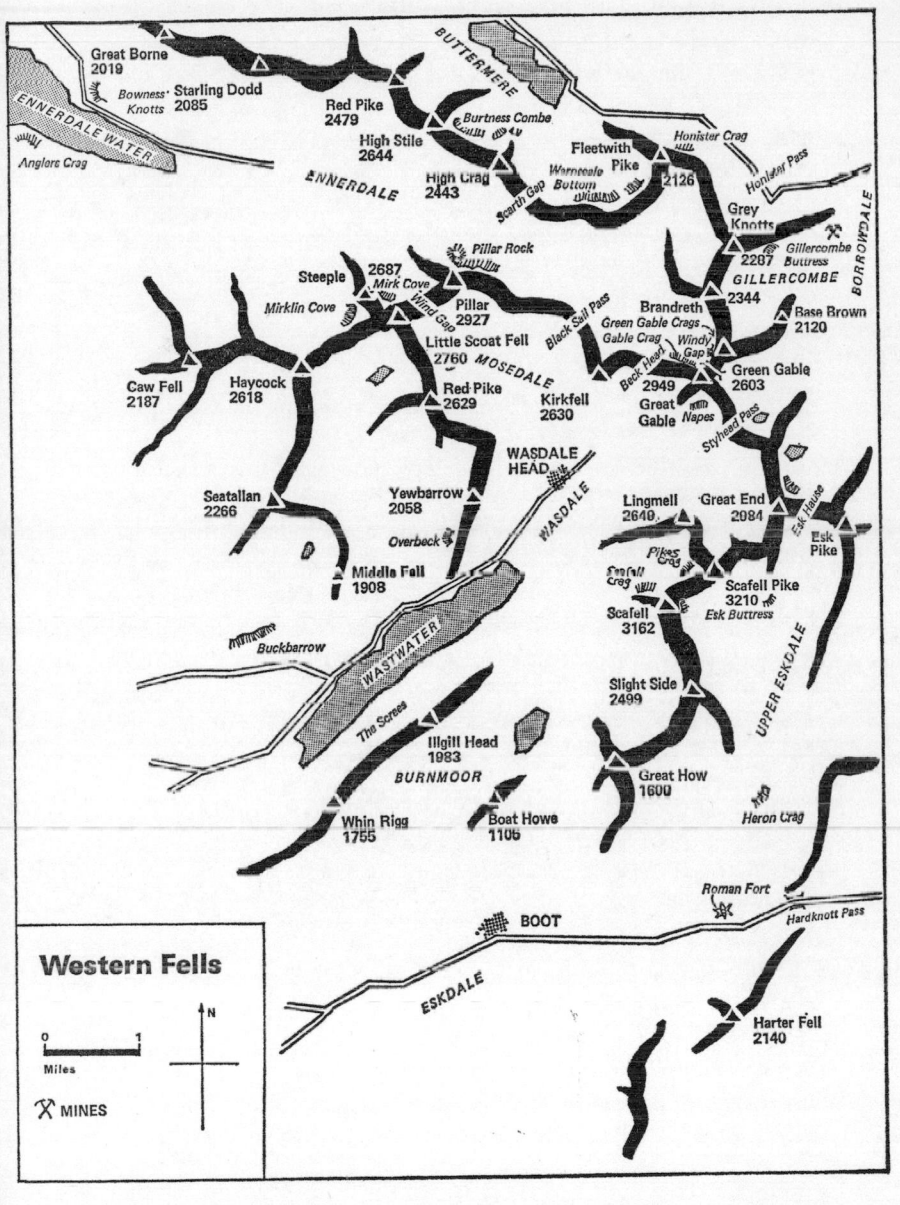

Great Borne
2019

Bowness Starling Dodd
Knotts 2085

ENNERDALE WATER

Anglers Crag

Red Pike
2479

High Stile
2644

High Crag
2443

Scarth Gap

ENNERDALE

BUTTERMERE

Burtness Combe

Fleetwith
Pike
2126

Warnscale
Bottom

Honister Crag

Honister Pass

BORROWDALE

Grey
Knotts
2287

Gillercombe
Buttress

GILLERCOMBE
2344

Pillar Rock

Steeple
2687

Mirk Cove

Mirklin Cove

Wind Gap

Pillar
2927

Little Scoat Fell
2760

MOSEDALE

Brandreth

Green Gable Crags
Gable Crag

Windy
Gap

Base Brown
2120

Green Gable
2603

Caw Fell
2187

Haycock
2618

Red Pike
2629

Kirkfell
2630

Back Heap

2949

Great
Gable

Napes

Styhead Pass

WASDALE
HEAD

Seatallan
2266

Yewbarrow
2058

Overbeck

WASDALE

Lingmell
2649

Great End
2984

Esk Hause

Esk
Pike

Middle Fell
1908

Buckbarrow

WASTWATER

The Screes

Sca Fell
Crag

Pikes
Crag

Scafell Pike
3210

Esk Buttress

Scafell
3162

UPPER ESKDALE

Ilgill Head
1983

BURNMOOR

Slight Side
2499

Whin Rigg
1755

Boat Howe
1106

Great How
1600

Heron Crag

Roman Fort

Hardknott Pass

BOOT

ESKDALE

Harter Fell
2140

Western Fells

0   1
Miles

N

⚒ MINES

rearing boldly above the wilderness of upper Eskdale, or better still, observe them in the evening light from Wind Gap between Pillar and Steeple, when they look really superb.

To move in closer is to focus again on the parts rather than the whole. On the western edge of the group we have the justly celebrated view of the screes across the expanse of Wastwater, one of the most dramatic mountain scenes in Britain, whilst on the eastern edge we have in winter the immense snow-ribboned bulk of Great End, the finest snow and ice climbing south of the Scottish border. To the south, Esk Buttress dominates the river of that name, whilst to the north, the immense snaking gorge of Piers Gill seems to rent the fells apart. Each of these in its own way, is incomparable. Each is dramatic, stark, bold. There is no lightening of texture, no concession to softness.

Of all the groups with which this book deals, none offers more to the mountain explorer than does this one. Simply to walk the main summits is nothing—except the somewhat dubious distinction of having climbed the highest peaks in the land, and it is a journey which even Wordsworth found easy. Similarly, those who enjoy the long sweep of a fine ridge will find nothing of that sort here: the Coniston Fells, or the Pillar group have more to offer in this respect. But for those who do not mind rough or unusual ascents, who are prepared to tackle a mountain head on and give it best from time to time—this is the very stuff that dreams are made of.

This sort of walking and scrambling needs more time than the straightforward kind, and it takes more out of you, too. For these reasons it is best to explore the Scafells from Wasdale Head, though I must confess that most of my wanderings hereabouts have been from other valleys, especially Borrowdale and Eskdale. Once, I remember, we had a glorious romp over the fells from Langdale, with the intention of climbing on Scafell Crag. We went up Rossett Gill to Esk Hause then over Scafell Pike to Mickledore, only to discover the crag running with water and most unappetizing. Somebody mentioned 'opening time' so we ran down Hollow Stones to the Wastwater Hotel, found suitable refreshment for an hour or so, then plodded up the track to Sty Head, and from there to Sprinkling Tarn, and so back to

Rossett Gill and Langdale. It was a grand day's walking despite the intermittent rain showers, but not really a recommended way of exploring the Scafell Group!

To get to know the group properly these exploratory walks must include the low levels as well as the high tops. The ways in and out, up, down and around are far more fascinating for spending a day than joining a mass of tourists on the summit cairn.

Take upper Eskdale, for example. Here is the grandest valley head in the Lake District, completely wild and unspoilt, where, even in these ubiquitous days, walkers are not overcommon. If you want to feel alone in the majesty of the fells, this is the very place, for it is surrounded by the highest and grandest of mountain ridges, sweeping round from Crinkle Crags in the east, by Bow-fell and Esk Pike to Ill Crag and Scafell in the west.

Below the crest, tiers of crags and outcrops stagger down the fellside to the valley floor, and even on occasions squeeze the river into a semblance of a gorge. All nature is here chaos and con-fusion, make of it what you will. Some of these lower crags are incredibly commanding: the unique flat prow of Heron Crag, for instance, the shambling Scottish-like rocks of Cam Sprout Crag, the superbly commanding Esk Buttress.

The path from Brotherilkeld farm follows the river fairly exactly and shares its various moods, only abandoning it when it cuts deep into the rocks to rush through a minor gorge. At the Great Moss, where the river meanders shallowly over wide beds of stone, there is time to stare and contemplate whether to con-tinue to Esk Pike (2,903 feet) or take one of the rough byways into the Scafells themselves. Esk Pike, of course, standing at the very head of the valley makes the logical terminus for such an expedi-tion, and being one of those fells unfortunate enough to be over-shadowed by more imposing companions, deserves the ascent. Certainly this is the best way up, and to return by Lingcove Beck from Ore Gap, having traversed the peak, is to do a tour of upper Eskdale that will live long in the memory.

Because Esk Hause, which is the true head of the valley, is so central to the Western fells, the variations on this walk are end-less, and each variation adds something new to your Lakeland knowledge and experience. It can, of course, be used as a means of ascending Scafell Pike itself, with a return down the steeper route to Mickledore and Cam Spout, or the walk can be continued by Sprinkling Tarn, under the impressive broken bulk of Great End, to Sty Head and a return made along the *Corridor Route* above Piers Gill and underneath Pikes Crag into Hollow Stones, overlooked by the dark, powerful buttresses of Scafell Crag, before climbing up to Mickledore and descending the Cam Spout track. But one word of warning on all these itineraries— they are tough going, fairly long, and not to be undertaken lightly, especially if the weather is less than perfect.

West of the main massif the fells roll away into moorland whose highest point are Illgill Head (1,978 feet) and Whin Rigg (1,755 feet), two summits at either end of the broad ridge overlooking Wastwater. As a walk the ridge is short and rather dull, but its saving grace is the fact that the north-western face of it falls sheer into the lake, forming the well-known Wastwater Screes. It is possible to look down on the lake like an eagle from its eyrie, and even take cautious peeks down the savage gullies of the screes.

To savour the screes to the full, though, it is best to return along their base by the rough lakeside track, though even this does not match the superlative views of these immense crags which you get from the narrow motor road on the other side of the Lake.

How impressive they are, these screes! Huge bulging bastions of rock tumbling down to the wide fans of scree which shoot at an incredibly steep angle into the lake. In total height they exceed 1,500 feet and about 1,000 feet of this is sheer crag—easily the biggest in the Lake District. The tragedy from the rock-climbers' point of view is that the rocks are broken, and moreover, desperately rotten. Only the *Great Gully* ('severe') receives much attention, and that too can be unpleasant, as Mummery found out when he made the second ascent in 1892, shortly after it had been climbed for the first time. Mummery was the greatest alpinist of his day, and a fair rock-climber, but his experience in Great Gully put him off Lakeland climbing for ever. "Climbing in the Caucasus", he said to his friend Collie, "was easy and safe; in the Alps too it was usually easy and safe, though sometimes difficult; but climbing as practised at Wasdale Head was both difficult and dangerous!" Strong words from a man who had made the extremely dangerous traverse of the Col du Lion on the Matterhorn, and who habitually climbed the rotten chalk of the Dover cliffs—but it gives some indication of the nature of the Screes. I blame Collie for Mummery's disenchantment: it could only have been the impish nature of this renowned climber which made him take Mummery to the Screes when there was so much better climbing to hand.

From the heights of Illgill Head and Whin Rigg the moors roll south to Eskdale and are disected by two rivers, the Mite and the Whillan Beck which give pleasant walks of the easier kind, leading up on to Burn Moor. From the edge of these moors Harter Fell looks particularly good, and despite its modest height reinforces its claim as one of the finest mountains in the district.

The track over Burnmoor from Eskdale to Wasdale is one of the most popular walks in the district. I wonder how many of the fell-walkers who happily wander over it know that it is an old corpse road, and that it is reputedly haunted? The story goes that a horse bearing a corpse once bolted as it crossed this lonely moor and was never recaptured: its spirit is said to haunt the moor still—not a pleasant thought for the imaginative soul caught out on Burnmoor in a mist!

I must confess that I have never experienced anything uncanny on this delightful moor, though in younger days I must have crossed it dozens of times in all sorts of weather. My favourite route was by the steep track up behind the *Woolpack* in Eskdale to Eel Tarn and then the decrepit planks of Lambford Bridge over the Whillan Beck and so to the tarn.

There is some indefinable quality about Burnmoor Tarn which makes it uniquely attractive. Size might have something to do with it, for it is one of the biggest tarns of Lakeland, but it cannot be the impressiveness of the surrounding fells because there are none worth the mention. Somehow it just looks right, and I remember how there always used to be a herd of cattle standing in and around the water's edge as if trying to prove that Landseer was right, after all.

But that was thirty years ago. The cattle were not there last year when I revisited the place, though I was surprised to find that the Burnmoor Lodge, that strangely isolated building which rivals Skiddaw House for remoteness, still survived, apparently as some form of mountain hut. It is good to know that vandals have not penetrated to Burnmoor.

I have gone on at some length about Eskdale, Burnmoor and the lower surrounding of this great group of fells because I wish to emphasize that there is a good deal more to Scafell than its crags and its height. As I mentioned earlier it is a region to explore.

Nevertheless, there can be no denying that the focus of all attention rests in the twin summits of Scafell and its Pike, and their immediate surroundings.

These are great fells, magnificent mountains, and to climb them as they should be climbed you need to give them a worthy approach, and test their mettle against your own. Of course you can stroll up Scafell Pike from Esk Hause; of course you can pant up Scafell from Burnmoor—but what is the sense in that, when they have so much more to offer? Might as well climb the Seven Sisters slag heaps at Wigan—in fact, the slag heaps are steeper.

Even Wordsworth found the ordinary route up Scafell Pike quite simple. He climbed it on a clear October day:

On the summit of the Pike, which we gained after much toil, though without difficulty, there was not a breath of air to stir even the papers containing our refreshments, as they lay spread out upon a rock. The stillness seemed to be not of this world. We paused and kept silence to listen, and no sound could be heard. The Scawfell cataracts were voiceless to us; and there was not an insect to hum in the air. The vales which we had seen from Esk Hause lay yet in view, and, side by side with Eskdale, we now saw the sister Vale of Donnerdale terminated by the Duddon Sands. But the majesty of the mountains below, and close to us, is not to be conceived. We now beheld the whole mass of Great Gable from its base—the Den of Wastdale at our feet—a gulf immeasurable; Grasmire, and the other mountains of Crummock; Ennerdale and its mountains; and the sea beyond!

Wordsworth's description of the summit view would do equally well today, except that seawards he would need to call attention to the white pile of the Seascale Atomic plant which is so obscenely prominent on the coast.

Such a majestic view and such a majestic mountain demands an ascent which is worthy of it. Eschew the highway, and take instead the tough but glorious ascent by Cam Spout from Eskdale (perhaps the finest way up of all) or at least traverse the Corridor Route from Sty Head before climbing the summit via Lingmell Col. Either way does more justice to the mountain, but there are others too, which your exploration will reveal. I have often thought, as a rock-climber, that a complete traverse of Piers Gill would be a unique way of climbing Scafell Pike—but I must confess that I have never put it to the test—the other attractions for rock-climbers hereabouts have always been too tempting. The gill has been climbed and though a lot of it is no more than scrambling, some bits are 'severe', and it is not a place for the inexperienced.

If Scafell Pike demands the grand approach, what then of Scafell itself; whose great crags frown down on to Hollow Stones and seem to defy access to all but the rock-climber? The easy ways, by Slight Side or from Burnmoor, are round the back, as it were, and though useful as safe ways off they are laboriously dull as ways of ascent and not at all worthy of the mountain.

The essence of Scafell is sheer rock, and unless you are prepared to rub noses with this rock, however modestly, you cannot possibly savour Scafell properly. Fortunately this demands no heroics on the part of the modest fell-walker, only a steady head and the sort of scrambling ability that would get him up Jack's Rake, for instance, or Crib Goch in Wales.

The most direct ascent, of course, is by Lingmell Gill to Hollow Stones from Wasdale Head. It is steep and exhausting on a hot day, but the cirque of rocks towards which the path toils gains in magnificence at every step until finally it is completely revealed, stretching round from Pikes Crag on the left to Black Crag on the right and dominated by the soaring central buttresses of Scafell Crag.

Every notable feature of Scafell Crag can be observed from Hollow Stones, and even if your energy is still not flagging after the steep walk from Wasdale Head, it is worth while to pause and identify these.

From Mickledore, the col between Scafell Pike and Scafell, the crag arcs upwards at first in a great crescent until its shape is lost in the serrated tops of the central portion. The most obvious feature of this left-hand side is the strange light-coloured slab which slopes up to the left like a grotesque ramp: Botterill's Slab. There then follows an extremely steep and bulging portion, where, if the light is right and your eyes sharp enough, you can detect a great flake of rock sticking to the buttress. This is Central Buttress, and it is sharply defined on its right-hand side by the longest gully of the crag—so long that it cuts way down past the line of ledges which runs below the other parts of the rock. The gully is Moss Ghyll. On its right is the tall Pisgah Buttress, followed by a narrow, savage-looking gully called Steep Ghyll below which the rocks seem to spray out into ledges. Next comes the Pinnacle, tall and narrow, though you may not be able to detect that it is almost separated at the top from the parent fell and has its own little summits called High and Low Man. Adjacent to the Pinnacle on its right is the wide gully of Deep Ghyll, and beyond that the bulky masses of Deep Ghyll Buttress and rocks of lesser importance. The right-hand end of the crag, from the foot of the Pinnacle on, is largely hidden by another crag called the Shamrock which stands in front of Scafell proper, and, depending on your observation point, you might just be able to detect the start of Lord's Rake, which goes up between Shamrock and the parent crag. Finally, and further right still, Shamrock gives way to Red Ghyll Buttress and Black Crag.

A very steep and loose scree shoot runs up from Hollow Stones to Lord's Rake, and on this side it is the *only* easy way to the top. However, it is preferable to continue up the track to Mickledore and meet the route coming from Eskdale by way of Cam Spout.

The difficulty about climbing Scafell from Wasdale is that you are forced to return by the way you came, more or less, and it is always much more satisfying to traverse a mountain than make a simple ascent. For this reason Eskdale again suggests itself as a better base for such a walk—though a very tough one, both in terms of physical stamina and nervous energy.

The start of this long, magnificent, walk is along the River Esk until it is possible to climb up the track by the rushing waters of Cam Spout Force and the final screes to Mickledore, below the grim crags of the Eastern Buttress. At the rocky col, the full grandeur of the cirque becomes apparent, though it would seem that there is no possible way on to Scafell itself.

A rock-climber, confident in his own ability, might be tempted to squeeze up the narrow rift that leads to Broad Stand and scramble to the top from there, but the only virtue of such an ascent is quickness—and the slippery sloping slab that is the 'bad step' of Broad Stand, puts it out of bounds for most people. Make no mistake, Broad Stand is a dangerous place—I once had a perfect climbing day taken up by helping to carry down two Boy Scouts who thought otherwise.

To reach the summit from Mickledore it is necessary to traverse below the crag to the foot of Lord's Rake, and there are two ways of doing this. The easiest is by a path which runs below the rocks and begins a short distance down from the col, or taking courage in both hands, you can follow the climbers' track, known as *Rake's Progress*.

Rake's Progress is a curious succession of ledges running directly beneath the climbs and above a band of lower crags. It is narrow and exposed but for the most part it carries a path and causes no difficulty. The main difficulty lies at a short stretch near the Mickledore end: here the *Progress* calls for a steady head and an ability to cross steep rock, though the holds are generous. In my opinion it is no more difficult than the harder bits of the Napes Traverse, but to each his own, and the problem, being at the Mickledore end, can either be faced immediately or not at all, as ability and prudence dictate.

Beyond the bad bit *Rake's Progress* quickly becomes more amenable and leads below the towering walls of Central Buttress and the deep gash of Moss Ghyll. Steep Ghyll comes next, but here ledges and outcrops lie at the foot of the climbs and cut them off from pedestrian sight. Indeed, the nearer you get to Lord's Rake, the less you see of the crag proper, but never mind, the *Progress* has at least given you a little taste of Scafell Crag.

At the end of the traverse a cross has been cut in the rock to mark the terrible accident of 23rd September, 1903, when a party of four climbers led by the redoubtable R. W. Broadrick (of Broadrick's Crack on Dow Crag) fell to their deaths whilst attempting to reach a feature in the rocks above known as

Hopkinson's Cairn. This climb is a severe and delicate route, even by today's standards, but in those days, when proper rope tactics were not understood and belays were minimal, it must have been desperate indeed. For some reason Broadrick had given up the lead to a man called Garrett and when he slipped and fell the others, spreadeagled across the rock face, could do nothing to save either him or themselves. As far as I am aware, the Scafell tragedy remains the worst single *rock-climbing* accident ever to take place in Britain.

It is disconcerting to a walker to have to pass this memorial cross just as he is about to start the ascent of Lord's Rake, especially as Lord's Rake too, has seen its share of fatalities, though for different reasons. The narrow, steep, scree-filled corridor has over the years become the favourite tourist route up the mountain, and there is no denying that it is the best way up for a fell-walker. The scree, however, can have its dangers and care should always be taken to advance circumspectly. In these days of large parties (the fells sometimes seem invested with roaming bands) Lord's Rake is one of those places where you should not go either with or behind such a group.

The Rake goes up in a straight line and the easiest way is to follow it to the bitter end until it debouches on to the scree of the parent fellside from where it is an easy matter to walk to the summit of the fell. There is, however, yet another interesting diversion for the more adventurous—the *West Wall Traverse* of Deep Ghyll.

This traverse leaves Lord's Rake just before a prominent little col. It consists of an easy shelf across Deep Ghyll Buttress and leads into the stony bed of the enormous gully above its two rock pitches. It is used by climbers to get to routes such as the popular *Woodhead's Climb*, which begin in the Ghyll, but it is equally useful as a direct way to the top of the fell, and once again, it gives that feeling of having really come to grips with the mountain.

I remember walking over Scafell with a Swiss lad called Rolf a few years after the War. We had come down the Rake and were resting at Hollow Stones, devouring some of Rolf's delicious salami, which he always carried in his back pocket as a cowboy might carry a chew of tobacco, when there was a tremendous outcry from the regions of Deep Ghyll. Glancing up we saw an incredible sight. Five or six youths were descending the ghyll and having missed the West Wall Traverse, were desperately involved with the rock pitches lower down. They were not roped and were further hampered by their enormous rucksacks. They shouted and bawled warnings and instructions to one another in a language which could only be German.

There was nothing we could do except watch the whole circus, expecting an accident at any moment. It was only by sheer good luck they all managed eventually to arrive at the bottom safely. I think Rolf suspected they were Swiss and was ashamed of such stupidity in a mountain race of people, for when they reached Hollow Stones he strode angrily up to their leader. "That was a bloody silly thing to do," he said, speaking in English.

The other drew himself up, literally beat his chest and cried, "But I was trained in Bavaria!"

Rolf gave him a pitying stare. "And I was trained in the Oberland," he said. "It was still a bloody stupid thing to do!"

It is much more interesting to stroll around the rim of Scafell looking down the gullies and at the impressive top of the Pinnacle which is almost detached from the fell, leaning against it like a lazy copy of Pillar Rock, than it is to visit the summit. The summit is just a cairn set well back from the rim in a waste of stones. The rim leads, by a well-worn climbers' path, down Broad Stand (Mickledore looks temptingly close) but unless you are a climber and accustomed to doing daft things in dangerous places, it is best to turn back at this point.

In fact all the ways down on this side of the fell have their dangers. Broad Stand because it is rather slippery and awkward, and the West Wall Traverse or Lord's Rake because their precise beginnings can be confusing to anyone not familiar with the ground. Lord's Rake in particular can be a trap. The tendency is to go down Red Gill in mistake for the real start, and though the two routes do eventually converge, the upper part of Red Gill is most unpleasant, not to say dangerous. In bad weather or mist, all these routes, either up or down, are best avoided.

But with our Eskdale base we have no such problems. From the summit an easy, though long, descent leads back over Slight Side (2,499 feet) to Cowcove Beck, and eventually, the *Woolpack*.

This traverse of Scafell is certainly one of the best mountain ascents south of the Scottish border, but, as I said earlier, it is not for the aged or infirm (though I know a couple of gentlemen in their seventies who could do it any day) and Scafell is potentially the most dangerous fell in the Lake District.

Tougher still, of course, is to walk the whole of the valley head —the famous Eskdale Ring. Where you start this long fell walk is left largely to your sense of honour; strictly it should begin and end at Brotherilkeld, but having done it once I must confess that the first few miles around the head of gloomy Moasdale (not to be confused with Wasdale Head's Mosedale) is a dreary slog quite alien to the rest of the walk. But once Crinkle Crags have been gained the going is superb and interesting all the way: Bowfell, Esk Pike, Great End, Scafell Pike, Scafell and Slight Side—a unique combination of some of the finest fells in Lakeland. The distance, in actual fact, is not excessive (about 12 miles) but there is a lot of up and down in it, and the terrain is seldom less than rough.

Most walkers would reckon the Scafell Ring a good day, though it is not exceptional, and to fell-runners would probably be a simple exercise. I once had as a companion at the camp site at Blea Tarn a man who ran down to Stool End in Langdale, up the Band, over Crinkles and Pike o'Blisco back to camp site— before his breakfast. The very thought of it put me off for the rest of the weekend!

The whole of the Scafell area is a firm favourite with climbers. Besides the obvious challenges of Scafell itself there are those on Esk Buttress, a stern crag in an isolated setting overlooking the upper Esk (Dow Crag on the O.S. Map) and the more recent discoveries on Heron Crag, lower down the same river. On the northern extremity of the range Great End bulks magnificently over Grains Gill, its two principal gullies giving some of the best snow and ice climbing in these islands, outside of Scotland.

But the chief of these subsidiary crags, to the average climber, is the beautiful Pike's Crag, which rears up in pinnacle fashion at the head of Hollow Stones, helping to make that place the impressive rocky amphitheatre it is. It is a spiky sort of crag, like those of the rock-climbing areas of Austria, though a good deal smaller than its Alpine counterparts, and a good deal sounder, for that matter. By local standards its climbs achieve a respectable length, 250-400 feet, but most of them are hardly serious in the context of modern rock-climbing. Instead, given a sunny day, they are routes of pleasant delight on good, clean rock. It is the sort of place you can sit and smoke a pipe in between pitches and nobody will think any the worse of you for doing it.

Pulpit Rock, the highest part of the crag, is one of those rocky tops which protrude above the parent fellside, so that once having attained it you have to scramble down again by a short wall. Not too difficult, but it is difficult enough to keep the summit as a preserve for rock-climbers only.

Pike's Crag is for those lazy pleasant afternoons when any urge to risk life and limb is at a minimum. Across Hollow Stones, however, you are constantly reminded of much sterner stuff: the massive buttresses of Scafell Crag, one of the greatest seminal rock faces of British climbing history.

It is an awesome crag, even to those who know it well and have climbed on it many times. It always seems sunless and threatening, and when it is wet (as it frequently is) it drips malevolence. Not all the climbs are hard, but they are all serious. Nobody messes about on Scafell Crag.

It is hardly surprising that such a crag has played a significant part in the development of climbing in this country, and has attracted the best climbers. After the easier gullies had been climbed, the first great route up the face was made in 1888 by Cecil Slingsby, Geoffrey Hastings, Edward Hopkinson and W. P. Haskett Smith (the day after the first ascent of Great Gully on Dow Crag: see Chapter 1) who scrambled up the easier lower part of Steep Ghyll and then made their way by an awkwardly overhanging chimney (now called Slingsby's Chimney) to High Man, the upper point of the almost detached Pinnacle. Though not particularly difficult, the route has exposure and the penultimate crossing of the knife-edge between Low Man and High Man gives a suitable Alpine quality, well in keeping with its originator, for Slingsby was not only a pioneer on British rock, but one of the leading alpinists of his day; a companion of the great Mummery.

The most coveted prize of those early days, when gullies were all the rage, was the deep, prominent gash of Moss Ghyll. The name is significant of the state of the gill at the time it was first climbed, but the boots of succeeding generations of climbers have removed most of the moss—though anyone who wants to see something of the original state can still do so by taking the forty-foot chimney of Pitch 3, which is now usually avoided.

This fine gully was first climbed by Professor John Norman Collie, Geoffrey Hastings and J. W. Robinson on Boxing Day 1892. Not only was it regarded as a landmark in gully climbing, it also gave rise to one of the most famous controversies in climbing history.

The party had got a considerable way up the gill when they found further progress blocked by a huge chockstone. Collie later described their quandary:

Our only chance was to traverse straight out along the side of the ghyll, till one was no longer overshadowed by the roof above, and then if possible climb up the face of the rock and traverse back again above the obstacle into the ghyll once more. This was easier to plan than to carry out; absolutely no handhold, and only one little projecting ledge jutting out about a quarter of an inch and about two inches long to stand on, and six or eight feet of rock wall to be traversed. I was asked to try it. Accordingly, with great deliberation, I stretched out my foot and placed the edge of my toe on the ledge. Just as I was going to put my weight on to it, off slipped my toe; and if Hastings had not quickly jerked me back, I should instantly have been dangling on the end of the rope. But we were determined not to be beaten. Hastings' ice-axe was next brought into requisition, and what followed I have no doubt will be severely criticized by more orthodox mountaineers than ourselves. As it was my suggestion, I must take the blame. *Peccavi!* I hacked a step in *the rock*—and it was very hard work. But I should not advise anyone to try and do the same thing with an ordinary axe. Hastings' axe is an extraordinary one, and was none the worse for the experiment. I then stepped across the *mauvais pas*, clambered up the rock still I had reached a spot where a capital hitch could be got over a jutting piece of rock,

Scafell Crag from Pike's Crag

and the rest of the party followed. We then climbed out of the ghyll on the left, up some interesting slabs of rock.

Making holds where none exists has always been a heinous crime in the climbing calendar (climbers turn a blind eye to necessary pitons though!) so Collie's action, self confessed, was regarded with disfavour. Nevertheless, the hold he cut was thankfully used by succeeding climbers, and the 'Collie Step' became part of history.

Collie was a bit like that though—unpredictable, roguish, and a sharp sardonic humorist. The story is told of how one day when he was climbing, his two companions held a loud conversation on the evils of tobacco, obviously intending that Collie should overhear it, for they knew he was a heavy smoker. He said nothing on the subject, but every time there was a difficult pitch to lead, he ostentatiously took out his pipe, lit it, and climbed with it in his mouth.

On the day following their ascent of Moss Ghyll the same trio made the first ascent of the notorious Great Gully of the Screes—not bad going for a Christmas holiday.

A year later another great climber made his appearance at Scafell. Owen Glynne Jones, despite his Welsh name, was to become the finest exponent of Lakeland rock-climbing during the remaining years of the century. A somewhat brusque personality denied him many friends, and in his formative climbing years he frequently climbed alone, doing some of the hardest routes of his day. So it was in January 1893 when he soloed Moss Ghyll. The fells were snowbound, the rocks cold and in places iced over. Not surprisingly Jones fell off at the Collie Step, and had he not arranged a rope in a sort of automatic belay he would have gone 250 feet to the scree below. As it was he cracked two ribs and suffered numerous bruises, though these injuries did not prevent him from attacking the pitch again and successfully completing the climb. As if to show the Ghyll who was boss he repeated his solo ascent two days later.

Jones's real pioneering on Scafell began four years later, after he had met and become firm friends with the two Keswick photographers, George and Ashley Abraham. Some interesting routes flowed from this partnership, though strangely enough

6

The Screes, Wastwater

the two climbs that are most popular with present-day climbers came when the trio teamed up with other partners. The Abrahams, with that intrepid inventor of Derbyshire gritstone climbing, J. W. Puttrell, made a long, elegant route up the rocks to the left of Botterill's Slab, and called it the *Keswick Brothers' Climb*. Jones, with G. T. Walker, exploring from the ledges above *Rake's Progress* at the foot of the Pinnacle, made the extremely delicate climb now known as *Jones' Route Direct from Lord's Rake*: a climb which involves as its crux a very exposed and off-balance mantelshelf move.

Jones and the Abrahams brought a hint of professionalism to climbing which did not go down well with the more conservative elements in the climbing world. In their Keswick shop the brothers sold photographs of Jones in action on the rocks (these could still be purchased until recently when the business closed) and in return they provided Jones with illustrations for his book, *Rock Climbing in the English Lake District*, the guide-book in which he laid down the standards of difficulty which have since been adopted, with some modifications, by rock-climbers throughout Britain.

Jones was well in advance of his time. He tried Botterill's Slab but was stopped by ice, and though he made some fine gully climbs elsewhere, he showed that open faces could be successfully attacked also. It was a tragedy to British climbing that he was killed in an Alpine accident in 1899 when he was at the height of his powers.

With face climbing coming into prominence it was obvious to anyone who knew the crag that the great Slab sloping up to the left of the Central Buttress would be a prize of major magnitude. It fell eventually to Fred Botterill, a Yorkshire gritstoner, and one of the most technically accomplished climbers of his day. The time was June 1903, and Botterill pushed out up the smooth slab carrying his ice axe and wearing his Norfolk tweeds in the approved fashion of the day. I doubt if anyone but a gritstoner could have done the climb that followed. The holds were small, the exposure extreme, and there were no resting places where Botterill could stand to bring up his companions. When he was a considerable way up he lost his ice axe, which went spearing down into Rake's

Progress—symbolic of the final rejection of Alpine values which this new route represented. There was still time for courtesy though: Botterill observed a party of ladies passing below the cliff, and as they looked up at him, he politely raised his hat. I find this action symbolic too, symbolic of the new balance climbing that was to put the sport on its modern progress.

Fred Botterill's climb is still rated as 'very severe', and though the present guide-books describe it as mild for its grade, one must remember that there has been seventy years of progress since it was first climbed. Botterill's great promise as a climber never matured: there was an accident on Gable in which his leader was killed, and Botterill was so upset by this that he retired from climbing altogether. Had he persisted he would most assuredly have rivalled the legendary Jones.

After Botterill's fine effort, the crag rested for almost a decade before anyone of comparable stature came along, but in September 1911, John Laycock, another gritstone expert, introduced a young friend to the crag who was to have a dramatic impact not only on Scafell, but on British climbing as a whole. Siegfried Herford was an undergraduate at Manchester University and had just begun scrambling on the edges of rock that fringe the bleak Kinder plateau in Derbyshire when Laycock had met him the previous year. The lad had such innate ability and promise that Laycock at once invited him to become a regular companion. That Laycock's judgement was rapidly proved correct is a matter of history. The tremendous sweep of Scafell so impressed the young Herford that he returned the following Easter with a new companion, George Sansom. Without previous investigation Herford immediately led a direct route from Lord's Rake to Hopkinson's Cairn.

This was an astonishing break-through. Hopkinson's Cairn had been placed on a ledge of the Pinnacle in 1887 by Edward Hopkinson when he and his brothers had tried to descend the Pinnacle, and it represented the limit of their descent. A virtually blank wall separated the Cairn from the easier ground near Lord's Rake, but the wall was such an obvious challenge that virtually every climber of note had tried to reach the Cairn from the Rake. All had failed, and it was whilst attempting this climb that

Broadrick and his companions had fallen to their deaths in 1903. Climbing in his stockinged feet for greater delicacy of hold, Herford ran out 130 feet of rope in a single pitch, now known as Herford's Slab, to reach the Cairn. Today, with modern aids, it can be done much more safely, but it is still not easy, and it shows quite forcibly the standard that Herford had achieved.

Elated by their success, Herford and Sansom returned in June to complete another of the incomplete Hopkinson routes—a face climb known for some reason as *Hopkinson's Gully*, though the 'gully' part is largely imagination.

A few months later they added a Girdle Traverse to the crag. This is a form of climb which instead of going *up* the rocks goes *across* them. It had been invented by Herford on the little gritstone crag of Castle Naze, and it had the obvious advantage of lengthening the amount of climbing that could be done. Nowadays all the major crags have their 'Girdles'.

The Girdle of Scafell was not excessively difficult, but it did give Herford a unique opportunity of exploring the full length of the crag. From a ledge on Central Buttress (the Oval) he saw a remarkable crack soaring up into a sharp flake, and recognized at once a new, difficult challenge.

A good part of the next summer was occupied in exploring around the Flake Crack. As Sansom had gone abroad after the first week or so, his place was taken by Jeffcoat, another of Herford's gritstone companions, and he it was who belayed himself on a curious ledge above the Flake (Jeffcoat's Ledge) whilst Herford, held by the rope, descended the Flake Crack.

Herford was convinced that the Crack could be climbed. The following Easter, Herford, Sansom, Gibson and Holland returned for assault, sad only in the knowledge that Jeffcoat was unable to be present. Herford and Sansom climbed the Crack on a rope held from above, but when they tried to lead it both men failed. Determined not to give in, they returned the following day, and by some complicated rope tactics managed to climb the Flake and reach Jeffcoat's Ledge. Herford led, the others following one by one, and they even managed to pick up a 'hitch hiker'— D. G. Murray, who had been watching them, and who was later to create the famous *Murray's Route* on Dow Crag.

Feeling they had done enough for one day they traversed off from Jeffcoat's Ledge. Two days later they returned to the Ledge, and this time with Sansom leading, climbed the delicate upper part of the buttress. George Sansom's part in the story of Central Buttress has never really been appreciated to its proper degree—many of today's climbers think that the delicate traverses above Jeffcoat's Ledge are technically quite as difficult as the Flake Crack.

Nevertheless, there is no doubt that the Central Buttress was Herford's climb. It was at once the boldest, hardest lead ever done on British rock, and a yardstick by which all other climbs were measured for years to come. Even today, almost sixty years later, it is still graded 'hard very severe' and remains one of the great climbs of all times.

What might Herford not have done had the First World War not intervened? Not yet 24 years old, he was killed by a sniper's bullet at Ypres.

After the War, the crag saw the advent of H. M. Kelly, who was to put up more new routes hereabouts than anyone else, but who never matched the greatness of 'C.B.' Kelly's finest achievement was the superbly exposed *Moss Ghyll Grooves*, starting up the Central Buttress side of Moss Ghyll.

By the '30s rock-climbers had become much more cosmopolitan, and a climber was as likely to put up a route in Wales one week and the Lake District the next. Scafell too was changing in its challenge. With the main face virtually worked out, climbers turned to the East Buttress; a sombre cliff running down towards Eskdale from Mickledore, and found here a new hardness to match their increasing powers. Colin Kirkus, predominantly a Welsh climber, put up *Mickledore Grooves* in 1931 on the East Buttress, and his close friend Maurice Linnell followed this by adding the superb *Great Eastern Route* the following year and *Overhanging Wall* the year after that.

The East Buttress began to dominate Scafell climbing and all the Lakeland experts gave it their attention. Jim Birkett added *May Day Climb*, the *Girdle*, *Gremlin's Groove* and *South Chimney*, and he was followed in the post-war years by the legendary Arthur Dolphin who put up *Pegasus* and *Hell's Groove*.

And the East Buttress remains the dominant crag today, with

new routes as hard as you are likely to find anywhere. It is the crag for the expert—there is nothing on these grim bastions for a man of modest climbing skill.

Nowadays, with fast roads and readily available transport, the distinction between Welsh and Lakeland climbers or between gritstoners and non-gritstoners, blur and ultimately vanish. Everyone climbs everywhere. Only the Scots, isolated in their northern fastnesses, have kept some semblance of regional identity. What is particularly striking, however, in the history of Scafell, is the part played by gritstone in its development. Herford is the outstanding example, of course, but there was Botterill, Kelly, Frankland, Kirkus and Dolphin, amongst others, who reached a high degree of gritstone skill which they transferred to Scafell and in so doing pushed up standards. Years later the same thing was to happen in Wales, and the whole standard of British climbing was to rise as a result.

Though Scafell Crag and the East Buttress are the mecca for rock-climbers, when winter comes and lays a mantle of snow over the central fells, the focus of activity shifts to Great End, the north-facing terminus of the Scafell massif. The crag is bold and black and the snow lies on it deeper and longer than anywhere else.

Steep snow slopes cover the long banks of scree which tumble down below the crag towards Grains Gill. Above this, the crag is seamed with a number of gullies, glistening white against the surrounding black buttresses, and two of them catch the eye immediately.

In the middle is the huge rift of Central Gully, perhaps the most famous snow and ice climb in England. It narrows to a deep channel in which the famous 'ice bulge' occurs—a twenty-foot convex wall of ice that is the crux of the climb. Towards the top, however, the gully opens out into an immense funnel which is easy to climb but has its own dangers in terms of avalanches. When the snow is unstable, Central Gully is a place to keep away from.

Further left is the long, challenging gash of South-East Gully; a rather more serious climb. . . .

Stuart Thomas and I set out from the Robertson Lamb Hut in

Langdale early one February morning to 'take a look at' Great End. We had both done the Central Gully in previous years, but neither of us had found an opportunity of tackling the South-East. Conditions seemed right: Stuart was on top form, though I, as usual, was less enthusiastic.

By the time we reached the foot of the mountain I was feeling desperately tired, through weeks of inactivity and the consequent lack of fitness. My spirits flagged; the day was grey and inhospitable, the low clouds heavy with a promise of more snow.

Stuart had raced ahead, across the steep slopes of ice and snow which are such a feature of Great End in winter, and now stood waiting for me at a black pinnacle of rock below the main face. I lurched across towards him, took a wrong line which involved me in some nastily verglassed ledges and beat a hasty, insecure retreat to my starting point. My gloom deepened. I was not even thinking straight; the veriest novice would not make a mistake like that! I cursed myself and the mountain, lurched out on to the steep slopes once more, crampons biting into the ice, and stamped my way over towards my companion. It took me two pauses before I reached him; pauses in which I leant heavily on my ice axe, feeling sorry for myself, wondering what a man of 40-odd was doing in such a place anyway.

"Well, what d'ye think?" It was Stuart's universal greeting under such circumstances.

"I think it's going to snow again," I countered, tossing the ball back into his court.

"Might as well have a look now we're here."

It was the traditional response and I had expected no other.

We roped up at the foot of the South-East Gully. The gully twisted up into the mist, a narrow ribbon of ice enclosed by rock, but the first pitch seemed straightforward enough: an ice ramp with a chockstone at its head. Stuart led off and it was not long before we were both standing above the chock. Now that battle was joined, so to speak, things felt much better. My spirits revived and my tiredness left me.

The gully bed was fairly steep, alternately hard snow and pure ice, so that there was little opportunity for us to travel together, Alpine fashion. Moreover, it began to snow, and soon little avalanches of powder snow were trickling down the gully bed, hissing and swishing. They could do us no harm, they were much too small for that, but they were a constant reminder of the hostility of the mountain.

After several pitches the gully divided into two, with the true gully forking off to the right and a subsidiary gully breaking away into the jumbled face of the crag on the left. The few hundred feet we had climbed were sufficient to transform the rocks into ice encrusted grotesque shapes, like giant meringues. Our way led to the right and to the principal obstacle of the route.

The bed of the gully reared up into a sheer wall fifteen or twenty feet high. It was draped in ice and on such breaks and ledges as existed fresh powder snow had piled itself in unwelcome heaps.

Stuart took the lead whilst I found a good rock spike for a belay. His way led over to the left where there was a groove between the obstacle and the retaining wall of the gully. It was steep, delicate climbing: hanging on with one hand whilst he cleared away powder snow with the other and chipped handholds in the ice beneath. Every minute or so he would be satisfied with his handwork and pull up one or two moves, his crampon prongs scraping into the ice as he sought for purchase with his feet.

After he had climbed vertically for a few feet up the corner he moved delicately out on to the upper part of the ice wall until he was able to surmount the lip and secure safe lodgment on the far side. I followed up the route, full of admiration at Stuart's neat little lead, for the ice in the groove was of poor quality; brittle, watery stuff without substance.

It began to snow even harder, and the gully, though never again matching the pitch we had just overcome never relented sufficiently to allow us to travel together. As we pulled out at the top, after a fine finishing snow pitch, we were alone in a white world of swirling snowflakes.

Visibility was down to about ten yards; not a white-out exactly, but bad enough. However, we thought we knew our way and confidently plodded towards the boulder-strewn shoulder of the fell leading to Esk Hause. Fortunately there was no wind: just swirling mist and gently falling snowflakes.

A line of cairns led us to the Hause, but though it had by this time stopped snowing, the mist was as thick as ever. It was time to get out the map and compass, for we had no idea of which direction to take.

There is something oddly satisfying about defying Nature at her worst, when you know that you have the upper hand. Adequately clothed against excesses of weather, armed with ice axe and fed with chocolate bars, there seems nothing that you might not dare Nature to do, and the harder Nature pushes the more exhilarating the experience and later, in the pub, the greater the 'victory'—though everybody is very self-effacing about it in true British style. "It's hell up there," somebody says, parodying an American film hero, and everyone laughs.

But the real truth of the matter is that the protagonists *are not equal* and never will be, and any superiority which a mountaineer may momentarily feel over his surroundings is totally illusory. Nature is inanimate, unfeeling, uncaring and one hundred per cent hostile and anyone who takes up its challenge romantically thinking otherwise is a fool. Man on the other hand, is a delicate living mechanism, subject to a thousand and one inperfections and failings, many of which, in high fells, could bring disaster.

The mountaineer's greatest enemy is carelessness and forgetfulness; failings which have caused the deaths of a great many skilful climbers.

Like not having a compass. We searched through the rucksacks, and though we found a map in its appointed place, neither of us had a compass. Normally, I carry a compass in the top pocket of my rucksack on all occasions, but it was not there this time—taken out for some purpose and never replaced. Sheer carelessness.

The loss of the compass tipped the scales in favour of the mountains. Without a knowledge of direction one could wander round for hours in such a thick mist, even become benighted, and though we both had protective down clothing, a night on the snowbound fells was less than attractive.

We tried every dodge we knew to deduce our direction but, except for one brief moment when a sudden gap appeared in the clouds, the mist was impenetrable. The gap revealed a high peak, glistening with fresh snow and totally unrecognizable. It looked more Alpine than Cumbrian, but it dashed our hopes by its very existence—there ought not to have been a peak in that direction!

The only sensible thing to do was get down below the mist level before nightfall and this was easy enough to do by simply following the lay of the land. As we broke free from the cloud we saw a long sombre valley stretched before us and for a few minutes we thought we had struck Langstrath and our hopes lifted—we could cut back over Stake Pass into Langdale and still be home for supper. But as we descended such sanguine hopes evaporated. The snaking river in its wild, wide valley could only be the Esk, and we knew it would be many hours before we finally reached home.

4

Gable and Pillar

IT IS not by chance that the memorial to those members of the Fell and Rock Club who died in the two wars was erected on the summit of Great Gable. When you think of the sites that might have been chosen—the summit of Scafell Pike, highest fell of all; the top of Pillar Rock, noblest of rock monuments—a stranger may wonder why Great Gable? The answer surely lies in the fact that of all the Lakeland fells, Gable represents the spirit of Lakeland. It is the quintessential fell; the one remembered when others are forgotten. Gable is as much romance as reality, like the Matterhorn, and just as the Matterhorn symbolizes the Alps so too Gable symbolizes Lakeland.

Who knows what it is about Gable that arouses such universal regard? The name perhaps, one of the most evocative in the area, or the associations with the Napes and Napes Needle? Whatever else it may be it surely cannot be the profile of the fell, for in this matter Gable is outclassed a dozen times at least. From most points of the compass the fell is either hidden or insignificant, and even the traditional view from Wasdale Head is scarcely more than average. You must climb Lingmell, or at least traverse the Corridor Route, to see the fell at its best.

Kirk Fell, the odd man out in this group of fells because of its regular conical shape, has no such problems. You look at it from Wasdale Head, admire its bulk, and symmetry, and leave it at that. This view gives the essence of Kirk Fell, for it hides nothing, and there is nothing to hide. From the north the view is different, the fell looks lumpy and even adorned with a modicum of crags, but it is less of the real Kirk Fell than that seen from Wasdale. In any case, neither Gable nor Kirk Fell ever form an integral part of the whole group. They are isolationist in attitudes, and are separated from the rest of the fells by Mosedale and the deep col of the Black Sail Pass. And another factor, strangely disturbing to the eye, is the odd baldness of Kirk Fell—a plain grass mountain set amongst a clutch of peaks whose rocky nature is legendary.

There is a case to be made out for not looking at all the group in one grand *coup d'œil*, but to treat Gable, Kirk Fell and the rest as three separate entities, when each then has its own magnificence.

Grandest of all, of course, is the ridge which includes Pillar, Steeple and Haycock, and the rather complex side ridges and corries which bolster these peaks from the south. The top of the Corpse Road over Burnmoor, above Wasdale Hall, or the summit of the Screes, give superb views of this massif.

Yet the best side of this ridge, from an observer's viewpoint, should be that of the north, overlooking Ennerdale. It does not seem to come off somehow: the best of the craggy bits seem to merge into the fellsides (even the great Pillar Rock) and it cannot compare, say, with the High Stile ridge as seen from the Buttermere Valley. Moreover, Ennerdale is itself a depressing place, claustrophobically blanketed with the dark pines of the Forestry Commission. Surely the time has come when we ought to ask ourselves whether these trees are really necessary? Can we afford to give up one of the principal dales of the Western Lakes to commerce? The trees around Thirlmere are bad enough, but those in Ennerdale are infinitely worse.

All in all, this is not a group of fells whose distant prospects are among its best assets. Rather is it a group to be seen at close hand, in parts, for more than any other group in the Lakes perhaps, the sum of the parts is greater than the whole.

Although Wasdale Head is the most convenient centre for the entire group, Great Gable is more frequently visited from Borrowdale. This is partly because there are more tourists in Borrowdale anyway, and partly because the access to the mountain by the Sty Head Gill is relatively easier, though longer, than the way up from Wasdale. Add to this the knowledge that it is easier still from a car parked at the summit of Honister Pass, and you can see why the steep slopes on the Wasdale side are shunned by all but the hardy walkers.

The Sty Head pass is worth closer attention, however, in so far as it ranks with Rossett Gill as one of the main arteries of the western fells. Between them they control the heights: Rossett Gill from Esk Hause, and Sty Head pass from Sty Head itself. They are like dipoles around which the fells revolve, or perhaps in city terms, they stand to one another as Piccadilly Circus does to Trafalgar Square.

In walking terms though, the comparison should not be too evenly made—it is much easier to walk up Sty Head Gill from Borrowdale than it is to walk up Rossett Gill from Langdale. Even the ascent to Sty Head from Wasdale Head, across the lower slopes of Gable, is not too strenuous: one of those places which seem to get easier every time you do it. At the same time it is rather exposed—a mere track trickling upwards across a very steep fellside—and it was with something akin to disbelief that I once came across a cyclist, struggling on the steepest bit, his cycle slung across his shoulders, and perspiration, as Shakespeare put it, "larding the lean ground he walked along".

I helped him up the slope. "I thought this was a pass," he complained between hard breaths.

"It is," I said.

"Then where does the road begin?"

"In Borrowdale."

I left him resting by Sty Head Tarn, contemplating the folly of using inadequate maps.

For those without cycles, however, the crossing of Sty Head Pass is one of the easiest and most interesting walks between any two valleys of the Lake District. Though the path up from Stockley Bridge is now cruelly worn into scarred ribbons, like the one up Mill Gill in Langdale, it does give superb views into Borrowdale. The tarn too, just before Sty Head itself is reached, is a lovely sheet of water, and then, hidden at first by a fold and corner of fell, the whole of Wasdale burst into view, the fields criss-crossed with their thick and numerous stone walls, a reminder that the life of a farmer in this dale is one of constant battle against rock.

Anyone worth his salt will descend into Wasdale, if only for a pint at the Wastwater Hotel: one of the handful of hotels in our mountains irrevocably associated with climbers. This is where the pioneers set out from when rock-climbing was in its infancy: Collie, Jones, Haskett Smith—between them they made the place something of a shrine. Modern climbers are much less polarized, and all these old centres have declined in importance, but nothing can take from them their place in mountain history.

To return from Wasdale Head to Borrowdale by any other route than Sty Head, is a much more strenuous undertaking than the Pass itself. Probably the most popular is to ascend the very steep spur of fell which Gable points down into the valley, known as Gavel Neese. This grassy nose is extremely hard going while it lasts, and when it gives out on to the scree between Gable and Kirk Fell, the best track is not readily apparent. But it is not long before it joins the path to the Drum House which leads directly to Honister, or a more ambitious descent can be made to Seathwaite via Gillercomb and Sour Milk Gill.

The whole of this track between Wasdale and Honister was once the pack-horse route for goods being sent from Borrowdale to Ravensglass for shipment. It is known as Moses Trod, supposedly named after an illicit whisky distiller called Moses who used the route to move his goods from his still on Fleetwith to the welcoming farmers of Wasdale. In those days, of course, Honister Pass was not the highway it is today, and this high level route, contouring behind Grey Knotts, Brandreth, Green Gable and Great Gable, was really an ingenious solution to a crossing of the fells—comparable in its way to the use which the Romans made of High Street, over in the east. From a casual glance at the map there seems little sense in it: that Sty Head would always be preferable, and yet it proves to be a remarkably level and quick way.

For anyone with a motor-car, it certainly offers the easiest way of all to climb Great Gable, and curiously enough, perhaps the best. Moreover, by the merest of deviations from Moses Trod, a number of other summits can be crossed *en route*: Grey Knotts (2,287 feet), Brandreth (2,344 feet) and Green Gable (2,603 feet), though of respectable height above sea level are perpetual reminders that height alone never made a mountain. From the Fleetwith Moor they are simple hummocks. They do not, of course, seem to belong to the group of fells we are considering at all, but who would climb them except as a way to Gable?

The views to the west from Moses Trod (or its alternative just mentioned) can only be described as sweeping. The fault, if any, lies in the fact that the going is so good underfoot, so easy, that one seldom stops to look. Ahead, the bulk of Kirk Fell and the huge black buttresses of Gable Crag draw the walker as if by a magnet.

Whether or not Grey Knotts and Brandreth are included in the walk, Green Gable must be crossed in order to attain Windy Gap, the col between Green and Great Gables. To do otherwise means a rough ascent up the Stone Cove side of the col, and anyway, why not have two fells for the price of one? From Wind Gap the path goes up, in parts quite steep and a bit rocky, but nothing to worry about for any average walker. The top (2,949 feet) is rather flat, and comes much more quickly than you imagine it will, which is the reverse of usual fell climbing!

If the top of Gable is not very exciting, more interest can be had by walking over to the Westmorland Cairn which perches on the crags of the same name, overlooking the Napes Ridges. All Wasdale lies spread out like a carpet below: the incredible criss-cross of stone walls on the green patches of the valley head, the hotel, church and farm buildings, and the road ribboning away to meet Wastwater. Steep fells embrace the little valley, and with the lake, seem to cut the dale off from the rest of civilization.

Having traversed Great Gable in every conceivable direction at one time or another, I find the way from Honister cannot be bettered for an ascent of this fell. Other ways have too many drawbacks for my liking—the ordinary way from Sty Head (the way the ponies came in Victorian times, bearing well-dressed ladies to as near the top as ponies could) is rather dull and you never see anything of the real quality of the mountain from start to finish; and the alternative way up to Windy Gap by Aaron Slack is claustrophobic and hard going—these are better as ways down, for anyone who wants variety. As for the western side, from Beck Head between Gable and Kirk Fell, this has interminable boulder slopes best left strictly alone.

There is a variant to the Fleetwith Moor approach which is much harder going but perhaps ever finer if considered purely as a mountain ascent. This is to start from Seathwaite and climb up the steep rocky track by the side of Sour Milk Gill—one of the best and most direct starts to any climb in the district. The rough track demands attention (especially near the top) but the gill itself is worth looking at from time to time as you pause in your labours. It really is a delightful waterfall—much better than Southey's oft-quoted waters of Lodore. In full spate it can be quite frightening, doubly so if you happen to be camped on the small camp site near the Gill foot!

The well-known Seathwaite Slabs are perched near the start of this ascent. They consist essentially of a flat plane of rock, perhaps thirty or forty feet high, tilted at an admirable angle for delicate rock climbing. As a place for beginners to learn the art of balance on rock I know of no better in the whole district. A morning spent here, under proper instruction, will teach you more about the basics of climbing than a whole week of thrutching up long, boring 'moderates'. There are some more rocks above the Gill, known as the Upper Seathwaite Slabs but these are too easily angled for anything except seeing how far you can traverse them without using your hands.

The Gill leads up into the secret hanging valley of Gillercomb, boggy underfoot but ringed with impressive crags which contain some of the best—and the worst—climbs in Lakeland for the modest climber. The long *Grey Knotts Face* with its unique letter-box pitch is a classic 'difficult', which some people find quite hard, whilst *Gillercomb Buttress* is a 'severe' grade climb, rather gentle for its standard, and equally popular. On the other hand, the long, rambling 'moderate' called *Rabbit's Trod* is scarcely a climb at all, and must surely rank as one of the worst routes in the country.

The way up to Gable lies along Gillercomb and out of the top end of the valley where the crags give way to grass contours sweeping round to meet Base Brown.

Many years ago a group of us youngsters came this way one

Great Gable

Easter, intent on climbing the Gables then traversing over by Esk Hause to Rossett Gill and Langdale. The day was crisply blue, the air sharp, the fells covered with a foot of good snow.

Our heavy framed rucksacks made the pull up by Sour Milk Gill rough going under the conditions and we looked forward to easier progress in Gillercomb. Judge our surprise when, arriving at the top of the Gill and entering the valley, we found that the whole sweep of the valley head round to Base Brown was rimmed with the most beautiful impenetrable cornice.

Impenetrable to us, that is, for we had no ice axes, crampons or ropes—we could not afford them, and even if we could, I doubt whether any were obtainable in those lean wartime years.

Of course, we ought to have turned back. There is no other logical way out of Gillercomb if the rim is impassable. But the thought of retreat did not appeal to us, and the rock buttresses seemed pretty free of snow, as did the gullies.

We chose a gully that offered a direct route to the top of the crags and soon we were involved in some desperate scrambling over verglassed chockstones. None of us at that time had undergone his rock-climbing apprenticeship, but I remember that we all seemed to enjoy this novel and highly dangerous ascent—as I look back on it I shudder at our boyhood ignorance.

Danger there certainly was. The top of the gully narrowed a bit and then opened out into a typical funnel shape. The funnel was lined in pure ice, totally without purchase.

I think that for the first time we began to doubt the wisdom of our action. By some crafty manoeuvring on the part of the others I had been pushed to the front, and I distinctly remember looking down between my legs at their upturned, expectant faces. They were poised in a wild variety of awkward positions, and below them, a long way below, was the floor of the valley.

A retreat down the gully was quite impossible and we seemed doomed to remain trapped in our icy slot until the eye of faith spied one chance. On the vertical left wall a stream trickled over from the moor above. It made the wall slimy but it did not seem verglassed, and I reckoned that the stream might have cut through the snow above leaving a wet but otherwise rocky exit.

It was not all that far, the climb up the wall, but it was slippery

7

Climbing on Gable

and awkward. If my theory proved incorrect, if the stream flowed *underneath* the snow, then I would have been in real trouble.

I pulled over the lip of the gully, and to my immense relief saw the black path of the stream, free of snow and ice. My hands were frozen with icy water, my trousers soaked, but I was safely up. Whether we continued our walk up Gable I cannot now recall. All I do remember is how thankful we all were to emerge from the gully. Though we said nothing at the time, I think we all realized, in the words of Wellington, that it had been "a damned close-run thing".

It is sad that all the best ways up Gable for a walker are round the back, so to speak, for they all omit the finest part of the mountain—the glorious jumble of the Napes.

The Napes comprise a series of rock ridges and outcrops jutting out from the stony fellside overlooking Wasdale. They do not reach up to the summit of the mountain—Westmorland Crags are above them—and for this reason you cannot look down from the mountain top upon their intricate crags and gullies, as you might reasonably expect. Nor for that matter can you see them properly from the valley below or from their flanks: from these viewpoints they are as nothing, mere excrescences which merge into the sombre rocky shades of the fellside. From Lingmell's top you get some idea of their complex attractions—if the light is in the right quarter, quite a good idea—but they really need to be explored at close hand.

I think it was Haskett-Smith who once described the Napes as one of the four finest climbing grounds in England, and though this is no longer the case, the Napes do retain something that is unique. The strange, close packed nature of the ridges have a lot to do with it; almost like Alpine ridges of the Chamonix sort but very much smaller of course; the total absence of gullies of the climbable kind; the weird sweep of red screes at Great Hell Gate, and of course, the Needle.

It is still a paradise for rock-climbers, provided they are content with climbs which are less than the modern extremes, but not only that, by a touch of mountain irony, the Napes also provides one of the finest, most exciting walks in Britain. Perhaps 'scramble' might be a better description since you certainly need to use hands as well as feet on this fantastic traverse. Call it what you will, it still ranks with the best of its kind.

The basic idea of the route is really simple: it is to traverse the foot of the Napes from Sty Head to Beck Head (done in the other direction it is not nearly as fine). Since the ridges of the Napes jut out from what is already a very steep fellside it is obvious that any such walk must be somewhat 'airy', and indeed so it proves.

The path slopes up the shoulder of the fell from Sty Head and soon reaches the huge tumbled boulders below Kern Knotts, a steep buttress with a flat, open-book corner on the left page of which is the unmistakable *Kern Knotts Crack*.

Although Kern Knotts has some much harder climbs nowadays it is because of this celebrated crack that the outcrop has become so well known. A few years ago a picture of a climber making an elegant ascent of *Kern Knotts Crack* was almost *de rigueur* for textbooks on climbing. Ever since the days of Jones and the Abraham brothers it has been one of the most photographed pitches of British rock.

The reasons for this are not hard to find. In the first place it is easy to reach, requiring no hazards on the part of the photographer, and in the second place, given the right lighting conditions, it can make a really spectacular picture.

It was regarded by some of the pioneers as too severe to be even attempted. J. W. Robinson, who climbed the much easier *Kern Knotts Chimney* with O. G. Jones on Boxing Day, 1893, told the virtuoso that if ever he climbed the Crack he would never speak to him again. Whether he kept his promise, I do not know, but Jones made the first ascent four years later with H. C. Bowen.

They avoided the lower part of the chimney by a neat little mossy traverse, which is still the most popular way of tackling it. The direct start (done the following year by the Welsh expert, W. R. Reade) is too strenuous for most tastes. Indeed this comment applies to all the lower part of the Crack, as far as the chockstone, and it is ironical that the Crack is usually 'climbed' by being avoided until the easier upper section can be reached!

Despite the fact that it is a very short route by local standards, more akin to the cracks of a gritstone outcrop, it has always been a popular route, and remains so to this day. Its popularity has led to the holds becoming highly polished through wear, and so anyone who approaches *Kern Knotts Crack* with the idea that it is a simple, old-fashioned 'severe', is in for something of a shock. It is, in fact, quite hard, and I have known more than one 'expert' retreat from the Crack and climb the (theoretically) harder adjacent *Innominate Crack* instead.

Round the corner is the deep straight gash of the Chimney which makes an alternative way up (and much longer) for those whose ambitions do not include the famous Crack. It is a good old-fashioned chimney climb of the best sort and well worth climbing.

Although it is not obvious to the walker, the track at Kern Knotts is actually traversing between upper and lower crags. In a short distance it traverses above another outcrop (Lower Kern Knotts West) and when this is passed, there remain numerous smaller outcrops and very steep scree almost the whole way to its far end. It is this juxtaposition of outcrop and scree which gives the walk its sense of spaciousness.

The track curves round the scree beyond Kern Knotts and soon becomes rocky, after which it moderates and rises towards the red screes of Great Hell Gate. Tophet Bastion guards the screes, and seen from here looks like a smaller edition of the Requin as seen from the Mer de Glace. For the first time you become aware of the singular nature of the Napes: that they stand out from the parent fell, rather than be part of it. A weird little pillar guards the narrows at Hell Gate, and if you have sharp eyes you might even pick out the so-called Shark's Fin pitch of Tophet Bastion, but the over-all impression is one of a steep scree shoot and a confused, exciting jumble of rocks.

This excitement, an uplifting of boyish spirits, is more noticeable at the Napes than anywhere else, with the possible exception of Pillar. I realize that rock-climbers have sterner tests, bolder buttresses, than any found on Gable, but there is something about the Napes which will revive flagging spirits in a manner which Scafell or Dow can never do. This is emphasized as the walk continues, and the intricacies of the ridges are revealed, bit by bit. Each corner of the track is a new experience, a new juxtaposition

of rock and sky and scree—but mainly of rock. Those who enjoy
the close acquaintance of fantastic rock architecture cannot fail
to be impressed, and the only snag, if it be one, is that the track is
so narrow that walking and looking cannot be safely combined.

There is absolutely nothing difficult or dangerous about the
Gable traverse, providing you keep to the lower track throughout
and are not tempted to go scrambling up inviting-looking gullies
and grassy ledges, most of which carry intriguing little tracks of
their own made by climbers taking short cuts and ramblers who
have got lost.

However, having said this, let me hasten to add that if you do
take the lower track you will miss the best part of the whole
excursion, for there is an upper way, which parts company with
the parent track just beyond Great Hell Gate and slopes up towards Napes Needle. There are two reasons for preferring this
upper path: one, it is the only way you will ever get a real view
of the Needle, and two: it gives one of the best scrambles in
Lakeland.

There is nothing quite like it elsewhere. It is more difficult than
Jack's Rake, much more difficult than Striding Edge or Sharp
Edge and longer than the difficult part of Rake's Progress on
Scafell. It differs from all these, however, in so far as each bit of
difficulty is followed by a relatively easy way off—or, as climbers
say, escape is possible at various points. It is immensely popular!
I have seen parties of fat (but fit) middle-aged ladies being guided
across it, and groups of excited schoolchildren. Personally, I
would take neither, but it goes to show some of the additional
hazards you are likely to meet on the way.

The track slopes up into Needle Gully below the obelisk itself,
but anyone who has a modicum of rock-climbing ability will
probably prefer the exercise known as 'Threading the Needle'—
that is, to scramble up the narrow gap between the Needle and
Needle Ridge to the sharp col, and from there descend into
Needle Gully. It is not really all that difficult and the holds are
generously large, if somewhat polished by the passage of
thousands of boots.

It is also possible to scramble directly up Needle Gully from
the lower path (most people do) but it is an annoying place for

loose stones, often heavily trafficked with careless people who send them slithering down on to unfortunates below.

From the gully a short scramble up the left-hand wall leads to a large platform known as the Dress Circle from where the traditional view of Napes Needle can be seen. On a fine week-end it is likely to be crowded, for watching people climb Napes Needle is an unfailingly popular pastime hereabouts. And why not? For once the observer can see precisely what the climber is trying to achieve: he can see the point of the exercise, if you will forgive the pun! Fortunately for the poor climber, forced to make his moves under these fishbowl conditions, the crux of the route is out of sight round the shoulder of the Needle and he can struggle with the mantelshelf unobserved, to emerge like a butterfly in sunlight, dramatically poised for the final moves to the top.

You cannot really see the Needle properly from anywhere else except the Dress Circle (though there is a dramatic view looking *down* on to it from Needle Ridge). Photographs of the pinnacle have been so impressed on our minds that anything but the traditional view does not seem right, somehow.

All sorts of hyperbole have been larded on this famous pinnacle, so that fact begins to merge with fantasy, and the place becomes a sort of tribal totem for homage by fell lovers. It is, of course, a free standing pinnacle (about 60 feet high) and as such fairly unusual in our British hills, though by no means unique. It is not especially difficult to climb, though wear is making it harder every year, and its chief advantage over its rivals lies in the fact that it is easily the most elegant of them all. It really is pointed, and anyone who has been to the top will tell you there is very little room there for a rope of three people.

The first ascent, solo, by Haskett Smith in 1886 is regarded by many climbers as the birth of rock-climbing as a sport, and if one had to choose a symbolic landmark for such an event, then the Needle might as well fill the rôle. But it was not the first rock-climb by any means—Needle Ridge itself was climbed two years earlier.

Quite apart from the first ascent, it is redolent of history. It was a photograph of the Needle in a Strand shop which inspired O. G. Jones to try his hand at climbing. In later years Norman Collie claimed that he rescued Jones from the Needle in those formative years—but there seems no foundation for the story, and it might well have been Collie just stirring things up in his usual manner.

But Jones and Collie did climb the Needle together on the first ascent of the *Lingmell Crack* (1892), the first occasion that another route up it, other than Haskett Smith's original route, was attempted. Others followed, Slingsby did a route, Herford put up the *Obverse* and even the notorious Aleister Crowley, self-styled Great Beast, made a new line. Oddly enough, despite the attentions of the famous, the most popular route nowadays is the *Arête*, discovered by a relatively unknown climber called Fowler.

Like all famous landmarks it has suffered its indignities too. People have stood on their heads on top of it, and it has been used for a rock-climbing 'race against the clock', won by Jerry Wright (who had climbed it hundreds of times as a guide) in some fantastically minimal time.

Cutting through all the mystique and brouhaha, the question remains, what is the Needle like as a climb, *now*? The answer, I think most climbers would agree, is surprisingly good. It is neat, elegant, and varied—and except for sheer difficulty, what more can one ask for from sixty feet of rock? In any case, one cannot entirely escape tradition—if you are a rock-climber, then fell-walking friends always ask, "Have you climbed the Needle?", just as people always ask alpinists whether they have climbed the Matterhorn. If the answer is "No", then you might as well shut up, even though you have just returned from *Dovedale Grooves*, *Central Buttress*, or some other major epic.

The Dress Circle is on Abbey Buttress and if you are lucky you may see someone climbing *Eagle's Nest Ridge*, immediately above your head. The Direct route is arguably the best climb on Gable: exposed and serious, though not technically hard by present-day standards. It was led by G. A. Solly in 1893—incredibly, the third route on the Napes, and a daring lead for its day.

Beyond the Dress Circle the traverse becomes more exposed and there are one or two awkward places, particularly a little slab at the start. Finally the path skirts below the Arrowhead Ridge (another fine pinnacle here) and reaches Little Hell Gate at the Sphinx Rock. Though the route is variable in places, it is only marginally so; remaining a high-grade scramble throughout.

Like its better-known twin, at the beginning of the traverse, Little Hell Gate is a long sweep of scree descending the side of the mountain. At this juncture the structure of the Great Napes becomes apparent: ribs of free standing rock jutting out from the huge scree mantle of the mountain, which enfolds them like a cloak. The top of the slopes is like a true mountain ridge, with its narrows and cols.

There is even a summit from which another and gentler ridge merges into the fellside below the upper rocks of Westmorland Crags.

Great Hell Gate is used as the way down from the crags by most climbers: a skittering scree run if ever there was one, not at all pleasant. It would, of course, be possible to reach the summit of Gable from the Traverse by either Great or Little Hell Gate, but only a masochist would knowingly embark on such a course.

From Little Hell Gate the Traverse continues below the White Napes to Beck Head, now much easier, and the walk can be continued right around the mountain back to Sty Head via Aaron Slack, but after the Napes, the rest is anticlimax.

Besides its individual climbs, the Napes is ideal as a place for the complete climbing circuit, where you go up one route and down another, something like an Alpine traverse. Ridges are essential if this sort of climbing is to make sense, and two of the ridges on the Napes seem specially designed for the beginner.

It was an Easter day more in keeping with the middle of August than March: the rocks were sun baked and shimmered in the heat. Brian Evans and I had walked up to the Napes from Borrowdale with our families, partly for pleasure and partly for business—he to make some sketches for a forthcoming guide-book and I to take some photographic slides to help illustrate a lecture on the history of rock-climbing I had been asked to give at Glasgow University. The bright sunshine ensured that our work was easily completed and we met below the Needle, with an hour or two to spare.

My son, Duncan, aged twelve, had been on one or two outcrop climbs but had never climbed on a higher crag, and it struck me that this was a fine introduction to the fells—a hot sun and long, easy climbing on genuine ridges. Brian liked the idea and so we set off up Needle Ridge, he and I leading through and Duncan acting as middle man throughout—a luxurious sort of climbing you can afford on these ridges where belays and stances are comfortably large.

I disappoint you if you are expecting a tale of intrepid daring or macabre accident. Ninety-nine per cent of climbing is not like that at all: it is a tale of enjoyment, simple, uncomplicated, even lazy. We pottered up the ridge and then, carrying the rope alpine fashion, walked the crest of the Napes to Arrowhead Ridge and pottered down that, over the Strid, then down the slabs by the Arrowhead itself to the path of the Traverse.

It was completely enjoyable—nearly six hundred feet of rock, none of it above 'diff.' standard. Of course, no rock-climber, and especially a young rock-climber, would be content solely with this, for challenge and difficulty play a large part in the game's attraction, but every now and again such a mountain circuit brings back the true enjoyment of the fells.

Can any two mountains be of greater contrast than Gable and Kirk Fell (2,630 feet)? What imp of the Gods ordained that they should lie next to one another, one crag-bound and scree covered, the other bald grass in a simple dome? At least, that is the way they appear from Wasdale, though less than justice is done to Kirk Fell to assume it has no crags at all—it even provides some rock-climbing on Boat How; one of the least popular of Lakeland's crags. Poor Kirk Fell! Hemmed in by Gable on the one hand and Pillar on the other, what chance does it have?

It is not even as though it was another Brandreth or Grey Knotts, which are so simple to ascend that a courtesy visit in passing is quite in order. Kirk Fell offers no concessions to popularity at all. To climb it involves steep unremitting toil no matter which approach you make: the path between Beck Head and Black Sail Pass consequently contours round the back and misses the summit altogether.

It also puts out of court what would otherwise be one of the finest ridge walks in the district—a traverse from Gable round to

Steeple and Red Pike (or Haycock, as fancy dictates). To include Kirk Fell destroys the character of the walk, simply because Kirk Fell is such a completely different kind of fell. There is an affinity of spirit between Gable and the others which Kirk Fell does not have: one feels that it has been misplaced by Nature—that it ought to be over Kentmere way, with its cousins, Ill Bell and Froswick.

But beyond the Black Sail Pass, the scene changes quite dramatically. A fine ridge runs up to the summit of Pillar, descends rapidly to Wind Gap, then rises again to Scoat Fell where branch ridges diverge from the main watershed to Steeple on the Ennerdale side and Red Pike on the Wasdale side. Further still, the ridge continues to Haycock but now it has become gentler, and soon it sprawls out in all directions to the humpy summits like Caw Fell and Seatallan.

It is Pillar, Steeple and Red Pike which command our interest in this part of the group—the head of Mosedale; that dark and brooding side valley stretching north-west from Wasdale Head. As a ridge walk it is short, and the ridges are not narrow in the sense that Striding Edge is narrow, nor are there any intrinsic difficulties as there are on Scafell, yet the rock scenery on every hand is so striking that a traverse of these fells has a sense of achievement that few walks can equal.

The head of Mosedale is itself a striking piece of scenery. If the walk is begun by ascending the good track up Black Sail Pass, there is ample opportunity for looking back at the magnificent cirque. This is by far the best way round, for though it brings you to the highest fell—Pillar—first, the others are in no sense an anticlimax.

The ordinary route follows the ridge from the pass exactly, leading without undue incident to the top. It is a fine ridge, noble of aspect and endowed with exhilarating views—yet it is not the way for a first visit. Anyone climbing Pillar for the first time must pay homage to Pillar Rock, the most visually dramatic crag in Lakeland. Not to do so would be like visiting the Louvre and missing out the *Mona Lisa*.

The Rock is on the Ennerdale face of the mountain, a considerable distance below the summit. From the ridge it is reached by the High Level Route, another of those adventurous traverse paths which are such a feature of the Wasdale fells. This one dips away from the ridge at a col beyond Looking Stead, and traverses below the crags of Green Cove and Hind Cove to the prominent memorial called Robinson's Cairn, built in memory of J. W. Robinson; a pioneer of rock-climbing and the principal discoverer of this way to the Rock. At this point, the full magnificence of Pillar Rock bursts into view.

The great rock fang rises from a pedestal of outcrop and screes sheer for almost five hundred feet. The structure of it is so audacious yet so superb, that it takes away your breath. Here is an immediate challenge to which anyone must make a response; nobody could be so insensitive as not to feel it. It is perhaps the only crag in the Lake District which would make even the most dedicated fell-walker wish, just for once, that he was a rock-climber.

The summit outline shows three distinct steps. On the right, with a wall plunging down into Pillar Cove is the broad step of Low Man. The crag then rises to the crenellated summit, High Man, and drops again on the left to a sharp gap (the Jordan Gap) beyond which is another 'top', Pisgah, which is connected to the parent fell by an easy ridge. In itself this would be enough to qualify Pillar Rock as a major crag, but by a superb piece of natural architecture another huge crag, the Shamrock, rises immediately in the foreground, half obscuring High Man, but giving the whole scene an extra three-dimensional aspect. No designer could have planned it better had he tried: it has the perfection of a medieval cathedral.

So you stand at Robinson's Cairn and stare in admiration, noticing new features every minute, but lost in wonder at the whole. Only slowly does it dawn on you that what you are looking at is but a part of what must really exist, for the Rock is obviously free standing, well away from the fellside, in which case there must be other faces to it, equally impressive. You feel an urge to go and see them, at once, as though this was some ancient memorial to be explored from all angles.

The trouble is that Pillar Rock does not reveal its secrets lightly, and the dramatic view from Robinson's Cairn is the most that the average walker can expect. To circumnavigate the crag, to see the East, North and West Faces in the course of a single walk is arduous and possibly dangerous for anyone who does not know the Rock. Pillar Rock not only looks like a fortress, it *is* a fortress, and well guarded at that.

It is not so much that there are no easy ways around and about the Rock, but rather that the easy ways have a habit of leading to places of increasing difficulty. You really do need to be quite sure of your capabilities before exploring hereabouts, for it is a sobering thought to reflect that most of the easy scrambles overlook enormous precipices.

There are no difficulties, however, about following the High Level Route beyond the Cairn, providing the weather holds good. The path dips to an easy ridge which leads up to a nastily steep scree shoot, which in turn gives access to the famous Shamrock Traverse. This is a broad ledge, high up on Shamrock, leading into the hollow of Great Doup which lies between the Rock and the summit of Pillar. It is an exhilarating traverse giving a sense of spaciousness and freedom, like similar paths in the Dolomites, though there is nothing intrinsically difficult about it, as there is with, say, Jack's Rake on Pavey Ark.

The Traverse gives a sense of involvement with the Rock (though it is a false sense really) because it leads to the heart of the matter. At the far end the south side is revealed as undistinguished knobs, with a hint of fearsome walls, partly hidden and waiting menacingly. A bowl of scree sweeps down to the funnel top of a gully between the Shamrock you have just 'conquered' and the main body of the Rock, but there is no hint from where you stand that the gully plunges sheer for four hundred feet. It is known as Walker's Gully, but do not be tempted by the name—it refers to a man who was killed there!

Pisgah, Jordan Gap, High Man—all look reasonably near, reasonably accessible, and those with the eye of faith can even trace an easy line across the 'sheer' face of High Man to Low Man. All very tempting, all perfectly possible—for those who really know what they are doing. But these are not ways for the merely adventurous: the risks are too great.

And in a sense so is the way round the base of the Rock. A good track leads off the High Level Route before Shamrock is reached and trails around below that massive crag, showing its fluted nature to good advantage. It continues below Walker's Gully and then enters on to the Green Ledge, a traversing line below the impressive North Face. So far all is well and the rock scenery almost overpowering, but to follow Green Ledge much further is to ask for trouble because it leads into the gully known as the Waterfall, and a very awkward crossing of this has to be made to reach the rocks of the West Face—so awkward indeed, that some experienced climbers prefer not to risk their luck.

Green Ledge is really a climbers' track, not designed for fell-walkers at all and it is best to pay heed to this fact. To overcome the difficulty it is fairly easy to descend before the Ledge is reached and enter into Pillar Cove, making a wide, circular sweep well away from the base of the rocks, before scrambling up the fellside again once the Waterfall Gully has been passed. But all this is very tiring and time-consuming (if the circuit of Mosedale is contemplated) and the North Face of the Rock is so fore-shortened by close proximity that it loses the quality which gave it its name.

True, the West Face is worth seeing once you have puffed your way up the fellside again. The best of the older climbs are on this side and it is not difficult to see why: clean sheer rock beyond compare; a much flatter face than its companions on the North and East, and no Shamrock to distract attention. Nevertheless, once the initial impact has worn off, the West Face does not have the artistic quality of the East and one is left with the conclusion that perhaps Robinson's Cairn is the best viewpoint after all.

In any event just to see the West Face it is not necessary to go to all this trouble because it can be reached by a simple if steep scramble across the back of Pisgah and down the steep scree gully on the other side. But where do you go from there? Back up the scree is the only answer for most people—or reverse the long circuit previously mentioned. Such to-ing and fro-ing is not conducive to a good fell walk, and the answer is, I suppose, that a lazy day spent pottering around the Rock and looking at it from all angles is the only satisfactory solution. Choose a good day, though—the environs of Pillar Rock are not places to visit when the mists are down.

It is enough on this first visit, however, to see Pillar Rock from Robinson's Cairn and to cross the Shamrock Traverse to Great Doup, from the far side of which a track goes up some four hundred feet of steep fellside to the top of Pillar itself (2,927 feet).

The summit comes as somewhat of a surprise, especially after a traverse of the High Level Route. Conditioned to rock scenery on every hand by the walk from Black Sail Pass you somehow expect a rocky, pointed summit. If this were Skye or Arran, the expectation would be fulfilled, but this is Lakeland where Nature always draws back at the final extravagance. It is as if, having created the great Pillar Rock, Nature felt suddenly ashamed of overdoing things and so made the summit of the parent fell a gentle grassy place.

The view is superb—one of the best in the district—ranging over the distant fells and then drawing nearer to encompass the darkling crags of Gable's forgotten side, and those of Kirk Fell too.

Nearer still, below one's feet as it were, is the wild corrie of Mosedale's head on the one side and the dark gloom of Ennerdale on the other. Best of all are the views of Scafell Crag and Pikes Crag seen down the full length of Mosedale and across Wasdale: to my way of thinking, one of the finest mountain views in Britain.

The ridge from Pillar plunges down steeply to one of the most incredible cols in the Lake District—Wind Gap. Seen from Mosedale, Wind Gap appears as a nick in a rocky skyline, yet an obvious nick and the only crack in an otherwise impregnable ridge. It is a true pass in the best Alpine tradition, for incredible though it may appear at first glance, there is a direct way over from Mosedale to Ennerdale by Wind Gap. Crags frown round the gap and seem to almost close it in, and yet the way is there, straight and narrow.

I once crossed Wind Gap. I was young and romantically brought up on tales of Whymper and Mummery, and I saw in Wind Gap a challenge. To me it was the Moming Pass, or the Col du Lion all over again, and in a sense I was right.

The day was extremely hot and I carried a full pack, walking

over Burnmoor from Eskdale with the intention of spending the
night at Gillerthwaite. A glance at the map will show you that
Wind Gap is the most direct route.

A glance at Wind Gap itself, however, will quickly convince
you that this is no ordinary fell crossing. My companions were
against me, but superior persuasive powers, aided by the knowledge that I was carrying the food, convinced them that the best
course was to accompany me.

In my worst nightmares I still think I am climbing up to Wind
Gap. Scree of the most abominable size and set at the ultimate
angle of friction is not the happiest of media for a fully laden
walker, and to tackle these conditions under a broiling sun made
them ten times worse. Up, grinding, panting, coughing and at
the Gap, collapsing. Thank God, the Ennerdale side was easier!

I have never been back to that treadmill, and time tends to
cloud judgement, but if the ascent of Wind Gap from Mosedale
is not the steepest path in the Lake District, I do not want to know
what is!

From Wind Gap a fine ridge, rocky on either hand, leads up
towards Steeple (2,687 feet) or to be more exact towards the
grassy dome of Little Scoat Fell (2,760 feet), for Steeple itself is
the lesser height, the sharply conical peak rising superbly across
the gap of Mirk Cove. If ever proof was needed that height alone
does not make a mountain, here it is—not one fell-walker in ten
has heard of Little Scoat Fell, yet there can be scarcely one that has
never heard of Steeple.

Is it the shapeliest fell of all? There is a case to be made out for it,
and there are none which combine shape with such grandeur of
setting. It is not difficult to climb, the short ridge from the col
between it and Little Scoat Fell is steep but nothing more, and
leads directly to the summit. On either hand are two of the
wildest, grandest corries you will see anywhere—Mirk Cove and,
confusingly enough, Mirklin Cove. Great rock buttresses sweep
down into these lonely recesses, and it is not surprising to learn
that these are now yielding a crop of fine long rock climbs—
indeed, the surprising thing is that they were not more thoroughly
explored earlier. Perhaps George Abraham hit the mark when
commenting on another part of this remarkably craggy ridge.

"Even rocks suffer from the drawback of being situated in a land of plenty."

Little Scoat Fell, which overlooks Steeple, is important because it marks a parting of the ridges. Straight ahead the main ridge continues to Haycock (2,618 feet) where it spreads in all directions to encompass the somewhat remote and little-visited fells stretching between the western ends of Ennerdale Water and Wastwater. Though not the sort of fells to excite much admiration (especially situated in such close proximity to Wasdale Head), they do cover a much larger tract of country than is generally imagined—at a fairly conservative estimate, between 30 and 40 square miles, and they include four tops over 2,000 feet, though only one of these, Seatallan (2,266 feet) is of any interest, and that only for those who are tired of the beaten track. Strangely enough there are two major crags on the fringes of this area which attract attention from climbers because of their accessibility: Backbarrow, overlooking Wastwater, which is scrappy and old-fashioned and the more popular Angler's Crag, overlooking Ennerdale Water, where there are some very good climbs indeed.

Most walkers will prefer to leave the main watershed at Little Scoat Fell in order to traverse the subsidiary ridge over Red Pike (2,629 feet). Here are spectacular views down into the bowl of Mosedale's cirque on the one hand, contrasted with the very much gentler valley of the Nether Beck on the other. Mosedale, especially in the late afternoon, is grimness personified, and the contrast with the gentle hollows containing Scoat Tarn and Low Tarn makes one wonder how it is possible for Nature to show two such utterly opposite faces in such close proximity.

The ridge itself is interesting if it is followed accurately, for the real crest is also the tip of the Mosedale crags. It is not a route for walking in a strong wind, nor with dogs and children, and the regular path is careful to avoid it altogether, even to the extent of missing out Red Pike's summit cairn.

At Dove Head, the attractive col between Red Pike and Yewbarrow, it may well be considered that enough ground has been covered in one day and that to continue further, instead of descending easily if somewhat steeply to Wasdale Head, would be

The Ennerdale face of Pillar

merely gilding the lily. Further, Yewbarrow (2,058 feet) is not strictly a part of the Mosedale circuit—it actually veers away to the south-west and forms part of Wasdale, so there is no competitive inducement to prolong what has already proved an exciting walk.

Yet Yewbarrow is just as interesting as that which has gone before, and providing you have the time and energy, another mile or so is not going to make much difference to your state of collapse! The fell is worth the effort, and this is really the only time to see it, because it is too short for a day out on its own and being already at Dove Head means you have broken the back of the steep ascent from the valley.

Nor is it as formidable as it appears. Stirrup Crag, one of those awkward rock bands which are for ever popping up to block the way of the walker, is all show. As George Abraham once said of Ben Nevis: "Smack it boldly in the front and it will collapse." Once beyond the crag the barrow-like summit ridge is easy walking until with a final gesture of defiance the crags at the Wastwater end seem to prevent escape. These—Bell Rib and Overbeck—are real climbing crags, but the way between them is fairly obvious, and the lakeside is reached in a few minutes.

As may well be imagined, such a unique natural curiosity as Pillar Rock was an object of attention long before the sport of rock-climbing was born. The Pillar Stone, as it was then called, was well known to shepherds of the district and its fame reached the early guide-book writers (though not, apparently, that collector of the curious tale, Harriet Martineau, who fails to mention it at all). Many people undoubtedly tried to reach the summit, but the first-known ascent was by a shepherd from Croftfoot in Ennerdale, John Atkinson, who climbed what is now known as the Old West Route on 9th July, 1826.

Atkinson's feat was recorded in the local papers, not without some confusion: reporters were apparently inaccurate in those days too. For one thing he was called variously 'a shepherd' and 'a cooper'—though what a cooper might be doing at Croftfoot is rather puzzling, and then again, it is not all that certain that it was the Old West he went up. Anyone who knows the rock would

8

Buttermere, with Grasmoor beyond

agree that the eastern side not only held similar opportunities for a daring spirit, but actually looks safer into the bargain.

All that we can be sure of is that Atkinson did make the ascent, and that it was recognized locally as being something of a feat. No doubt prompted by Atkinson's erstwhile fame, three other shepherds also made the ascent in the same year.

They were well ahead of their time. Their daring produced nothing but local recognition, for there was no corpus of interested outsiders who recognized the feat for what it was, and nobody ready to repeat the challenge.

It was twenty-two years before the first tourist ascent— Lieutenant Wilson, RN, and two more years before the next, but from 1850 onwards the trickle grew to an ever-increasing stream.

In 1872 the rock was visited by a distinguished group of Alpinists including Frederick Gardiner and Richard Pendlebury—the same Pendlebury who was later to make the sensational first ascent of the Marinelli Couloir on Monte Rosa.

Mostly, however, the visitors were simply adventurous travellers. Ropes were never used, of course, and these enterprising men and women must have shown considerable courage, especially in an age when most people who visited the district still employed a guide to conduct them from one valley to the next.

One such visitor was that incredible character the Reverend James Jackson, the parson of Rivington in Lancashire, who climbed the Rock in 1875 at the age of 79 and called himself the Patriarch of the Pillarites. Jackson was one of those remarkable eccentrics who seemed to flourish in Victorian days. He was a tough old bird who once walked 60 miles in under 20 hours, and even climbed up his own church to repair the weather-cock; though anyone who knows Rivington church will realize that this is not quite so desperate a feat as it might appear. It did not stop Jackson from celebrating with one of his doggerel verses:

> Who has not heard of Steeple Jack,
> That lion-hearted Saxon?
> Though I'm not him he was my sire,
> For I am Steeple Jackson!

Unfortunately this likeable old character was killed in 1878 whilst trying to repeat his ascent of Pillar, having apparently fallen down the crags of Great Doup.

The Rock was already beginning to influence future generations of great climbers, though rock-climbing as a sport was unknown. In 1869 Lawrence Pilkington climbed to the top when he was 14 years old, assisted by his elder brother Charles. Who can say how much this experience decided the climbing career of a future President of the Alpine Club?

But as was so often the case with the great Lakeland crags, it was the arrival of Walter Haskett-Smith in 1882 (four years before his celebrated ascent of Napes Needle) that marked the start of real rock-climbing on Pillar. Haskett-Smith saw what he considered to be a perfectly obvious way to the top of High Man from Jordan Gap, and climbed it. As with all his early climbs he did it alone, and added a second route nearby for good measure. In fact for eight years he had the Rock to himself so far as climbing was concerned, though obviously the routes he could attempt were limited in scope and difficulty. His brother Edmund was with him from time to time and they succeeded in climbing a considerable way up what was later to become the famous *North Climb*. Each was climbing separately, since they did not know of the use of a rope for climbing purposes, and they had a narrow escape when a block came away.

Perhaps with Pillar more than most crags it is remarkable how the standard of climbing improved with a bang. Gullies were the natural lines used by the pioneers, and Pillar has gullies which are more difficult than any others in the Lakes: more difficult even than those of Dow Crag, its only serious rival in this respect.

In 1890 Geoffrey Hastings and Charles Hopkinson arrived on the scene, led there no doubt by the indomitable J. W. Robinson, who knew as much about Pillar as most men. Though it was midwinter, they climbed the difficult *Shamrock Gully*, and in the following summer Hastings returned with Slingsby and Haskett-Smith to climb the *North Climb*, which Haskett-Smith led. The famous Nose pitch—the crux of the route—defeated them, however, and they were forced to escape by some devious and rather hair-raising antics into the easy upper part of Savage Gully: a legitimate way for many climbers even to this day. It took the climbing genius of Solly (of *Eagle's Nest Direct* fame) to overcome the Nose by a hand traverse some months later, leading a large party which included Hastings and Slingsby. The Hand Traverse is still the hardest way of doing the Nose; Joseph Collier found another and more direct way which was slightly easier, a short time afterwards.

These two climbs alone (both are still 'severe' in standard) would have been enough, but a few years later, towards the turn of the century, a further spate of new climbs added to the prestige of the Rock. The Broadrick brothers succeeded in making a start to the conspicuous *Walker's Gully*, where others had failed. It was an encouraging incentive to tackle what had long been an outstanding problem of the gully era, and a few months after the Broadricks' fine attempt, the great Owen Glynne Jones led a party to the top.

Apart from *West Jordan Gully*, which was climbed in 1898, nobody had considered the fine rocks of the towering West Face. Pillar was primarily the gully crag *par excellence*, and the experts were so engrossed with these that, the *North Climb* apart, much of the rest went untouched. This was remedied in 1901 when George Abraham led a party up the *New West Climb* (a delicate compliment to John Atkinson's scramble which was known as the 'Old West').

The Abrahams have never received their just acknowledgement as leaders in the break with the old gully climbing school, possibly because they were overshadowed by technically more proficient climbers such as Jones, Botterill and Solly, but it is remarkable how the Keswick brothers' names appear in so many of the first open face or buttress climbs of those pioneering years. The *New West* on Pillar is a case in point, and though they made many more difficult routes, it is doubtful if any excel this one in line and situation. It rises straight up the sheer West Face for almost three hundred feet, picking its way amongst the difficulties in a remarkable way so that, despite everything, it is technically only in the 'difficult' grade by climbing standards, which in these days of 'extremely severe' climbs is very modest indeed. Nevertheless the climb remains one of the great classic routes of all time: some would say the best of its grade in Britain.

A few months after this break with tradition, the last of the great gullies was conquered when Claude Barton led a rope to the top of *Savage Gully*. It was an astonishing feat (still graded 'very severe') and a fitting climax to the gully epoch.

In 1906 Fred Botterill, another climber whose contributions to standards have never been fully appreciated, led the *North-West Climb*. It was an open face climb of the Abraham type, but of a much harder standard—even today it keeps its 'very severe' grading. In the short space of five years Pillar had witnessed not only the birth of a new concept in climbing but the final success of the gully epoch and the ultimate standards for the new face climbing.

It was the crag's greatest period, beyond doubt; the time when it contributed most to the national climbing scene. In the years which followed almost every climber of note added something to the Rock, and though many of the new routes are fine climbs and much harder than those mentioned (especially the recent ones) Pillar has never reached the importance that it had at the turn of the century. The mantle of progress shifted towards the East Buttress of Scafell, to the Eastern crags like Dovedale and Castle Rock of Triermain, and sadly for the Lakeland climber, to Snowdonia.

5

The Buttermere and Newlands Fells

ARE there any two valleys in the whole Lake District so starkly contrasted as Ennerdale and Buttermere? Separated as they are by a narrow ridge they are yet worlds apart in mood and appearance: Ennerdale, long and narrow, cloaked in its sombre shroud of firs; a place where, symbolically at least, the sun never shines and no birds sing. Then the vale of Buttermere, broad and angular, containing lush meadows and a prosperous village, with the two lakes of Buttermere and Crummock Water glinting in a summer's sun. In a pilgrim's progress this is the Promised Land, to be reached after crossing Ennerdale's Slough of Despond.

Perhaps in other chapters of this book I have been unwilling to say overmuch about the views, either from or of the fells concerned, except occasionally to point out those which I have considered particularly outstanding. This is because I consider views in general to play only a minor role in fell-walking: a pleasant backcloth to an interesting activity. Wide views are almost always disappointing (Ruskin's dictum again!): the best mountain views are from moderate elevations. Better still, and the real inner truth about walking in the Lakes as distinct from anywhere else, is the intimate vignette encountered at the bend of a beck, or corner of a crag. A red-berried rowan clings tenaciously to a crack in some rocky outcrop, a beck eddies mysteriously deep in a hidden pool—these are the true scenic delights of the fells.

And yet only a fool could ignore the broader canvas. There are times and places when it is staggeringly beautiful.

I mention this in connection with Buttermere because I believe there is a greater *variety* of scenic beauty here than almost anywhere else in the district: Borrowdale alone can stand compare. Lovers of Langdale and espousers of Eskdale may well blanch at such a statement of what is patently sheer prejudice—and yet I would still deny them their favourites. The variety here is really quite astonishing: the fells are amongst the showiest in the district.

Consider some of them. The marvellous views towards the head of the Buttermere valley seen from the western shore of the lake; Fleetwith Pike dominating the central background and the tortured ridges of the High Stile range dropping down to the trees which fringe the right-hand bank. Or turn the other way and gaze over Crummock Water towards Mellbreak and the little known but dominant Sourfoot Fell, with Grassmoor bulking large on the right—if you were to paint such a picture from imagination the critics would accuse you of gross sentimentality. Yet it is true, it is *there*.

Again, and quite differently, walk up into Warnscale Bottom. The scenery is much closer this time: frighteningly close. Was there ever such another awesome corrie? Then what of Newlands' Vale, by way of contrast, the Elysian Fields of the Lakes? And, if you must have the grand gesture, what of the view from Grasmoor, surely the finest panorama of the whole district?

All the scenic qualities for which Lakeland is justly famous are distilled and concentrated into this area.

As for the fells themselves, there are three quite distinct groups and several little outliers, none of which has any real connection, or indeed, anything in common, with the others. To the south of Buttermere the High Stile ridge rises in impressive corries then loops and dips to join the rim of Warnscale Bottom, which culminates in Fleetwith Pike and Honister Crag. The deep gash of Honister Pass, with its quarries and motor road, effectively separates these fells from the Newlands fells immediately to the north, and the narrower motor road over Newlands Hause itself separates the latter from the huge and complicated fells of the Grasmoor group.

At the heart of all three groups is the village of Buttermere, comfortably settled on the alluvial plain between its two lakes. It is, in theory, the logical centre from which to walk these fells and yet in practice it turns out not to be so. The principal valleys of the Newlands and Grasmoor fells are on the opposite side of the watershed: the mountains turn their backs on Buttermere and run away towards the vale of Keswick. Only big Grasmoor itself gives of its best on this side, and grand though it is, it is not enough. Walking the Grasmoor or Newlands fells from Buttermere always gives me the feeling that I am doing things the wrong way round. With the High Stile ridge, of course, it is a different story. Buttermere is the only logical starting point—to climb these fells from Ennerdale is not only a steep and weary slog, but it reveals nothing whatever of their true nature.

The High Stile ridge begins in the west with Great Borne (2,019 feet)and continues as a broad uninteresting ridge to Starling Dodd (2,085 feet) and then rises to meet the higher Red Pike (2,479 feet), High Stile (2,644 feet) and High Crag (2,443 feet) before descending to the col at Scarth Gap, the principal pass from Buttermere to Ennerdale. At a rough estimate this is some six miles of walking but Great Borne is an inconvenient starting (or finishing) point and usually only the second half of the ridge is done, that is to say, Red Pike, High Stile and High Crag.

Certainly it is the better half, and yet I have always had a sneaking regard for Starling Dodd, the perfect plum pudding hill. What a ridiculous shape this fell is, especially when seen from Ennerdale! Poor old Starling Dodd, skirted with dark firs below and bald pate above, yet retaining a singular dignity.

My affection once—only once—took a practical turn and I climbed directly up from Gillerthwaite. Once out of the trees it proved to be steep but very easy going and I was on the top in no time at all. Nevertheless, I find it hard to credit the dalesman who told me that during the war a plane crashed on the Dodd and the rescuers managed to drive a jeep up the fell.

The Buttermere side of the Dodd is much less steep, though several times as long. The great attraction here is Scale Force, spraying down into its dark, ferny, ravine. Waterfalls have a perpetual fascination, but there are few in the Lake District grand enough to excite the imagination (the best are in Upper Eskdale). Scale Force does have atmosphere and position, though, and it is reputed to be the highest fall in England—a rather dubious claim, I would have thought. Nevertheless, it has been one of the wonders of the district from the earliest tourist days when they did it in style by arriving across Crummock Water in a boat.

There is no great difficulty in visiting Scale Force *en route* for the High Stile ridge—the diversion is negligible, since it is preferable to walk the ridge from Red Pike to High Crag, rather than the other way round. It makes a pleasant afternoon stroll—no more—and the walking is both fine and easy, with spectacular views all around. With luck and good eyesight you might even pick out Pillar Rock across Ennerdale.

I remember once, during the latter end of the war years, when I was still what is known disparagingly as a callow youth, three of us had walked over the Robinson Group from Honister Youth Hostel one warm June day and dropped down the fellside for a pint in the Fish Inn at Buttermere. My companions were afflicted with one of those bouts of idleness that come over us all at times, but which are particularly annoying to anyone in the party who is feeling ready for a hard day. Perhaps it is a condition of youth: these days it is usually me that is the lazy one! Anyway, when I suggested that we might return along the High Stile ridge and Fleetwith back to the hostel, I was met with discouraging grunts. Two to one, I was outvoted, but fortunately there is nothing democratic about climbing: nobody was ever voted up a mountain. Their alternative plan of simply walking back up the pass appalled me, for no fell-walker (and especially a very young one) likes walking along a road. I rounded on them hotly, rashly boasting that not only would I do the ridge alone, but would beat them back to the hostel into the bargain. They looked at me as if I was mad; which of course, I was.

Small bets were placed. As a concession, they magnanimously granted me the right to *run* the entire course, whilst they promised to walk, slowly and sedately, as befitted gentlemen on a warm afternoon.

So off I went at a rapid jog up the rocky track on Red Pike, rucksack and all. I was as thin as a whippet in those days, so the uphill run hardly raised a sweat, despite the hot sun. I paused for a moment on the summit of Red Pike and then set off steadily along the ridge, feeling good and very certain of winning my bet. Over High Stile, over High Crag—no time at all—then a burst of speed down to the col of Scarth Gap. And that is when I came unstuck—a lurch, an ill-judged landing, and over I went, at considerable speed.

Fortunately I landed fairly well, without suffering any cuts or bruises, but two steps forward told me I was done for—I had twisted my ankle.

The joyous run now became the painful crawl, and anyone who has had to walk on a bad ankle will know just how painful it can be. Every few paces the throbbing grew to such a pitch that I was forced to sit and rest until the pain ebbed sufficiently for me to go on again. There was no question now of going over the Fleetwith Moors, I turned down the path towards the valley, and then straight down towards Warnscale Bottom and Gatesgarth farm. At the beck, I took off my right boot and bathed the swollen ankle in the cold stream. Then somewhat relieved, hobbled towards the farm.

Cars were not all that frequent in those days of petrol shortage and the offer seemed to me like manna from heaven. He was going up the pass and could drop me off at the door of the hostel.

As the car wound up the steep road, bitter thoughts crossed my mind. Time had galloped away since my accident, and my friends would be already at the hostel waiting to greet my belated arrival. If they saw me arriving in a *car*—why, I would never hear the last of it!

So I asked to be dropped off a little short of the building, and made my entrance trying to look all unconcerned. But what could I say? Youth takes these things very hard.

They were not there. I could scarcely believe it. Even a one-legged dwarf could have walked up the pass from Buttermere in the time which had elapsed.

They came in about an hour later, and were obviously quite put out to see me washed and changed, waiting to greet them. Being crafty young men, they had spent a quarter of an hour or so in Buttermere actually calculating how long it would take me

to run the ridge and cross Fleetwith and their calculations had
shown them that they had ample time for a cup of tea at Gatesgarth Farm. They must have been finishing their tea when I got
the lift.

"But how on earth did you do it?" they asked.

"Oh, just got a move on," I said, modestly.

I never did tell them the true story, but I generously waived
the bet!

One of the attributes of the High Stile ridge which has seldom
been stressed, is its usefulness as an introduction to ridge walking.
It has all the qualities that anyone tentatively undertaking fell-
walking requires: neither too high nor too long, a succession of
attractive summits without much loss of height between them,
and a sense of being on a real ridge. In good weather it is a ridge
to be enjoyed without any fatigue or sense of danger; it avoids
the boredom that make some ridges 'a drag' in the mountaineer's
phrase book, yet is not so 'airy' as to disquiet a novice. Nor is the
navigation tricky: you could hardly have a simpler ridge formation, and the start and finish are close at hand—always an important point with beginners.

The corries on the Buttermere side of the ridge are amongst the
most attractive in the Lakes, especially the well-known Burtness
Comb with its variety of crags for the rock-climber. Here the
expert can tackle steep routes such as *Eagle Front* on the rather
grim looking Eagle Crag, or the less ambitious can spend the day
combining routes on the lower crags, where one climb seems to
lead on to the next, in a rather superior Pavey Ark fashion. Just as
the Ridge tends to be ignored as an introductory walk, so the
Burtness climbs have never had their fair share of praise as rock-
climbs for novices. Perhaps in these days of instant everything, the
steep walk up into the comb is too much trouble for the embryo
climber—why bother when Shepherd's Crag or Scout Crag are
so near a road? Nevertheless, for those who prefer solitude and
surroundings of grandeur, Burtness Comb is infinitely preferable.

Beyond Scarth Gap (once called Scarf Gap) the great cirque of
Warnscale Bottom opens out. From Gatesgarth it is an easy walk
into this superb corrie—perhaps the easiest to reach, and certainly

one of the most impressive, corries in the district. Black walls of
rock hem it in on every hand, especially at the valley head where
the crags are cleaved by ferocious looking gullies.

A number of new climbs have been done on these crags in
recent years. Many are hard, but there are some interesting easier
routes on Striddle Crag, which melts so effectively into the background on the left that it can scarcely be seen.

Striddle is a very peculiar crag indeed. When Brian Evans and
I went to take a look at it, it seemed to us, as we clambered up
the steep fellside, that the crag was nothing but a nondescript
collection of outcrops forming part of the larger scree. On arrival,
however, we discovered an easy angled crag of considerable size,
which gave us a pleasant climb on good rock, at about 'severe'
standard. True, the lines were variable from pitch to pitch, but
the pitches themselves were interesting and the rock very sound.
It reminded me very much of Eel Crags in Newlands—and the
descent too, was just as difficult as the descent from Eel Crags; a
complicated matter of wending in and out of a deep gully.

Striddle, of course, is at the back of Fleetwith Pike so to speak.
The Pike throws down a long spur towards Buttermere which is
an interesting scramble, but the real glory of this underrated fell is
Honister Crag, looming ominously over the pass of that name.
It has always been one of the tourist sights of Lakeland, and
though the cynics may sneer at its popularity and accessibility, it
remains an impressive piece of rock.

Here and there on the crag can be seen the workings of the
slate quarriers, for Honister slate had always been highly regarded by discerning architects. The knapping sheds are close by
the top of the pass and it is interesting to watch the men at work
there, splitting the slates with an uncanny eye for the correct
cleavage. In a mechanized world such as the one in which we
live, it is good to see the skill of a craftsman employed directly
on to natural material: to fashion nature, using only crude tools
and native intelligence—that is real skill.

Over one hundred years ago Harriet Martineau was equally
impressed with the quarrymen of Honister:

The dark, stupendous, almost perpendicular, Honister Crag

frowns above; and as the traveller, already at a considerable height, looks up at the quarrymen in the slate quarries near the summit, it almost takes his breath away to see them hanging like summer spiders quivering from the eaves of a house.

These quarrymen are a hardy race, capable of feats of strength which are now rarely heard of elsewhere. No heavily-armed knight, who ever came here to meet the Scot (and there were such encounters on this spot in the ancient border wars) carried a greater weight, or did more wonders in a day than these fine fellows. The best slate of Honister crag is found near the top: and there, many hundred feet aloft, may be seen (by good eyes) the slate-built hovels of some of the quarrymen, while others ascend and descend many times between morning and night. Now the men come leaping down with their trucks at a speed which appears appalling to strangers. Formerly, the slate was brought down on hurdles, on men's backs: and the practice is still continued in some remote quarries, where the expense of conveyance by carts would be too great, or the roads do not admit of it. Nearly forty years ago there was a man named Joseph Clark at Honister who made seventeen journeys (including seventeen miles of climbing up and scrambling down) in one day, bringing down 10,880 pounds of slate. In ascending he carried the hurdle, weighing eighty pounds; and in descending, he brought each time 640 pounds of slate. At another time he carried, in three successive journeys, 1,280 pounds each time. His greatest day's work was bringing 11,771 pounds; in how many journeys it is not remembered: but in fewer than seventeen. He lived at Stonethwaite, three miles from his place of work. His toils did not appear to injure him: and he declared that he suffered only from thirst. It was believed in his day that there was scarcely another man in the kingdom capable of sustaining such labour for a course of years.

In some places where the slate is closely compacted, and presents endways and perpendicular surface, the quarryman sets about his work as if he were going after eagle's eggs. His comrades let him down by a rope from the precipice; and he tries for a footing on some ledge, where he may drive in wedges. The difficulty of this, where much of his strength must be employed in keeping his footing, may be conceived: and a great length of time must be occupied in loosening masses large enough to bear the fall without being dashed into useless pieces. But generally speaking, the methods are improved, and the quarries made accessible by tracks admitting of the passage of

strong carts. Still, the detaching of the slate, and the loading and conducting the carts, are laborious work enough to require and train a
very athletic order of men. In various parts of the district, the scene is
marked by mountains of debris, above or within which yawn black
recesses in the mountain side, where the summer thunders echo, and
the winter storms send down formidable slides into the vales below.

The quarry workings extend to both sides of the pass, ravaging
the fellsides in a manner which seems entirely nineteenth century.
The top of the pass offends the eye, for the workings, though
centuries old, have not acquired that abandoned look which can
make even the most unlikely material picturesque. It is not really
a place to linger long, though the slopes of Dale Head do have a
very fine and steep crag with a number of hard climbs, the best
known (and easiest) of which is the classic 'severe' called *Honister
Wall*.

From a fell-walking point of view this north-eastern rim of the
valley, consisting of the three peaks, Dale Head (2,473 feet),
Hindscarth (2,385 feet) and Robinson (2,417 feet), is not nearly as
satisfying as the High Stile range. The approach (from the
Honister side) is ungainly and the walking rather monotonous,
relieved only by the superb views it gives across the Buttermere
valley. Indeed one could say that the scenery makes the walk
worthwhile in this instance, though it is made even better by
including the long spur of fell which runs northwards from
Honister and terminates at Cat Bells (1,481 feet), and which
forms the western limit of the Borrowdale valley.

The Cat Bells ridge, pock-marked by the curious landslip
where a giant is reputed to have clawed away at it, has always
been a popular walk with tourists from Keswick, who seldom
venture much further than Cat Bells itself. It justifies itself as a
walk because it is a true ridge, a good one, and one which offers
excellent views of Derwentwater, Borrowdale and Newlands,
which is precisely what a tourist requires. Beyond Cat Bells, the
interest increases and so does the variety of views, which range
from the broad sweep over Borrowdale towards Keswick, to
intimate glimpses of fearsome crags and gullies plunging down
into Newlands.

Combining both the Cat Bells ridge and the Dale Head ridge

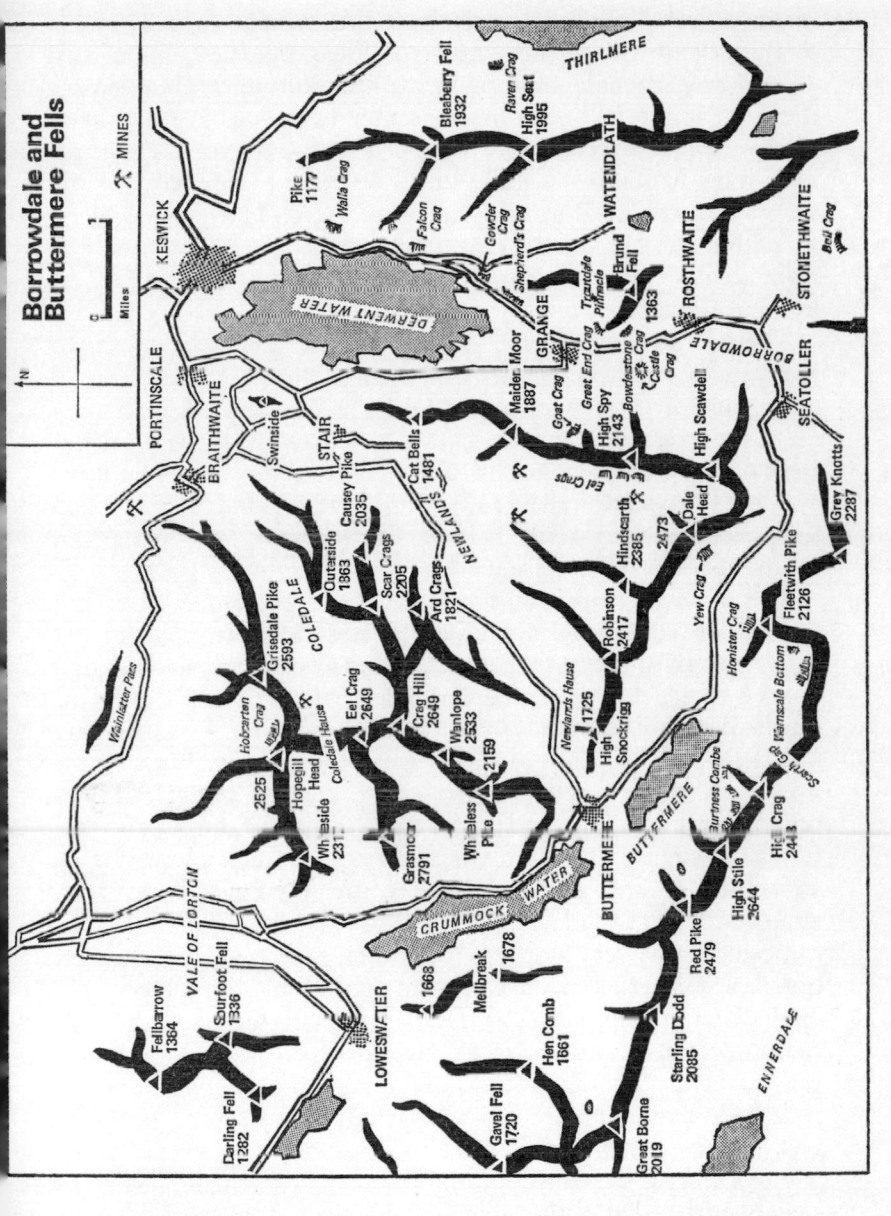

Borrowdale and Buttermere Fells

makes a fairly long walk—say about fifteen miles from Keswick to Buttermere village allowing for detours, but the going is easy all the way, though some may find the pull up to Dale Head's summit, at the half-way mark, rather fatiguing. For the keen photographer, especially one equipped with both wide-angle and long-focus lenses, it is a walk not to be missed—not only for the views it gives of Borrowdale, Buttermere, Newlands and so forth, but also because the two halves of the ridge are virtually at right angles one with another and so guarantee a variety of lighting situations.

There is no doubt in my own mind that the full walk from Keswick to Buttermere is the best that the Newlands fells have to offer, but for those who might find this too much for one day there are several alternatives. One is to follow the ridge from Cat Bells to the prominent col of Rigg Head and descend from there into the Newlands valley following a very good track (which later becomes a cart road) back to Little Town, and the narrow motor roads of the Swinside area.

This walk is equally good in either direction, and in any event the vale of Newlands is not a place to miss. Here are remnants of mining activity going back to Elizabethan days and earlier; best known of which is the Goldscope Mine, whose cave-like entrance can be distinguished easily near the foot of Scope End, the long northerly spur of Hindscarth forming the western flank of the Upper Newlands valley. This mine yielded both lead and copper, with small quantities of silver and gold as an extra bonus. It was closed about a hundred years ago, though there was an abortive attempt to reopen it shortly after the First World War, along with the Dale Head Mines. These ventures failed not because the veins were worked out, which they most certainly are not, but through lack of adequate capital and machinery. An application to reopen the Dale Head Mine, considered particularly rich in copper, was made in recent years by a mining company, but was refused on the grounds of damage to the environment.

Equally interesting are the crags fringing the valley, especially Eel Crags, which make such an impressive eastern skyline. Miner's Crag is the name given to the Buttress which rears up so steeply at the head of the valley on this side: steep and with rock not above suspicion. Lower down the valley are Waterfall Buttress, Red Crag and Grey Buttress, the three prominent crags which stand out amongst a welter of lesser outcrops and steep, nasty gullies. Despite their somewhat broken appearance they offer some remarkably inescapable climbs in the harder grades. The climbing, possibly because of the wild surroundings, seemed to me to be rather serious in nature and of an unusual kind for Lakeland. There is something of the expedition nature about it, despite its brevity, and the return to the foot of the crags is likely to prove almost as difficult as the way up. They are certainly amongst the most difficult rocks in the area to get down: definitely not for bad weather. Perhaps this, allied with their comparative remoteness, has prevented them from earning the popularity they deserve.

The summit of the ridge above Eel Crags is known as High Spy (2,143 feet); a curious D-shaped summit entirely ringed by crags and outcrops. The vertical arm of the D represents the long line of Eel Crags overlooking Newlands; the curved part represents a series of huge buttresses overlooking Borrowdale—the most impressive part of the western flank of that valley.

The casual visitor to our hills may well wonder why it was that the pioneers of rock-climbing devoted their energies to high crags such as Scafell, Pillar and Dow when there are so many more crags which are much more easily accessible. Logically, one supposes, the valley crags would be climbed first, and the higher crags later—especially in view of the transport inadequacies of those days.

The reasons why such was not the case are not simple, being compounded from many factors, historical and technical. Primarily though, the sport of rock-climbing developed from alpinism— that is to say, from mountain climbing—and though the pioneers realized that rock-climbing was done for its own sake, they felt bound to respect the mountaineering traditions upon which their sport was based. I am quite sure that this was totally unconscious on their part; that they never questioned the concept.

In any case, the high mountain crags were the biggest, cleanest and, by and large, best that were available. One must remember that there was only a handful of climbers anyway, and they were

9

unlikely to find even the popular crags crowded. Rock-climbers were a 'club' in the proper meaning of the term, most of them well known to each other. The big crags were more than sufficient.

The walks up to the crags were nothing to people brought up in an era when walking was regarded as the usual means of locomotion: twenty or thirty miles would not have been regarded as exceptional for a brisk walk. There is the well-known story concerning Edward Whymper, who once remarked to a friend that he thought a good walker was one who could average thirty miles a day. "Fair", replied the friend, pointing out that Charles Hudson could average fifty!

Another point is that most of the pioneers regarded rock-climbing as a kind of secondary activity: a rather poor substitute for the real climbing in the Alps. Some were even rather ashamed of it. Even the great Owen Glynne Jones longed to make a name for himself as an alpinist, and had little regard for his own out-standing rock-climbs.

It is small wonder then that such men were not concerned with the valley crags, even choosing to ignore such noble bastions as Gimmer and Troutdale Pinnacle, which could certainly hold their own with most mountain crags. There were occasional exceptions, very rare, and usually the result of independent minded souls like the Abrahams who were responsible for opening up the popular Milestone Buttress in Wales and odd climbs like Mouse Ghyll on the Borrowdale crags of High Spy.

There was too, a secondary reason for the neglect of valley crags—many were uncommonly hard to climb, and it is doubtful whether the earlier pioneers would have met with much success even had they tried. Strangely enough, parallel with the developments in the Lakes and Wales, another group were developing climbing on the gritstone edges of Derbyshire. J. W. Puttrell and his friends had no Alpine traditions behind them: they climbed rocks simply because they liked rock-climbing, and the 'holdless' nature of gritstone quickly led them to bring technique to a fine art. It was only when the gritstone tradition fused with the others that rock-climbing took a major step forward and began to break the shackles of its mountain ancestry.

The old crags of the high hills were not 'played out' (there are still major routes being made on Pillar and Scafell, for instance) but the net was cast wider: Gimmer, White Ghyll, Shepherd's and many other crags previously ignored grew in importance.

Standards rose fantastically, especially during the last twenty years. A recent issue of a climbing journal, commenting on a new route, described it lightly as "surprisingly mild—just an average Hard Very Severe". That is to say, about the same standard as *Central Buttress* on Scafell—for years one of the hardest climbs in Britain!

Such standards demand new attitudes as well as new crags, though the latter were inevitably discovered. Standards of acceptability were thrown to the winds and 'anything goes' is the new motto in climbing.

One of the crags that came late on the climbing scene was Goat Crag on the Borrowdale side of High Spy. It has all the features that earlier climbers would have found repellent: grassy, without proper form or readily distinguishable lines, and leading nowhere in particular. Bold enough looking from a distance, it is positively repugnant at close hand—and yet it has provided some of the hardest, longest climbs in the district.

Bentley Beetham, for ever searching for new routes on new crags, climbed on Goat Crag during the war, but Beetham found little here that accorded with his ideas of climbing. It was not until 1965, when the North Buttress was opened up by Les Brown with his fantastic *Praying Mantis*, that Goat Crag sprang to prominence. The crag was at once attacked by an active Keswick group which included Paul Ross and Mike Thompson, with the result that a whole series of difficult new climbs were created, and Goat Crag became, for a year or two at least, the *avant-garde* playground of the Lakes.

There are several interesting variations to the walk along the Newlands fells, especially for those whose journey must preferably end where it began. The upper Newlands Vale has already been suggested as a means of return after traversing the Maiden Moor ridge, but for those who wish to extend the ridge walk, yet have no desire to descend to Buttermere, a grand alternative is to cross Dale Head, continue to Hindscarth, and then descend the long and fairly narrow northern ridge of that fell on a good track which eventually leads to Low Snab and Little Town. Longer still is to complete the ridge by walking to Robinson, then descending either the northern spur of that fell (High Snab Bank) or the Scope Beck, but this gives a circular walk which is rather too much for most tastes: in bad weather High Snab Bank can be tricky and the Scope Beck is to be preferred on the grounds of safety.

Beyond Robinson, Keskadale and the Newlands Hause, which bears a narrow motor road, separate the fells I have been describing from those which build up in complicated folds to Grasmoor. The road over Newlands Hause is much the quickest way to Buttermere from Keswick by motor-car, providing the driver knows the intricacies of the roads around Swinside, is good at cornering and has a sharp set of brakes. It is a highly popular tourist route, and motorists like to pause at the summit of the pass (where there are unusually good parking facilities) and look at Moss Force, one of the prettiest waterfalls of the district. For walkers, however, Newlands Hause is anathema—the risk of being run down by a car is much too great for comfort.

It cannot always be good weather. It was one of those grey August days when Duncan and I left the car at Stair and walked up the well-marked path, worn through the bracken, that leads to Causey Pike.

Though Causey Pike is not particularly high—just about 2,000 feet—it occupies a prominent position at the end of a long ridge running down towards Newlands from Crag Hill, a thrusting ridge that separates it from all its neighbours, and this, together with the fact that seen end on it appears sharply pointed, gives the fell an importance that it might otherwise never have got. It is visually attractive—the sort of fell that even the most casual traveller could scarcely fail to notice.

In fact, Causey Pike sometimes seems omnipresent. You can hardly climb a fell in the Keswick area without Causey Pike sticking up like a sore thumb somewhere on the scene. It acts as a universal point of reference on such occasions: you know the sort—"Well, that's Causey Pike so that other must be——" One thing is for sure—nobody ever mistook Causey Pike for anything else. It would almost certainly be a scene stealer, too, were it not for the closeness of the much finer, more elegant Grisedale Pike.

Like the other fells around Newlands, Causey Pike and its companions were once the scene of much mining activity and right at the commencement of our walk that day, at the entrance of Stoneycroft Gill, we could discern an almost obliterated ditch that could only be the remains of some ancient rake workings. Rakes were always the easiest way to win the precious ore from the hard rock, because they usually showed in the surface out-crops. It was merely a question of extracting the ore by following the line of the rake, digging it out to whatever depth it happened to run. It was almost certainly the earliest type of mining, because it was so obvious and simple, and many rakes exist which are centuries old. There are rakes in the Low Peak area of Derbyshire which were worked in Roman days, and which are still being worked—though nowadays the quest is for barytes or fluorspar, not the precious lead ore that the Romans sought.

Sometimes, as in Stoneycroft Gill, almost all sign of the once prosperous industry has gone, except for such traces as the rakes, or some incongruous road like the one here; obviously too wide and well made to be just a fell track, yet nowadays leading to nowhere.

We turned away from the gill and climbed up to Sleet Hause, on the crest of the ridge below Causey Pike. Already we were aware of the popularity of our chosen route: people coming down and going up in great numbers, like the stairway in a busy department store. There was a sort of savage satisfaction in look-ing up at the final rocky peak and thinking: "There you are—it serves you right for being such a little show off—people come and trample all over you!" The trouble is, though, I believe Causey Pike enjoys it.

It is the tourist ascent *par excellence* from Keswick. Just as Skiddaw is the Mont Blanc of that town, Causey Pike is its little Matterhorn. You actually do need to use your hands as well as your feet to reach the top: just about.

Not that the ascent is in any way difficult. The way is well marked by thousands of boot scratches, the angle is not nearly as steep as it appears from below, and the holds are as big as buckets. Nevertheless, as Mallory once said, apropos a somewhat higher hill, it is there—and for those who normally never set foot on anything steeper than an escalator, it forms a real, interesting, but safe challenge.

We scrambled up the rocky front, stepping aside now and again to allow those who were descending to pass. One middle-aged lady was obviously enjoying her descent, making noises of self-satisfaction as she successfully negotiated every steep bit, as well she might for her progress was handicapped by the huge walking-stick she carried. I felt like advising her to chuck the damn thing away, but who am I to interfere with the idiosyncrasies of others, especially on Causey Pike?

The top of Causey Pike proved to be just one of a succession of tops which hummock out along the ridge like a serpentine monster. Nevertheless it was satisfactorily small, seemingly inhabited by predatory sheep who begged shamelessly from the tourists. They are probably the only sheep in the world raised on Mars bars.

Newlands lay below, and on either hand the dour little valleys of Stoneycroft Beck and Rigg Beck; cheerless places. Newlands Pass itself was obscured by Ard Crags (surely a name invented by climbers?), a singularly pure little ridge leading from nowhere to nowhere and not connected to any of the better-known fells round about. Immediately below the Pike, beyond Sleet Hause, the remaining half-mile of ridge ran out like a purple carpet, so thick was the heather.

But the glory of Causey Pike, and of all this long ridge as far as Grasmoor itself, is the tremendous panorama of Lakeland. The Vale of Keswick, Skiddaw and Saddleback, Derwentwater and the interlocked masses of the western and eastern fells. The Langdale Pikes can be distinguished as readily as they can from Windermere. For once the scene is not merely widespread, but aesthetically pleasing as well: for my choice, the finest panoramic view in Lakeland.

Westwards from Causey Pike we followed a good track over the hummocky crest of the ridge which here reaches a slightly higher elevation and carries the name of Scar Crags. On its southern flank broken crags drop into Rigg Beck whilst on the north, steep fellside slopes away into Stoneycroft Gill. The going was good and we made rapid time to Sail Hause after which the steep pull up the red shale path that shoots directly up the flank of Sail, put a stop to our gallop.

The Hause is itself of interest in so far as it is the logical crossing place from Stoneycroft valley to the valley of the Sail Beck, the easiest way for a walker to travel from Keswick to Buttermere if he is to avoid the traffic of Newlands Hause. A cobalt mine used to operate on the Stoneycroft side of the Hause, and it was for this that the luxurious mine road which is such an incongruous feature of Stoneycroft Gill, was constructed.

From the summit of Sail the desolate head of Coledale can be seen in all its dereliction. The Force Crag mine has scarred the landscape to an unusual extent, spoiling the appeal of the unusual two-level cirque that could have been so attractive. The waterfall still gushes, of course, but the mine buildings, which are of modern construction, are an eyesore. The trouble is that Force Crag mine seems to open and close at the slightest drift of the economic breeze, and not until it is finally decided that the mine is uneconomic can anything be done.

No doubt there will come a day when the buildings and machinery are taken away, and nature will soon cover what remains in a cloak of antiquity, but there is always cause for concern where modern buildings are introduced into mining sites. In the old days the mine buildings were made of stones hewn from local quarries and roofed with local slate, so that even when they were first erected they suited the landscape, were part of it. Left to decay they melted into their surroundings. But the modern building materials, concrete and asbestos, have no part in these fells and will never adapt. This is why they must be removed once their usefulness has gone.

Sail (2,530 feet) is really quite a good fell in its own right but is too much surrounded by its betters. Crag Hill (Eel Crag) towers over it on the west and detracts from its height, and the long Causey Pike—Scar Crags ridge makes such a good introductory part of the walk that Sail itself becomes a mere extension of it. I doubt if anybody ever climbs Sail for itself, though it certainly cannot be ignored—the pull up from Sail Hause to the top, though fairly short, is the most exhausting of the entire walk.

From Sail a magnificent little ridge, full of rock outcrops and narrow, connects with Crag Hill. The path teeters along the ridge then scrambles up amongst steep fellside and rocks to the barren plateau of the summit.

Crag Hill (2,749 feet) is the true hub of these fells, with ridges branching in every direction. Causey Pike via Sail and Scar Crags to the east, Wanlope and Whiteless Pike to the south-west, Grasmoor to the west, and then northwards, across Coledale Hause, the ridges of Grisedale Pike, Hopegill Head and Gasgale Crags. Seen from almost any direction it is a fine-looking fell too, for despite its uninteresting summit the sides are very steep and live up to its name. Not that any of this does the fell the slightest good in public esteem because, unfortunately for Crag Hill, Grasmoor is higher by some fifty feet!

The name, too, detracts from its appeal—an unusual state of affairs in Lakeland where almost all the fells have superb names. For one thing it is seldom called Crag Hill at all, being known to generations of fell-walkers as Eel Crag, though the Ordnance Survey insist that Eel Crag is the subsidiary summit above Coledale Hause. But I ask you—Crag *Hill*, of all names! Why not Crag Fell? Of all the higher fells of Lakeland, is this the only one to suffer the indignity of being named a 'hill'?

There was nothing to detain us on the summit, which is a particularly unappetizing wasteland, so Duncan and I descended into the wide depression (one can hardly call it a valley) which divides Crag Hill from Grasmoor. The tracks hereabouts have an interesting way of taking the most direct route to the summit, irrespective of gradient, as we had noticed on Sail, and the one up Grasmoor was no different from the rest. We toiled up until at last the great plateau that is Grasmoor eased the strain and we were able to stroll across it to the summit cairn.

Almost everything above Grasmoor is incredible. There is nothing else like it in the whole of Lakeland. It is a peak without a summit (or at least a *proper* summit), offering instead a broad

Borrowdale in winter
The Grasmoor Fells from Eel Crags

sloping plateau of splendidly springy turf, which ends in extremely steep edges all round its rim, except where it joins with
Crag Hill, and even that is steep enough for the tastes of most
walkers. The cairn too, is not the usual sort, but is like an open-air
dining car, or a small cottage in a derelict state, all compartmented
so that you can nibble your lunch without having to indulge in
conversation with any other party. Very civilized. Yet Grasmoor
is not a civilized fell: it has more of the atmosphere of the ancient
cultures than any other fell I know, like something from *The
Hobbit* or *Elidor*.

It eschews drama, just as Causey Pike revels in it, and yet it is
one of the most impressive of all the fells; its immense bulk
always recognizable on the western skyline when seen from other
fells. And those steep sides! Uncompromising sweeps of scree and
crag—especially Grasmoor End, overlooking Crummock Water,
with its enormous gullies. On the rare occasions when winter sets
hard on this face, what a tremendous snow- and ice-climbing
ground it is. Then the gullies run up in ribbons of snow with
green and black ice bulges interrupting their smooth passage.

From the plateau, the wide ranging views over the fells rival
those from Causey Pike, whilst downwards is the map-like picture of Crummock Water, Loweswater and Buttermere, with the
pretty little 'lost' valley of Rannerdale acting as a foreground. But
then walk across the plateau, as we did, and the picture changes in
startling manner. All the softness that is Buttermere's vale vanishes
and is replaced by the sombre Gasgale Gill which runs up to Coledale Hause from the west. Across the Gill the steep grey slopes of
Gasgale Crags seem like the ashes tipped from a giant's foundry.
It looks like world's end.

As we sat finishing our sandwiches a whisper of mist drifted
over the cairn, threatening rain. We packed the rucksack and set
off towards Coledale Hause at a brisk pace, skirting Dove Crags,
which are Grasmoor's contribution to the general desolation of
Gasgale Gill. Though broken, these crags are impressive and
would make an even finer winter climbing ground than Grasmoor
End, perhaps, though I know of nobody who ever tried them.

As we reached Coledale Hause the rain began to sprinkle down
in intermittent showers. Below lay the ugly ruins of the Force

Spinup on Lower Falcon Crag

Crag mine and the long valley of Coledale stretching away to Braithwaite village. Some old open shafts with derelict fences were another reminder that these fells had once been the scene of labour as well as recreation, but we were in no mood to pause long for reflection on Man's eternal struggle to make a living, for the weather was worsening every minute.

Nevertheless, it seemed a pity to leave out Hopegill Head (2,525 feet) because not only is it a fine peak but it was within easy reach—easy, that is, in distance, though the steep haul up from Coledale Hause made us pant for breath.

At the summit we promptly turned around and scurried down the slopes by the edge of Hobcarton Crags to the col which gives such an impressive sight of this great rock cirque, whose walls plunge down into the pine-forested little valley of Hobcarton. What an impressive valley head this is! Splintered slate tufted with grass and bilberry and seamed with two great gullies, the principal one of which—Hobcarton Gully—gives a fine but rather difficult snow and ice climb. I understand that rock-climbs have also been done on these crags, but the prospect of climbing vertical shattered slate certainly does not appeal to me, nor, I suspect, many climbers. Except in a hard winter, when frost can be expected to give some stability to this 500-foot face, and snow makes the gully feasible, Hobcarton Crag is best left alone.

The path teeters by the brink of the crag, playing hide-and-seek with a broken stone wall. At the col it meets a distinctive gap or notch, where the edge is firm and flat enough to peer over into the depths, and then begins to rise up shaly slabs and scree towards Grisedale Pike. We found the pull up this, our final peak, surprisingly easy. A subsidiary summit revealed the looping ridge running up to the top and in no time at all we were there, looking down on Braithwaite and the huge dark plantations that engulf the Whinlatter Pass.

Grisedale Pike (2,593 feet), like Causey Pike, stands forward at the end of a ridge and thus has all the advantages of eminence which such isolation confers. Not only that but the peak is of classical pointed shape formed by the summital juxtaposition of three ridges in the best alpine tradition. This alpine quality is reinforced too, by its skirts of dark trees on the Whinlatter side, and it does not need much imagination to picture Braithwaite as an alpine village sheltering in the lee of the mountain.

Like Causey Pike, the chief feature which makes Grisedale Pike such an attractive-looking mountain is the steepness of the final few hundred feet to the summit on the east or Braithwaite side, but Grisedale Pike is an altogether bigger mountain than Causey Pike and so the effect is more noble. Again, resorting to alpine comparisons, Grisedale Pike could be said to be the Weisshorn of the district.

In winter, with a good snow cover, Grisedale Pike looks at its best, especially on one of these frequent clear winter days when the sky is blue and the atmosphere frozen into crystal clarity. Then, of course, the ultimate alpine comparisons become valid, for everything is to scale and numerical height means nothing. It was the great pioneer Oberland guide, Mechior Anderegg, whom on seeing Snowdon in winter, expressed astonishment that it could be climbed in a single day. He would have felt precisely the same about Grisedale Pike.

The rain drifted away, thank goodness, as we scrambled down the steep track which is the start of the west ridge. This is the tourist route of the peak; the most direct way from Braithwaite, extremely popular, and a much better ascent than most tourist routes. In reverse, once the initial steep part had been negotiated, it turned out to be a swift descent along a ridge which projected like a finger pointing towards the village. Much of it was level, all of it was easy.

Above the village the ridge is known as Kinn, which is the German for 'chin', and one wonders whether the name came from German miners who were numerous in these parts during the sixteenth century. The same name is applied to similar jutting ridges in parts of the Alps.

I think it is the contrast between the three groups of fells which make up this north-western corner of the Lake District that gives it such a special visual appeal. That, and the ever-present lakes, for there are more lakes here than anywhere else—Buttermere, Crummock Water and Loweswater all lie within the folds of the area, and it looks down on to the western shores of Derwentwater and Bassenthwaite as well. Strangely enough, as if there was a surfeit of water already, there are very few tarns, and with the possible exception of lonely Floutern Tarn, none of special merit.

Tourists from Keswick regularly climb Cat Bells, Causey Pike and Grisedale Pike, and in that sense the area is a popular one, but the high ridges in general do not seem to attract the same number of walkers as do those of Langdale or Coniston. Perhaps the situation will alter now that the motorway reaches Penrith.

Beyond the major fells I have described in this chapter lies an extensive fringe of 'lesser' fells whose heights are in fact only marginally lower than those of their better-known brethren. For the most part, it must be confessed, they make rather dull walking, though some of them—Sourfoot Fell (1,336 feet) for example— give unusually picturesque views which might well interest the keen photographer. Only one of these outliers is really worth a special effort to reach and climb and that is the unique Mellbreak, overlooking the western shore of Crummock Water.

Like Harter Fell in Eskdale, Mellbreak is quite isolated from its companions: there are no connecting ridges with other fells, and so it must be climbed for its own sake. Fortunately it has twin summits, a north summit (1,668 feet) and a south (1,676 feet) almost a mile apart, so that it is a little ridge unto itself, as it were. Steep crags almost encircle the fell, and give it a unique appearance when seen from, say, Rannerdale or Loweswater village, but it can be climbed very easily (and boggily) from the Scale Force track. The fell deserves better than this, though, and all true fell-walkers will prefer to traverse the mountain from Loweswater village to Buttermere. Like the traverse of Yewbarrow in Wasdale, there is scarcely a pleasanter way of filling in a half-day.

6

The Borrowdale Fells

SOUTH from Keswick and the beautiful shores of Derwentwater, Borrowdale penetrates deep into the heart of central Lakeland. It is arguably the longest and widest of all the valleys—much longer and wider than one remembers. From the head of Langstrath to Keswick is all of fifteen miles and, incredible to susceptible senses, from Maiden Moor to High Seat it is a good four miles across. Arguably, because length and width can be varied, depending upon what one takes as criteria. Nevertheless, it is big enough to allow a much greater diversity of landscape than any of the other valleys and therein lies the secret of its great charm.

If we admit (and I think we should) that every valley in the Lake District has a high measure of beauty, we are forced to concede that the beauty takes a subtly different form in each. Wasdale's beauty is not Kentmere's beauty, but it would take a bold man to assert that one was superior to the other, or that either was superior to, say, Eskdale. What we can do is to try and rationalize the attractiveness of each, and though this is a pedantic exercise not to be encouraged (beauty should sweep the senses not affect the mind) it is not too difficult to do. The physical scenery of almost all the valleys is constant. To progress up such a valley is to have a fixed picture at which you can look for hours as you tramp forward, altered only by the moods of the weather or by some bend in the road that shows a different angle, as you might get from tilting a mirror.

But not Borrowdale. Borrowdale is a movable feast of scene and colour. The skyline is never the same for long, and the various branch valleys which go to form the whole are as unlike as the proverbial chalk and cheese. Troutdale is Borrowdale, but so is Langstrath; Watendlath is Borrowdale, but so is Comb Gill. Where else in this lovely district does beauty and diversity go so magnificently hand in hand?

Small wonder that Borrowdale has so many admirers: it is almost a kingdom unto itself.

The beauty of this valley is so incredible as to be almost unfair: it obsesses the mind, clouds the judgement. The place is so *right* that to question it at all arouses feelings of guilt. The trouble is that it can be so overweening that you end up mistaking Borrowdale for Lakeland; the part for the whole. Borrowdale addiction is the most widespread disease amongst Lakeland visitors.

Ironically enough the high fells play only a supporting role in all this, for Borrowdale is not like Langdale or Wasdale; there are no Bowfells and Scafells here. Indeed, what there is generally belongs more rightly to somewhere else—the western flanks of the valley, from Cat Bells to High Spy, are really an integral part of the Newlands fells, whilst the heights to the west of Seathwaite in upper Borrowdale belong logically with the Gables. With what, then, are we left? The long eastern flank, extending from Castlerigg right down to Thunacar Knott: a range so set back from the valley itself for a good deal of the distance that it cannot even be seen. That—and Glaramara. Glaramara is the crowning glory of Borrowdale; the one fell which owes allegiance to nowhere else, but belongs one hundred per cent to the valley it dominates so proudly.

These then are the high fells of Borrowdale, those of 2,000 feet or more. Hardly enough to deserve a chapter to themselves, despite Glaramara: and in any case, many have already featured elsewhere in the book. Yet Borrowdale deserved its chapter because these same high fells sweep down into lower outliers and a series of magnificent crags which no writer about the Lakeland scene could afford to ignore. 'The valley crags' was the disparaging name given to them only a few years ago to differentiate them from places like Pillar and Scafell. Yet who today could say they are not part and parcel of the high fells? Is a climb on

Troutdale Pinnacle not as valid a mountain experience as a climb on Scafell?

There are valley crags elsewhere of course, and valley walks too, if it comes to that, but nowhere else do they assume the same significance as they do in Borrowdale. Borrowdale is the one place where the valley dominates the fells, rather than the other way round.

Borrowdale shares with Buttermere and Newlands that scenic quality which makes them so outstanding, except that here most of the good views are much more intimate and enclosed affairs. The grand gesture, the great sweep, is not so common or so good. Only two or three spring to mind as being of outstanding quality —the view down the valley from the neighbourhood of Taylor Gill Force, towards Seathwaite and the Borrowdale Yews, with the widening patch of brighter green beyond; the view into the heart of Comb Gill from near Longthwaite; Glaramara and upper Borrowdale from the Bowder Stone; and, inevitably, Ruskin's famous view of the Jaws of Borrowdale as seen from Friar's Crag—the celebrated 'fourth finest view in Europe'.

And of these only the last is to be compared with the majestic quality of the Buttermere views. Where Borrowdale scores, it can be again emphasized, is in the wide diversity of intimate scenes—that sudden unexpected burst of magnificence which can perhaps be properly seen from only one small area. Take Watendlath, for example. This is a pretty hamlet no matter from where it is viewed—but seen from the track to Rosthwaite it becomes more than that, it becomes outstandingly picturesque. In Borrowdale this sort of thing can be refined and refined almost to the point of obsession—Shepherds Crag looks attractive from the roadside, for instance, but the view of the Chamonix buttress from the top of Donkey's Ears Climb is uniquely so. There are dozens of similar examples: a lifetime could be spent collecting such vignettes throughout the seasons.

The fells along the western rim of lower Borrowdale, over Cat Bells to High Spy, provide one of the best ridge walks in the district, though, as I explained in the previous chapter, the finest continuation is to carry on over the Robinson group to Buttermere or return by the Newlands beck. Nevertheless, for a shorter day and one of equal interest, it is easy to descend into Borrowdale down the stony track past the derelict Rigg Head Quarries and along Tongue Gill.

The path is unusually wide, due to the old quarrying activities, and this, no doubt, is what led us to call it the 'Old Toll Road' in our youth, when we used it frequently as a way from Grange to Seatoller. It really is a remarkable route, for it keeps well above the valley bottom, skirting along the fellside to the narrow col between Castle Crag and Low Scawdell, then descending to the river and finally to Grange. The scenery is astounding throughout, and to follow this path from Grange to Seatoller is to undertake what is possibly the finest low-level walk in the Lake District.

It also offers the only pedestrian way to the top of Castle Crag, that spectacular volcanic plug which forms part of the Jaws of Borrowdale. The way up is easy—a matter of minutes from the main track—and the top is more satisfactory than many a larger fell. It is a typical eyrie—space all round, the crag isolated from the rest of the dale by plunging tree-girt crags. It overlooks one of the prettiest parts of the valley; the river, trees and rocks blending magnificently.

Whether or not there was ever a castle on the summit is open to conjecture; there is no trace of it nowadays. All that remains are the weathered rocks of the old quarries, with their levels and caves. It was in one of these caves that Millican Dalton lived his strange existence between the wars. Dalton was a 'hippy' before hippies were known. He dressed in home-made clothes which gave him the appearance of a frontiersman, and sailed the Derwent with a raft of his own construction. In summer he wandered the Lakeland fells (he spent the winters in a cabin in the Epping Forest) and was something of a rock-climber, his greatest discovery being the unique Dove's Nest in Comb Gill. Despite his strange ways Dalton was accepted as a 'character' in Borrowdale, and his carefree life style was probably envied by many. To some he appeared as sage and philosopher, though it must be admitted that there were others who disliked him. He died in 1947 at the age of 80 years.

Across the valley from the Cat Bells ridge, a long chain of fells rise at Castlerigg and continue almost due south for ten miles to join the Langdale Pikes at Thunacar Knott. Taken in its entirety it would offer one of the longest and straightest ridge walks in the district, but I doubt if it is often done this way, for the sad fact is that for boring walking it has no equal. Some of the individual fells have a certain appeal—Bleaberry Fell (1,932 feet), High Seat (1,995 feet), Ullscarf (2,370 feet) and High White Stones (2,500 feet) are the principal tops—but the approaches and the ridge itself are nothing more than boggy slogs. None are worth the effort of climbing on their own account, neither for the views they offer (minimal) nor for the exercise they afford—if it is exercise you want, there are much pleasanter ways of getting it than tramping these sodden grass ridges. The two highest summits—Ullscarf and High White Stones—are best visited during the course of other walks. High White Stones, for example, forms the suitable goal of a walk up Easedale, and Ullscarf can be accommodated during a crossing of Greenup Edge, one of the traditional trade routes from Grasmere to Borrowdale.

The northern heights of this long ridge are less easily gained, and until quite recently I had never visited them for I knew their reputation as a non-event. Nevertheless, second-hand opinions are no substitute for the real thing, so one fine April day Duncan and I walked up the good track from Rakefoot, disputing possession of it with a flock of sheep being shepherded on to the moors above the farm, then struck up by the banks of the Brockle Beck into the wilderness known as Low Moss.

The moss is a large shallow bowl, whose highest rim is formed by Bleaberry Fell. No doubt the place is a nightmare in the height of the rainy season, but we were fortunate enough to cross it at the tail end of a long dry spell, and found the conditions much better than we had expected. Only the distance discomfited us— it was two miles of steady plodding before the steep slopes of Bleaberry Fell were reached.

Seen from Low Moss, Bleaberry Fell is an attractive little peak —easily the most attractive in the entire range. It has an asymmetrical profile, and enough rocks to give it an impression of being craggy—though, as is often the case, the crags proved largely fictitious and we had no difficulty in zig-zagging a way up through them to the summit.

10

I believe the summit was the last piece of dry ground we touched until we reached High Seat, a mile or so to the south. Bog—black bog and green bog—was our fate between the two tops, and we were more than ever thankful for the dry weather this time. What it must be like in wet weather I shudder to think. Aesthetically too, the wire fence and iron notices of the Manchester Corporation Water Board, added to our sense of disenchantment.

At High Seat we had had enough and cut steeply down by Raise Beck into Watendlath.

Can there by any other hamlet in the Lake District as well known and easily recognizable as Watendlath? I very much doubt it. Watendlath is every man's instant Lakeland. Along with Tarn Hows near Coniston, it must have featured on almost every Lakeland calendar ever produced. And why not? Why not acknowledge beauty when it stares you in the face, no matter how much it may have been popularized by the camera?

Hackneyed—yes, we must admit that. The hamlet has perhaps suffered from over exposure (if you will forgive the pun) but it is still one of the supreme visual experiences of the district. Then too, there are always the seasonal changes to be taken into account—true of all Lakeland views—and these show different facets of the familiar scene. Go and look at Watendlath in the snow: the experience is rewarding.

The hamlet is connected to Borrowdale by an extremely narrow road which joins the main valley at Ashness Gate. There is a car park at Ashness Gate and another in the hamlet, but it must be confessed that of all the Lake District roads this is the one which ought to be closed to tourist traffic: there is no possible justification for using a car to visit Watendlath.

There actually is such a restriction under active consideration, but at the time of writing the cars on this narrow road must be considered a hazard by anyone who wishes to walk up from Ashness Gate to the hamlet—a great pity because the walk up leads to some remarkable viewpoints over Derwentwater. Best known, and in the same league of photographic reproduction as Watendlath itself, is the view from Ashness Bridge; a lovely pack-horse bridge about half a mile up the road from the lowest car park.

Here also, for those with time to spare for exploring, is one of the most accessible and interesting of ravines—Ashness Gill.

The lower part of the Watendlath valley is well wooded and the trees extend up to and over the line of crags which separates the valley from Borrowdale. There are tenuous paths here, some of which lead to rocky promontories where bird's-eye views of the lake can be obtained. Higher up, the little valley becomes remarkably rocky, with low, steep outcrops on every hand, some of which have been investigated by rock-climbers in search for new climbs, though not, I think, very seriously as yet.

This traditional way up to Watendlath is full of incidental interest but the actual hamlet itself is not seen to advantage from this approach. By far the best approach is over the shoulder of Brund Fell by the well-marked track from Rosthwaite: a steep walk at first, but the whole journey is only a little over a mile and so could scarcely be called strenuous. Once the col is crossed and the descent embarked upon, the tarn and the whitewashed cottages form an increasingly comprehensive picture of this idyllic spot.

But exploration is ever the keynote in Borrowdale: a theme which stands repeating because it is so crucial to a proper appreciation of the place. Watendlath is no different in this respect from other parts of the dale: once the well-known tourist sights are seen (and probably recorded) eschew the homage-beaten paths of Judith Paris and go exploring the outcrops and rugosities of Grange Fell, of which Brund Fell (1,363 feet) is the highest point. Here is a mixture of rock and heather, trees and crags in gloriously uncertain profusion—just the thing for a lazy half-day in summer.

Lazy half-days in summer. Perhaps that epitomizes lower Borrowdale for most of us: only when we get beyond Rosthwaite does the ambience change. The crags, too, are affected by this aura of laziness, though many of the climbs are hard and serious. Sometimes it breeds a guilty feeling—I remember a few years ago attending a conference of climbing instructors which was held in Borrowdale. One after another these worthy (and in some cases eminent) gentlemen rose to their feet and made impassioned pleas for the High Mountain Ideal. We must teach our pupils the Beauty of the Heights (they said). Let us have less of this outcrop scrambling (they said). Let us concentrate on places like Scafell and Pillar, the true Grails (they said). It was all very uplifting and heartening, until one quiet little fellow rose to his feet. "Hands up," he said, "all those who were climbing on Shepherd's Crag today!" And every hand went up.

Climbers are more honest with themselves about their sport, these days. Now that derelict quarries form popular local climbing grounds, and when there are almost as many people climbing on sea cliffs as on mountain crags, you cannot pretend that rock-climbing should only be done on the great crags of the high fells. It was always nonsense anyway—climbing belongs wherever there are rocks to climb.

Rock-climbing has shaken itself free from the constricting shackles of greater mountaineering, and in doing so has enriched the latter. Once climbing gained its independence, it turned, *voluntarily*, towards the high fells and gave them a new lease of life. The high standards won on the outcrops and valley crags have been transferred to Scafell, Pillar and the other great crags until they too bristle with climbs of the most extreme character. There is no evidence to show that the growth of outcrop climbing has had anything but a good effect on mountaineering as a whole.

Of all the valley crags, those in lower Borrowdale are probably the most diverse and certainly the most beautiful. Beauty, of course, is not necessary for good climbing (*vide* some of the popular quarries) but it is a bonus worth having whenever possible.

A comparison with Langdale is inevitable, since it is the great rival of Borrowdale in this, as in other respects. Both have their devotees, and both are quite different. The crags of Langdale retain much more of the mountain atmosphere than do those of lower Borrowdale—which is probably why they were developed earlier—but those of Borrowdale are more intricate and varied. There is a friendliness about the Borrowdale rocks brought on, I am sure, by the leafy nature of the valley, and the intricacies of the landscape. Langdale offers everything at once, like a naked siren; Borrowdale knows how to play the dance of the Seven Veils.

Climbing began in lower Borrowdale at a fairly early date, due principally to the ubiquitous enthusiasm of the Abraham brothers.

Their routes, however, were of little worth, and the most surprising thing about this epoch was the utter failure of anybody to discover Shepherd's Crag. Then, in May 1914, another Keswick photographer, Ralph Mayson, with his climbing partner Mallinson, climbed *Troutdale Pinnacle* and *Bowderstone Pinnacle*: two truly outstanding discoveries which remain to this day amongst the best of the easier Borrowdale climbs.

The First World War put an end to exploration in the valley for a time, but then in 1921 Bentley Beetham and C. D. Frankland, two Yorkshire gritstoners, climbed the short but conspicuous *Woden's Face* near the Bowderstone. For Beetham, a schoolmaster who was one of the earliest exponents of 'outdoor activities' for his pupils, it began a life-long association with the valley crags.

Beetham's name must for ever be associated with Borrowdale. He it was who turned the valley into a major climbing centre, and he did it practically single handed. His best route was unquestionably *Little Chamonix*, on Shepherd's Crag, which he climbed in 1946 and which is perhaps the one route in the lower grades to equal the earlier climbs of Mallinson and Mayson. But Beetham's contribution was more than that of a mere innovator of a few good climbs: he has the almost unique distinction for modern times of being the sole and undisputed discoverer of a major crag. By sheer luck, or a quick eye for detail, believe whichever you wish, Beetham discovered Shepherd's Crag.

The discovery of Shepherd's Crag was an outstanding event in itself, but Beetham had the wit to put his discovery to good use. He was quick to realize that though the crag was a big one by local valley standards it was not continuous, as the great crags of the fells tended to be, but broken by ledges which made easy escape possible at the end of most pitches. Beetham ignored this: he simply strung the pitches together, *pretending* they were continuous. It was to this lack of continuity that most of the critics of valley climbing objected. They claimed it made the climbing artificial, but others pointed out that such a criterion was false; taken on that basis almost *all* climbing in Britain is artificial, since there is invariably an easy way up.

This perspicacious use of Shepherd's, as much as the finding of the crag itself, was Bentley Beetham's great contribution to British climbing. It opened new horizons. Unfortunately, Beetham himself took the idea to extremes—he began to search the fells looking for odd outcrops he could string together and call a climb, and some of his discoveries bordered on the ludicrous. Because of this his reputation suffered badly amongst later climbers, especially as he included all his routes, good, bad or indifferent, in the guide to Borrowdale rock-climbs which he edited for the Fell and Rock Club. A dalesman who was also a climber once summed it all up with a sad shake of his head. "The trouble wi' Bentley," he said, "was he was allus looking for another Shepherd's."

Although nobody could rival Beetham's connection with Borrowdale, if only because he held the palm for so long and was such an innovator, Paul Ross has come close to doing so. Ross dominated the valley climbing during the '50s, bringing it into line with modern developments elsewhere by a series of hard climbs on the major rocks such as *Obituary Groove* and the *Shroud* on Black Crag. Perhaps his finest contribution was to open up the largely overhanging rocks of Lower Falcon Crag with routes such as *Funeral Way* (he seems to have been in a morbid frame of mind at this time!), *Hedera Grooves*, and *Spinup*.

Ross dominated the valley, but he was not alone in setting high standards. George Fisher (of climbing shop fame) had preceded him with routes such as *Kransic Crack* at Shepherd's, and there were others like McHaffie and Les Kendall who played important parts in developing the rocks. Strangely enough, some of the best climbs were snatched by 'offcomers' and one thinks particularly of Vaughn's *Fool's Paradise*, Wilkinson's *Brown Crag Wall*, Veever's *Ardus* and Peascod's *Eve*: all post-war routes of fine quality. The greatest blow of all to the locals was Les Brown's snatch of *The Praying Mantis*: an extreme climb which did much to establish the popularity of Goat Crag, which lies across the valley from the other rocks.

The intensive, one might say single-minded, development of Borrowdale by Beetham and Ross has resulted in a wide variety of climbs of all standards from the easiest to the hardest, which has transformed the valley into the most popular of all Lakeland climbing grounds.

The lower Borrowdale crags extend from Walla Crag at the entrance of the valley to Bowderstone Crags on Grange Fell. They are not continuous but near enough to each other, and so masked by trees, as to give that impression: there are twelve separately identifiable outcrops in a space of some five miles. Not all are of prime importance, of course, but from north to south, Lower Falcon, Gowder, Shepherd's, Troutdale and Bowderstone are all crags of interest.

Climbers' paths run below and amongst all these rocks, making them easily accessible to anyone who cares to investigate them— and they are worth looking at, even by non-climbers, for the architecture of the rock and the sylvan nature of their settings. Being so readily accessible, too—in most cases only a few minutes' walk from the road—they are of interest to the photographer who likes to take action pictures, but who balks at the thought of carrying a camera bag and a collection of lenses up to the crags of the higher fells.

From this point of view the most open, and to the observer, the least interesting, is Lower Falcon Crag, reached in a few minutes' walk from the car park at Ashness Gate. The crag is a conspicuous landmark as you drive into Borrowdale—very stark and bold, though once directly below it on the road, it loses impressiveness. Falcon Crag proper, which is above it on the left and separated by a dramatic looking cleft too large to be called a gully, is far more impressive and it is not until you walk up to the rocks that the serious nature of Lower Falcon becomes apparent.

There are no easy climbs on these rocks; *Hedera Grooves*, a 'mild very severe' which takes the conspicuous central groove, is the easiest to hope for and enjoys a reputation of being the 'ordinary route' for most climbers. *Spinup*, at the left-hand end, traverses across to join the finish of *Hedera Grooves*, and the two routes are perhaps the best known on the crag. *The Niche* and the *Girdle Traverse* are much harder.

Though there are climbs on the upper crag, too, they have never enjoyed the same popularity. The trouble is that the rock is not always trustworthy, and indeed Lower Falcon itself sometimes needs handling with care—a friend of mine had quite a fright when a huge chunk of the Girdle Traverse came away just as he stepped off it!

The Falcon Crags stand out boldly on open fellside, but once you have moved down the valley a short way, past Ashness Gate and the road to Watendlath, the trees of Grange Fell begin to enclose everything in their all-enveloping blanket.

Gowder is the crag which rises so stupendously from the trees behind the Lodore Hotel. It is best observed from the hotel car park, and from this place it is easily the most impressive looking crag of lower Borrowdale: tall spires of rock, the sight of which would quicken the pulses of any climber. They are reached by the path to the Lodore Falls; a path carefully guarded by a toll gate, though climbers seem to regard this simply as another obstacle to be avoided, like a bad pitch. The rock and falls can be visited during the same short walk, but both prove rather disappointing on due acquaintance. The rocks look much better from a distance and Southey's famous waterfall is only at its best when it is in spate after a heavy downpour.

Nevertheless, from a climber's point of view Gowder Crag is important because of *Fool's Paradise*, a magnificent 'v.s.' climb which has the distinction of being the longest in lower Borrowdale—over 400 feet. It goes up the left-hand side of the tall buttress then traverses across to finish up a fine chimney pitch: the whole climb being steep and exposed. Though it is not hard by present-day standards, it is still not a climb for novices. Many knowledgeable experts would include *Fool's Paradise* in their list of the best dozen climbs in Lakeland.

From the Lodore the main road climbs up a steep little rise, then runs more or less straight and level for half a mile to the Borrowdale Hotel. Between these two hostelries lies Shepherd's Crag; most famous of all the Borrowdale outcrops.

Shepherd's is remarkably well hidden by its screen of trees, despite being the most readily accessible crag of them all. Ways up to it from the road are numerous, and indicated by man-made breaches in the roadside banks, each major incursion leading to a specific part of the rocks, for Shepherd's is a long crag and a lot of time can be wasted if you come up to it at the wrong point. However, only an expert can be so precise and most climbers are content to approach the rocks from one or other end, where the paths are better than average.

The reasons for the continual popularity of Shepherd's Crag are the wide variety of climbs of all standards except the most extreme, and the extraordinarily high proportions of good climbs to bad. In fact, almost every climb here has some merit, or it fulfils some special need in the education of a novice.

Even the curious traveller, who has no intention of embarking on a roped climb, but merely wishes to observe the place, is well favoured at Shepherd's. It is possible to reach the crag at the Brown Slabs and, follow the climbers' path along the base of the rocks to the stone wall below Jackdaw Ridge, scramble up the easy gully just beyond this point, then walk back along the broad and pleasant Belvedere, above the climbs, to the top of Brown Slabs from where a rather steep, earthy path descends to the starting point. There is no danger in such a perambulation, providing books are worn and reasonable care taken, and the views from the Belvedere make it very worth while. If someone happens to be finishing *Little Chamonix* at the time, you will have a close-up of rock-climbers in action of the kind usually denied to non-climbers.

The principal rocks at Shepherd's Crag lie in three distinct groups between which are broken, tree-invested slopes and a handful of minor routes practically nobody bothers with. I remember years ago I searched in the jungle next to Brown Slabs for a moderate climb of Beetham's known as the *100 foot Slab*. It was only when I was above the slab, that I realized I had climbed it, it was so broken: it must take the prize as being the worst of Beetham's routes, worse even than the celebrated *Rabbit's Trod* in Gillercomb.

The first group of climbs, at the northern end of the rocks, is the Brown Slabs area. It is a right angle of rock, the left wall of which is very steep and contains several high standard climbs. The classic, however, is the 'hard severe', *Brown Crag Wall*: one of the best climbs on Shepherd's. Round the corner, the rocks lie back in steep flat slabs which have been the nursery for literally thousands of novices. The holds are capacious, but the climbs are surprisingly exposed. The *Arête* is a neat little route for any novice.

Trees crowd the rocks beyond the slabs until a little bay shows a strange crack line in the contorted crags, and beyond that again, a very bold, almost evil-looking buttress. This is the celebrated *North Buttress*, once regarded as the hardest climb on Shepherd's Crag, a position which has slipped away from it in latter years as climbing standards have risen. The buttress is an unusual climb for Shepherd's, especially in the lower two-thirds which are reminiscent of some of the Welsh valley crags. Some route finding ability is necessary and the rock (a few years ago, anyway) not all that sound. The *Direct Finish* is certainly the crux—steep and strenuous, and it used to be done with the aid of two pegs, though I have no doubt it has been done without any artificial aid since those days. Not only is it a good climb, but *North Buttress* is also interesting as being one of the few Lakeland climbs in which Don Whillans played a rôle on the first ascent.

Despite its downgrading, *North Buttress* is still a hard climb by many people's standards, but fortunately the buttress is also a landmark for a collection of particularly good climbs nearby—taken all round, probably the best climbs on the rocks for the average climber. Two are of particular interest and have long been known as minor classics—*Eve* ('very severe') with its delicate little traverse, and *Ardus* ('severe') which takes (more or less) the great corner crack, then, just as further progress looks impossible, boldly traverses out to the left across a wall to finish up a little crack. There can be few climbs anywhere so short in length—135 feet— yet so exposed.

From North Buttress a walk across the screes brings you to *Kransic Crack*, the unmistakable great flake crack which was obviously designed to be climbed. George Fisher was the first to do it (1952) and for a few years it became a test piece for experts, though it is much too short to be anything more: more like a gritstone 'problem' than a Lakeland climb. This is the Chamonix area, so called from a climb of that name, and the undoubted classic is Bentley Beetham's *Little Chamonix*: only 'v. diff.' in standard, but one of the best climbs of that grade to be found anywhere.

Once again a bay of scree separates these climbs from the final buttress. Here the best-known route is *Donkey's Ears*, a name which has no meaning until you reach the middle of the climb where two large rocks stick up at angles just like the ears of some enormous stone donkey. Some of the individual pitches are good, but the climb as a whole is too easy to escape from—there is always an easier alternative to the proper route. I was once very glad of this: a young lady I was leading up the climb insisted on falling off the celebrated hand-traverse, which though not difficult needs to be done quickly before the strength drains out of your arms. After the fifth attempt had ended in a feminine "eek!" and a sudden tug on the rope, I decided to call it quits and showed her a much easier alternative. Usually, it is a bad thing to deny a learner the chance of doing a pitch, no matter how long he or she may take, because it undermines their confidence, but in this case I made an exception since each attempt simply sapped away her arm strength even more. In a hand traverse, most of your weight is taken by your arms because there are no real footholds, and if you do not do it after a couple of attempts you are not likely to do it at all.

The final rocks, just around the corner from *Donkey's Ears* has some climbs with steep but not too difficult starts, then long stretches of easy climbing to the top. They are ideal for teaching novices rope handling and belaying in perfect safety.

The climbs I have mentioned are only a fraction of those available on this universally popular crag. Shepherd's has become the Stanage of the Lake District: the climbing ground of Everyman. Those who prefer solitude, or who disdain to climb under the critical gaze of the knowledgeable onlooker had best keep away— but to do so means missing some wonderful routes, and climbs like *Ardus* or *Little Chamonix*, are not worth missing on any account.

With Shepherd's Crag the choice of climb is so wide and varied that to choose one route and proclaim it best of all would be ludicrous. With other crags this is not always the case: sometimes a particular climb proclaims itself by quality and situation to be *the* route on the crag.

Such is the case with the next crag up the valley from Shepherd's. Black Crag rises impressively at the head of the little Troutdale; a side valley cutting into Grange Fell from Borrowdale.

Scenically, it is one of the finest crags in the district, and even if you have no intention of climbing, a walk up Troutdale on a summer's afternoon, possibly (if energy allows it) continuing over Grange Fell to Watendlath, is a walk to be remembered.

The crag itself is big and bold, more after the fashion of upper Borrowdale than the valley crags we are at present concerned with, except of course, that it has its screen of trees. But no amount of trees could hide a crag like this one: it rears out of them defiantly, shrugging them off as a lion might shrug off persistent flies.

There are a number of good climbs on this crag, some of them hard—but few would deny that the route of the crag is the famous *Troutdale Pinnacle.*

Nobody seems to agree about the standard of this climb, except that it is somewhere between 'very difficult' and 'severe', but everyone agrees that it is one of the best routes in Lakeland. It goes up a succession of grooves on the right-hand part of the face then boldly traverses across the exposed upper slabs to a prominent rib on the left. The traverse looks sensational, but in fact comforting holds make it technically quite simple. The final rib turns out to be the 'pinnacle' itself: a truly alpine-style *arête* of the best sort, and it is here, just as the top is almost within grasp, that the crux move comes—an awkward little step in a groove that catches most people unawares.

Like *Fool's Paradise* on Gowder, *Troutdale Pinnacle* is one of the longer climbs in lower Borrowdale—375 feet—and each, at its own level of attainment, is probably the best in the valley.

But for sheer length, if that is to be the only criterion, the crag which faces Black Crag across Troutdale can hardly be rivalled. This is Great End Crag, a prominent landmark, well seen from Grange Bridge, and a most exciting looking crag. Alas! All is not what it seems. The trees which form an attractive surround for most Borrowdale crags here make an almost impenetrable jungle, and reaching the climbs might turn out to be as difficult as climbing them. Some of the climbs, when you find them, are quite hard, and of course, they are long—but there are no other redeeming features. The longest of all (one of the longest in the Lakes) is the 'moderate' called *Mountain Way*, 770 feet; though there is some doubt as to whether it is really a climb with a lot of walking involved, or a walk with some climbing in it. The whole area is recommended as a practice ground for anyone contemplating an exploratory trip up the Amazon.

All around this part of the valley the trees assume command. They sweep round unchecked both below and above Grange Crags, forming an effective screen for the car park near the Bowderstone Quarry. Quayfoot Buttress pokes up above the quarry: another crag with an assortment of routes fighting the trees, and a thoroughly dirty and unpleasant place. Much better is to walk along the good path from the car park to the Bowderstone itself.

Though the walk is a short one, it is not without interest: typical of these Borrowdale nooks and crannies that can only be explored by poking about in them. The quarry itself is an interesting bit of rock architecture where a number of unusual climbs have been made. A short distance further on is Woden's Face, an unusual isolated slab that contains two or three steep little climbs of a 'mild severe' or 'very difficult' nature. These routes are genuine boulder problems with small holds, and a summer's day will generally see a group of novices learning the finer points of balance climbing on them.

The finale of this short stroll is, of course, the famous Bowder Stone itself, one of the archetypal Victorian sights of Lakeland. The stone is an immense boulder which has presumably rolled down from the crags above many centuries ago. Access to the top is by ladder or the slippery 'north ridge', but the whole boulder now has a somewhat careworn look about it. From nearby, though, there is a splendid view of upper Borrowdale.

Above the Bowder Stone, and almost completely hidden by trees are the Bowderstone Crags to reach which involves a steep toil up a mass of large boulders. Most of the routes are hard to identify and not particularly entertaining, but *Bowderstone Pinnacle* (an easy 'v. diff.') has always been a favourite of the valley. The climb is fairly short, but the pitches are interesting and well worth doing. Most of the other climbs hereabouts can only be described as weird.

Shortly after Rosthwaite has been reached Borrowdale changes in character. The valley divides its energies into several head-waters. The main valley continues to Stockley Bridge where it receives the waters of Styhead Gill and Grains Gill, but another branch diverges to Stonethwaite, then Greenup and Langstrath. Between these two main branches of the valley lies the Glaramara massif: one of the finest fells in Lakeland.

Glaramara is a little world unto itself. Steep fellside separates it from lonely Langstrath and even steeper slopes look down on Borrowdale and Grains Gill. To the south it is connected only with Allen Crags (2,572 feet)—itself one of the most isolated summits in the district—whilst northwards are the ring of crags overlooking Comb Gill. It is so aloof, yet so near to a popular tourist valley that the two facts hardly seem compatible—which is true? Is it as isolated as it appears or is it all make-believe? Well, I have spent as much time on and around this mountain as I have on any other in the district and I really do believe that Glaramara has managed to cut itself off from the world at large. Even in high summer, these fells are never overpopulated. In winter, they are often yours alone for the asking.

This may be because Glaramara has no worthwhile ridge connections and so can scarcely form part of a long ridgewalk, and yet, as is so often the case in Borrowdale, it makes within itself an area of intense interest. Furthermore, it is a mountaineer's mountain, never completely tamed in any aspect.

I have climbed it in all seasons and all weathers. Two of the worst gales I have ever encountered in Lakeland have caught me descending the rough flanks of the fell into Langstrath: once with my wife after a visit to Tarn at Leaves, a lovely high-level pool on the northern ridge of the massif, and the second time after a rain-soaked struggle across the hand-traverse of *Corvus* with Ed Adamson, but I have also enjoyed many days of hot sunshine, climbing or walking with a few chosen companions on this fell.

One of the finest mountain days of my life was spent on Glara-mara. We did not do anything particularly daring or strenuous, yet in the end the sum total of our experiences added up to immense pleasure.

At that time Arthur Hassall had a little hut in Borrowdale: a converted platelayers' hut which he had managed to get permission to keep at Chapel Farm and a group of us occupied the hut one winter's week-end and we had as a guest a Spanish climber whom we had discovered wandering disconsolately in Preston, of all places. The Friday night had been spent in the back bar of the Scafell Hotel playing a vicious card game called 'Seven and a Half', and what with that and the ale, none of us were feeling too good when Saturday morning came round. We cooked a desultory sort of breakfast, whilst our Spanish guest champed at the bit impatiently.

"It is nearly eleven o'clock," he complained. "In Spain we set out much earlier than this!"

"That's because you move so slowly," we said, encouragingly.

But he had a point, so we got our gear on and stamped out into a crisp white snow-filled world.

We tramped up Comb Gill, a superb hanging valley made even more magnificent by the snow. Great black rocks, ribboned in white, rose on either hand whilst ahead of us the huge bulk of Raven Crag loomed like some giant peak of the Oberland.

At the head of the valley the Gill becomes a ravine which in summer is a tumble of boulders descending from the aptly named Comb Door: a typical Alpine *porte* or sharply defined gap in a rock ridge. The boulders now resembled a stream of Christmas puddings each covered in white sauce, but on either flank the steep walls of the gill seemed interesting. At first the snow proved softly unstable but we managed to work our way up from ledge to ledge until, at about 2,000 feet, we emerged on to a slope of steep compacted snow in which we were able to kick steps.

We climbed up to the Door, passed through it, and gazed upon a magnificent panorama of white mountains. The gentle curves of Ullscarf were like white breasts beyond which towered the Helvellyn range. Peak after peak stood sharply etched, fading into blues in the extreme distance where, like some final sentinel, the Pennine giant of Cross Fell rose as a white cone, forty miles away. Over all was a sky of pale washed blue, arcing from horizon to horizon. We all stood transfixed: I doubt if any of us had seen a view of such overpowering magnificence before, even in the Alps.

The air was not only clear, it was sharply cold into the bargain and once we had recovered from our surprise at the view we looked to the way ahead. A steep little ice wall showed us a direct way to the top of the subsidiary summit called Comb Head. We put on rope and crampons and soon were scraping our way precariously upwards. It was short but warming work, and once we were on top Glaramara revealed yet another surprise. What in summer is an uninteresting hollow between Comb Head and Glaramara proper now lay revealed as an arctic valley beyond which the final cone reared up in splendid fashion.

We plunged down into the valley and were soon attacking the summit cone. Much to our surprise it proved a lot steeper than we had expected and it was not long before we had fallen into line, each following the leader's steps as he kicked remorselessly upwards. Then, just as the slope seemed endless, a final few steps brought us over the rim—right to the summit cairn.

What a magnificent ascent it had been! Quite definitely the most elegant winter ascent I have ever made of a Lakeland peak, superior even to the Hall's Fell ridge of Blencathra.

We did not linger. The cold was extreme and despite my woollen mitts I began to feel the numbing onset of frostbite. We headed straight for Grains Gill, dodging the outcrops and finally glissading down to the valley. As evening fell we tramped back through Seathwaite, well content with our day's work. Our Spanish friend was suitably impressed.

Even in summer Comb Gill is a remarkable place. It is the perfect hanging valley, and it is surrounded on all sides by the most incredible crags, most of which have been climbed and all of which are fairly easy. Only the massive Raven Crag offers more serious climbing: the rest are rocks for novices to explore at their leisure. Most of them have been charted in guide-books and some are quite well known, but really they are best tackled in a spirit of pioneering adventure, under the guidance of a competent leader.

Apart from Raven Crag, only one set of rocks deserves special mention—the unique Doves' Nest. This can be seen way up on the left as you walk up Comb Gill. It looks like a normal crag but

Above Shepherds Crag, Borrowdale, at the end of the climbing day
Skiddaw from the Latrigg path

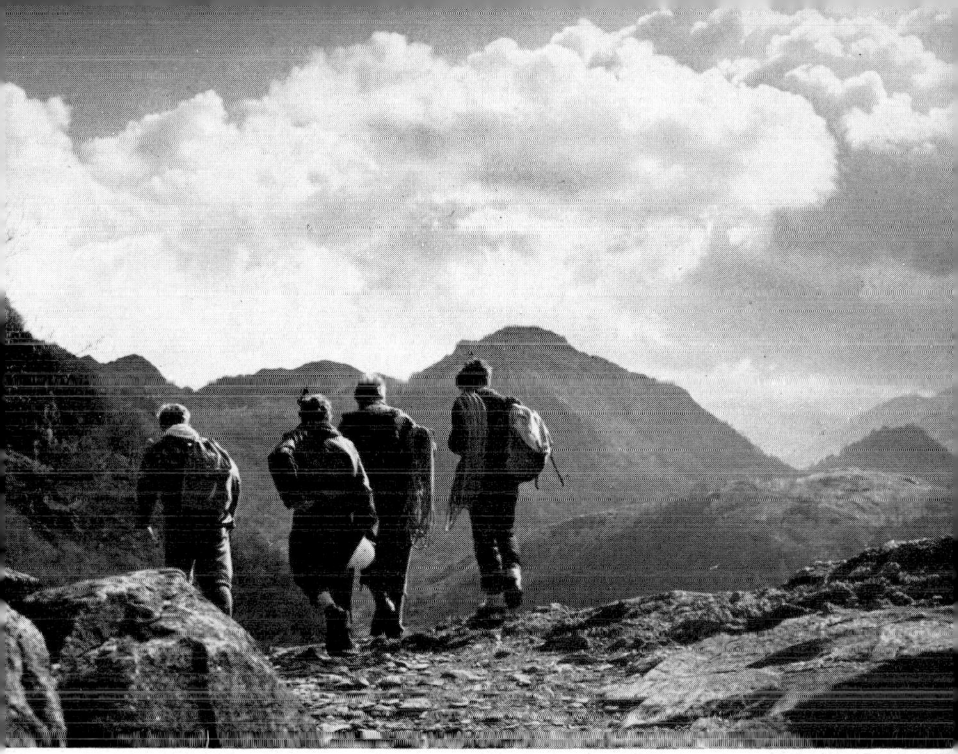

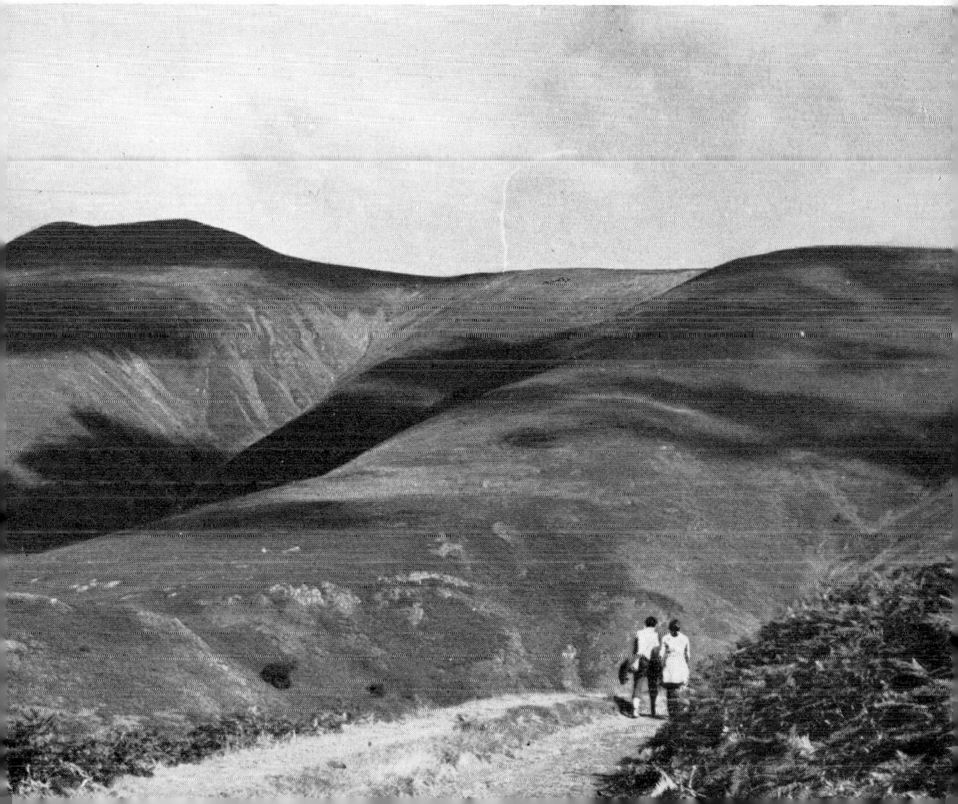

it is far from being that: in some past age a whole rock face became dislodged from the fellside, slipped a few feet then came to rest. The result is a gap between the visible outer surface of the rocks and the inner core, but as might be expected from nature, the gap is an irregular one and the final result resembles a series of caves penetrating into the mountain.

Access to the caves can be made in several ways, but the 'he man' entry is well to the left and is known as the *Rat Hole*. It comprises a very narrow, low hole in the rocks through which it is just possible for a body to squirm. This gives entrance to a remarkable cleft in the bowels of the fell, no more than a few inches wide and about forty feet high, lit by an aperture at the top through which daylight filters eerily. The trick is to squirm upwards towards the daylight: there is no danger of falling, the rock grips too tightly for that, but anyone of more than modest girth will find the way up to be utterly exhausting. It is more like potholing than climbing.

The *Rat Hole* is something of a claustrophobic experience which some people find quite unnerving. It leads to the big gully from which it is possible to enter the rest of the caves. These are quite different. They are much more commodious than the *Rat Hole*, but they are so dark that a torch is necessary for their exploration. One word of warning at this point: the climbing involved in the exploration of these caves is about 'diff.' in standard, and has to be undertaken by torch light. A rope is an obvious precaution and some climbing ability too—otherwise they are best left alone.

It must be confessed that the caves are not very extensive, but they are amusing. From them it is possible to crawl out on to the front of the buttress and climb up by a neat little route called *Face Route*, which leads to the top of the crag.

But these are just fun rocks: the serious climbing of Comb Gill is concentrated on the massive face of Raven Crag which dominates the little valley to an almost overpowering degree. To look at Raven Crag from the floor of the valley is to see an immense shield of rocks, riven by deep gullies, but soaring up purposefully to an apex. Under the right conditions of weather and lighting (especially in winter) it can be one of the most impressive crags in the district.

11

Blencathra
Back o' Skidda'

The truth, unfortunately, is much less exciting. Closer inspection shows the crag to be of reasonable angle and very broken—a bit like Lliwedd in Wales, or perhaps the upper part of Pavey Ark; neither analogy is perfect, but anyone who knows those crags will have some grasp of the formation: nevertheless, it is not possible to wander at will over these vast rocks, though it might seem that way at first glance. The rocks are cunningly contrived into a series of blind alleys, channelling the climber along certain well-defined routes. As it happens, these are mostly in the easier grades, and it soon becomes apparent that Raven Crag has only a little to offer the 'hard man'.

For those of more modest ambition, however, there are some long climbs (up to about 500 feet) of a satisfying nature. Best of all is undoubtedly *Corvus*, a 'difficult' grade climb which has rapidly established itself as a classic of the district, comparable with *Bowfell Buttress* in Langdale, though not quite so difficult. Like *Bowfell Buttress*, too, *Corvus* is a mountaineering route; which is to say it has that genuine feel of the mountains about it raising it above the mere technicalities of a rock-climb. Indeed, technical achievement is slight on a climb like *Corvus*—yet there is something much more satisfying about it than there is about some of the short, illogical 'very severes' which fill in the odd niches of our crags. It is unfortunate that there is a tendency these days to concentrate solely on technique in rock-climbing and climb likes *Corvus* are sometimes scoffed at by hard young men who, one suspects, come to the crags for all the wrong reasons.

Comb Gill is the key to Glaramara. The ordinary route to the summit follows the gill for a short distance before sloping away up Thornythwaite Fell, which is really a long spur of the parent mountain. It is an easy ascent, but extremely pleasant and never boring: in fact, if you take the final few feet by the 'direct' track there is an interesting little rock step to overcome, reminiscent of the so-called 'bad step' on Crinkle Crags.

For most walkers this way up, from Mountain View Cottages, is likely to be the only practicable way, and it also serves as the best way down. Unless you are prepared to put up with some fairly rough going, Glaramara does not lend itself to a traverse. All other ways up and down the mountain are either long, or tough, or both. Only a masochist would try to climb the fell from Langstrath or Seathwaite, though a competent snow and ice man might find some interest on these slopes in a good winter. As for the ascent from Langdale via Rossett Gill and Allen Crags, I can only say that it is one of the longest and most arduous ascents in the Lake District—and especially if a return has to be made by the same route.

The trouble with making a simple ascent of the fell is that it is hardly sufficient to fill a summer's day: indeed, it can easily be accomplished before lunch. If something more is wanted then probably the best idea is to traverse the ridge to Allen Crags, descending from these to the head of Langstrath, and following the latter valley back to Stonethwaite and Borrowdale. This is a round journey of about twelve miles and, done in this direction, too full of interest to be fatiguing. The ridge itself is a switchback of knolls and tarns which until quite recently was both confusing and tiring, though a line of cairns has now done much to help create a path which makes the traverse simpler. From Allen Crags the main track goes to Angle Tarn, and from there the long but easy walk down the well-named Langstrath provides an interesting return journey.

Langstrath is famous for its pools and its crags and both are worthy of examination. The pools at Tray Dub, Swan Dub and Blackmoss Pot are deep and inviting on a hot summer's day and in this respect Langstrath beck offers better opportunities for the avid mountain bather than any comparable stream, with the exception of Eskdale. Such frivolities, however, are not to everyone's taste and the bashful traveller may prefer to hurry past with averted gaze, fixing his strongly masculine eyes on the crags which cluster near the foot of the valley.

Here is the famous *Sergeant's Crag Gully*, first climbed by O. G. Jones and J. W. Robinson in 1893; for long regarded as something of a test piece in gully climbing, though it now earns only a 'v. diff.' grade of difficulty. On the rocks near the gully, and on Heron Crag, which is next in line down the valley, Bentley Beetham made a number of climbs in the '40s but they never really caught popular fancy. Shortly after this, W. Peascod, a brilliant Lakeland climber of the immediate post-war years, rediscovered Eagle Crag, that great bastion of rock which forms the cornerstone between Langstrath and Greenup Gill. A few poor gully climbs had been done on this crag in the early years of the century, but the buttresses themselves were much too forbidding for the techniques of those days. Peascod opened up with *Falconer's Crack* ('v.s.') and followed it a fortnight later with *The Great Stair* ('v.s.')—a series of huge steps on the left-hand side of the crag, and the slightly easier *Postern Gate* ('h.s.'). It set a new standard of difficulty for Borrowdale: *Falconer's Crack* was regarded as the hardest route in the district.

It was confidently thought that Peascod had worked out all the feasible lines of attack on this formidable crag, and nine years passed before Mike Thompson put up *Green Wall*, another 'v.s.'. With Thompson was Peter Lockey who saw what looked like another possible line of attack a little to the right of *Green Wall*. The following year Lockey returned with Paul Ross, then 19 and already a name in Borrowdale climbing, and, sharing the lead, they climbed the incredibly difficult *Post Mortem* ('extreme'): at once the most technically difficult route in the area.

In the years which followed a number of other hard climbs were added to Eagle Crag, though none, perhaps, quite to match the quality of *Post Mortem*. For a brief spell the crag was the 'in place' for *avant-garde* Borrowdale climbers, vying for attention with Lower Falcon Crag—but then Goat Crag was discovered and the tide of innovation swept away. Nevertheless, along with Goat Crag and Lower Falcon Crag, it forms one of the three major Borrowdale crags for hard men.

Langstrath debouches into the Stonethwaite valley: one of the prettiest corners of Borrowdale. The hamlet of Stonethwaite nestles under the crags and woods of Rosthwaite Fell and has the good fortune to have no through road. Instead, a pretty path leads up past the strange-looking Lining Crag to Greenup Edge and Far Easedale—an easy way to climb Ullscarf or High White Stones. This crossing of Greenup Edge has long been a traditional way from Grasmere to Borrowdale or vice versa, and the contrast between the savage sternness of Far Easedale and the sylvan valley of the Stonethwaite beck makes it one of the most enjoyable walks in the district, despite the bogginess of the short middle

reaches. Really it is quite like Pilgrim's Progress, travelling
through the Valley of Despair and the Slough of Despond, than
by breasting the final slopes of Greenup, The Promised Land
comes into view.

Borrowdale finally trails away up by Seathwaite, Grains Gill
and Styhead Gill. Here, at the side of the lovely Sourmilk Gill
cascades, are the remains of the famous Borrowdale Plumbago
Mines, once one of the richest properties in the kingdom. Plumbago is graphite or black lead of the sort used in pencil manufacture, and it was these mines which formed the basis for the
Keswick pencil industry.

There was a time [writes Harriet Matineau] when the value of this
plumbago was so little known that the shepherds used it freely to
mark their sheep: and next, the proprietors were obtaining from
thirty to forty shillings a pound for the lead of one single 'sop'
which yielded upwards of twenty-eight tons. Those were the days
when houses were built at the entrance, where the workmen were
obliged to change their clothes, under inspection, lest they should
be tempted to carry away any of the precious stuff in their pockets.

Harriet makes it sound more like a modern diamond mine than
one producing such mundane stuff as the lead for a simple pencil.
But of course she was right: the mines had to be well guarded at
the height of their prosperity and poachers were by no means
uncommon. At the time of which Harriet writes, a pound of
black lead would have paid a farm labourer's wages for a month.

Attractive though Seathwaite may be, it does not really compare with the middle reaches of the valley. The real magnificence
of upper Borrowdale rests so utterly in Glaramara that everything
else must be counted as anticlimax.

7

Skiddaw and Blencathra

"My neighbour Skiddaw" is how the poet Southey referred to the great mass of fell overlooking his home town of Keswick, and the phrase is an apt one indeed, for no other mountain in Britain so dominates a town as Skiddaw does Keswick. Seen from the shores of Derwentwater it fills the horizon with its bulk, and from Castlerigg, or better still, Low Rigg between Dale Bottom and St John's in the Vale, it seems to sit brooding over the little town. There are few views which draw the comparison of scale between the great bulk of the fells and our own puny man-made constructions, as this one of Skiddaw and Keswick.

The two are as one; inseparable twins, so that the thought of one is always linked with the other. Ben Nevis, far higher and a much nobler mountain, does not do the same for Fort William because they are too much set apart by Glen Nevis, nor does Snowdon dominate Llanberis to any great degree, and even within the confines of the Lake District itself neither Ambleside nor Windermere have anything to rival it. Perhaps the nearest to match it is Coniston—but there the dominating mass is a whole range of fells, which act more like a general backcloth and do not have such an air of singular dominance.

It is not only its nearness to Keswick but also its isolation from the other fells which give Skiddaw such a dominant air. Even its nearest neighbour, Blencathra, is separated from it by the wide valley of the Glenderaterra beck, whilst the lake of Bassenthwaite and the vale of Keswick separate it from the Lorton and Grisedale

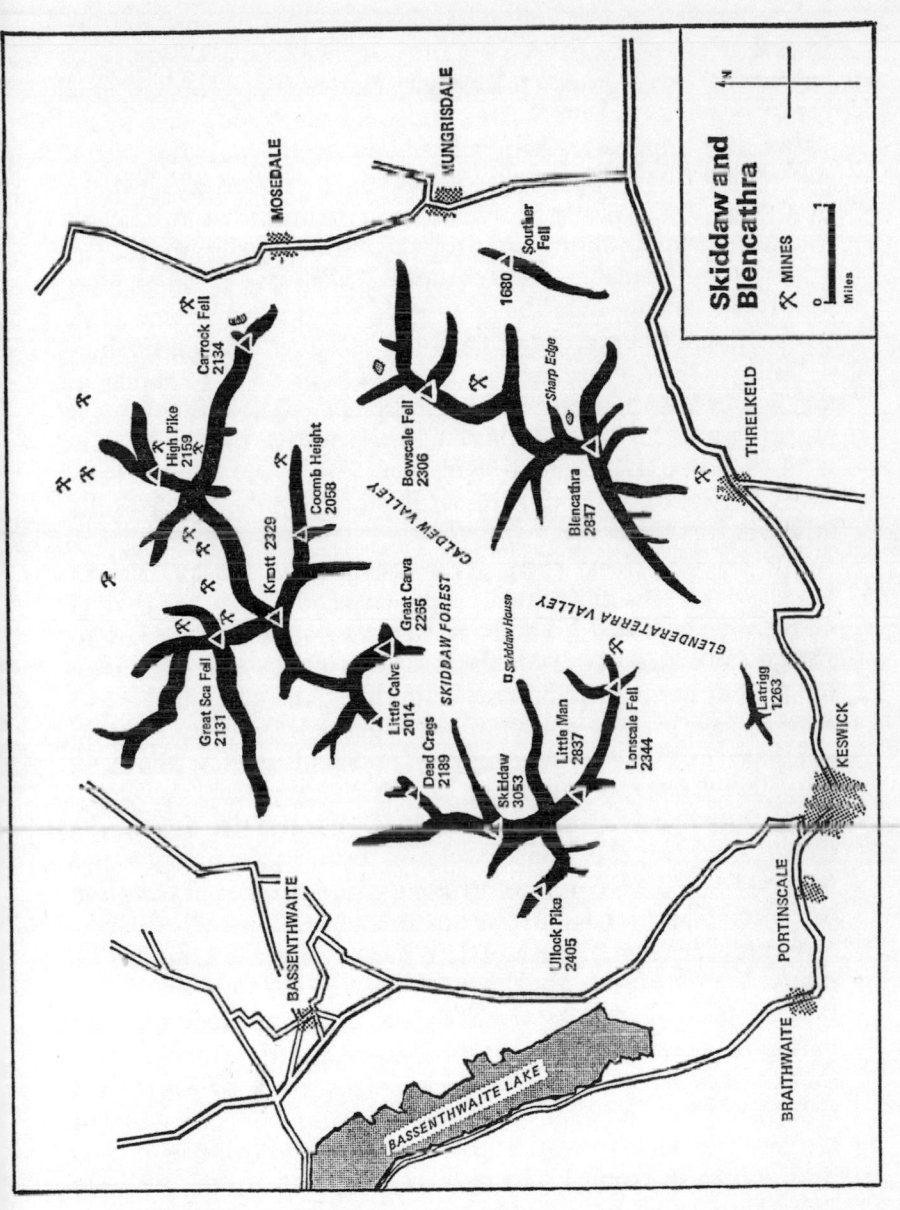

Skiddaw and
Blencathra

fells in the west. South, too, it has no challengers of eminence for several miles.

". . . it asserts itself to Keswick visitors like a bishop at a bazaar," wrote Graham Sutton, and went on to add, "It is bland rather than impressive. Its position does it no good: full in the sun's face, all day long, so that it lacks the definition and majesty that transverse shadows would give. It lacks colour too, at all events in the midsummer months when most pilgrims see it . . ."

The artist Pennant, two centuries earlier, saw it differently. He saw it "smiling over the country like a gentle generous lord, while the fells of Borrowdale frown on it like a hardened tyrant."

Both are right, of course, for Skiddaw is bland and smiling in fair weather. Perhaps this is why the average fell-walker finds it so unappealing? It is one of those fells which have the unfortunate distinction of only being climbed once—just to say one has been there. A pity, considering that it is the fourth highest peak in the whole district.

The trouble is that there are so many negative qualities to Skiddaw that it is difficult to arouse any enthusiasm for it all. I know quite well that if I were to suggest a walk up Skiddaw to any of my mountaineering friends, even on an 'off day', they would stare at me incredulously as if I had gone quite mad. Most of them have been regular visitors to the Lakes for years, but I do not think any of them have ever been up Skiddaw. Poor Skiddaw, it is rather that sort of mountain.

The only positive thing that it does is show its best face to the world at large. The popular view—from Derwentwater and preferably on a fine autumn evening—is also far and away the best view. Close at hand, it has no attractive features whatsoever, except for the craggy north-eastern serrations of the Ullock Pike ridge—but those can only be seen from near the summit.

Skiddaw is climbed by hundreds of people on every fine day during the season, though 'climbed' is perhaps too strong a word for the normal ascent from Keswick, because there is a path broad enough to take a marching army all the way to the top. It is one of the few fells where, on the ordinary ascent, it is impossible to miss your way even in mist or rain. To do so would not only show an extraordinary degree of incompetence, but hint at an over indulgence in alcohol—though even that is no excuse really: the Wordsworth and Southey families and their friends got pretty tipsy when they climbed the mountain to light a bonfire in celebration of Waterloo, and they seem to have got down all right. (Ironically, it was Wordsworth, the teetotaller, who had spilt all the drinking water, forcing them to drink neat rum!)

The path has been well defined for at least two hundred years but that did not prevent Harriet Martineau from making her description of the route a pretext for a long sermon on mountain safety which would make even our modern zealous mountain rescue men protest:

> There must be a guide, be the day ever so clear and the path ever so plain. Once for all let us say, in all earnestness, and with the most deliberate decision, that no kind of tourist should ever cross the higher passes, or ascend the mountains, without a guide. Surely, enough lives have been lost, and there has been suffering and danger enough, short of a fatal issue, to teach this lesson.

Mind you she does concede that "The ascent of Skiddaw is easy, even for ladies, who have only to sit their ponies to find themselves at the top, after a ride of six miles." That really *is* the way to do it!

Nowadays, most people reduce the distance by half by driving up Gale Road which runs from Applethwaite to a gap behind Latrigg where, at the end of the road, a sort of car park has been fashioned in the rough ground. It cuts out the preliminaries and makes the ascent brutally direct, but it also cuts out the walk around Latrigg itself, and this is not only the most beautiful part of the whole route but it also offers superb views over Borrowdale and the Vale of Keswick—frequently missed because too many walkers never pause to see what lies behind them: the backwards view is often unexpected and enchanting.

In fact one need not go too far up the Latrigg path (which starts from Spooney Green Lane, a short distance along the road behind the railway station) to enjoy this superb view. Keswick lies spread out and beyond it the silvery lake with the famous Jaws of Borrowdale closing in at the head. Further away still lies the jagged promise of the central fells, all blues, greys and mauves. To the right, the green Vale of Newlands runs up into the Derwent Fells, the wooded knoll of Swinside dividing the entrance and the shapely peaks of Grisedale forming the flanks. The whole picture is one of an idyllic lake and a tumbled mass of romantic blue hills: one of the finest, if not *the* finest, view in the whole district.

It is worth the walk to Latrigg for this view alone—but it is not necessary to continue to the top of Skiddaw, of course. The way up the main fell begins very steeply, and comes as something of a shock. Wasn't this supposed to be *easy*, the tourists ask? But the steep bit is short and soon gives way to a broad and gentle path which leads all the way to the top.

It is at this very point, where the path becomes easy, that Skiddaw plays its only trick; a pathetic subterfuge which never-theless catches out a good many tourists. On the left is a sharp peak of stones with a prominent cairn which looks so obviously summit-like that many people quit the broad track and make directly for the cairn. To their surprise they find that it is not the top at all—another cairn appears a short distance further on, and on reaching this they discover to their dismay that they have climbed a different mountain altogether—Little Man (2,837 feet) —and that a broad, discouraging gap of about a mile separates them from the real summit of Skiddaw.

The direct route keeps strictly to the path, but the ascent of Little Man makes an interesting enough diversion and the walk from there to the summit is quite simple and broadens the view, giving a good impression of the steep slopes down to Millbeck and then a look at the superb edge of the Ullock Pike—Long Side Ridge, which comes up from Barkbeth to join Carl Side and, eventually, the south summit of Skiddaw. In a hard winter, this would make a superb route of ascent for any competent moun-taineer—a fine, natural line of alpine quality.

The summit of Skiddaw (3,053 feet) is a long stony ridge, broad, rounded and entirely fitting to such a mountain. The view on a perfect day (preferably winter) is astonishingly wide, from the Galloway Hills to—where? Let us say, the southern and central fells of Lakeland at least—beyond that it is largely speculation and imagination. Harriet Martineau claimed she could see Lancaster Castle, Carlisle Cathedral and Snowdon—well, all one can say is that she must have had extraordinary good eyesight. Certainly the view is wide, but optimum conditions are rare. Cloud and mist obscure the view on poor days and heat haze on fine summer days —unless you do as John Keats did and climb the fell before breakfast.

To the north and east there is quite a different view. Once you have breasted the initial steep slopes and reached Jenkin Hill, there opens up a scene of wild desolation unmatched elsewhere in the district. For the first time one can see that Skiddaw really is separated from its neighbours. There are no connecting ridges as there are with other fells; no continuum of high-level walking.

Three deep and wide valleys meet in a wild hollow beneath the eastern slopes of the fell. One, the shortest and narrowest, is the Glenderaterra Beck which divides Skiddaw from its great neighbour, Blencathra. It runs steeply northwards from the valley of the Greta. Another, wider and almost without form, comes in from the north-west, and the third, longest and most desolate of all, the valley of the River Caldew, bites deeply in from the north-east. They meet in the vast bowl-like hollow of Skiddaw Forest wherein can be seen the dark patch of conifers which marks Skiddaw House; one of the most isolated dwellings in Britain. Sharp eyes might pick up the ribbon of road trailing away from the house towards the Whitewater Dash in the north-west, but apart from that, in all this great wilderness—about forty square miles of it—there is no other human sign to be observed. If it is a particularly fine day, a couple of walkers might be seen on the lonely road, but such a sight is not common, for 'back o' Skidda'' as it is called, is far removed from the common round.

The long, lonely valleys catch the eye first, and only afterwards does one look at the fells themselves. What an unprepossessing bunch they are, to be sure! Because Skiddaw is higher than any of them, and much higher than most, they seem almost like a range of anthills. Only Blencathra makes a show of eminence, but can it be the same fine mountain that throws down such impressive ridges above Threlkeld? It hardly seems possible that those long undulating slopes above the Caldew valley can be part and parcel of one of the finest fells in Lakeland, yet it is so, and the realization leaves a distasteful feeling in the mind; as though

Blencathra was somehow a fraud. We never like our idols to have feet of clay.

And what of the Caldbeck and Uldale fells, cut off from Skiddaw and Blencathra by the deep valleys? They look no part of Lakeland, more akin to the bleaker parts of the Pennines or the dull hills of Galloway. Mound upon mound they undulate away to the north, and only the distant characteristic summit of Carrock Fell seems of any consequence. They do nothing to inspire a walker, and it seems not unnatural that they should be rarely visited . . . which is, perhaps, why I went there.

It was a baking August day when Duncan and I, having toiled up Skiddaw amidst a throng of tourists, looked out over the hollows of the forest to the brown and purple fells beyond, lumpily progressing towards distant Carrock. 'Back o' Skidda'' looked just like the Pennine moors with which we were familiar, but we knew that here we would find none of those soul-destroying peat groughs, or channels, which make Kinder and Bleaklow such nightmares. Carrock Fell, six miles distant as the crow flies, seemed suddenly much nearer and I for one wondered whether we had misjudged matters: whether a day spent rock-climbing would not have been a better proposition than a walk over such a dull-looking moorland. My son too, was not very taken with the scene—but then, he had been against the whole project from the start and had been muttering darkly about the delights of Shepherd's Crag all the way up Skiddaw. For a thirteen-year-old to whom half a dozen words constitute a major speech when out on the fells, this boded no good: he even put his objection into the way he walked, deliberately adopting the 'guides pace' (for which he knew there could be no rebuke) when normally on a track like that up Skiddaw he would have gone like a bomb.

I offered to take the rucksack, but I ought to have known better —the rucksack was something he had claimed ever since we had started walking together, and he had no intention of losing possession on a mere stroll. He coolly declined my offer, giving the impression that if he must suffer, he would suffer in a proper and fully equipped manner, like a Praetorian guard going to his doom.

At first the descent into the forest was simple enough, all smooth grass and gentle angle along the broad spur of Skiddaw that descends to Hare Crag, but lower down, in Candleseaves Bog, we met the heather and the mire that we were to know only too well before our walk ended. The heather in particular was brutish stuff, like wading through glue, and where there was no heather there was tussock grass of the most bone-jarring quality. Proper walking was quite impossible, and it was with a sense of relief that we finally staggered on to the pack-horse road which runs a lonely course to Skiddaw House.

A couple of walkers came past us on the road heading for the dark hollows of Dead Crags and the romantically named water-fall of the Whitewater Dash. If anything they served to point up the desolation of the scene—the bare hills (Skiddaw looks at its worst from here) and the isolated pair of cottages that make up Skiddaw House, where a shepherd lives mid-week performing what must surely be the loneliest job in Britain.

But for us the road was merely a crossing point. We followed it for a few yards and then struck directly up the fellside towards the summit of Great Calva (2,265 feet).

If the going in the bowl of the Forest had been rough, the ascent of Great Calva was doubly so. Never had I experienced such a tiring, heartbreaking mixture of heather and bog. There were even groughs—baby ones compared with the Pennine monsters, I will grant you—but groughs nevertheless, and frequently concealed by heather. At least the Pennine groughs are plainly visible, with nothing sneaky about them like these Calva horrors. We staggered to the summit, worn out with our fight against raw nature.

In shape and position, if not composition, Great Calva is a fine little fell, a cone-like bastion standing proudly out into the bowl of the Forest, separating the Dash beck and the River Caldew. It is neither particularly high, nor steep, yet such is its position that it commands everything round about. It is the centre and literal hub of the 'back o' Skidda''.

The view from Great Calva is not particularly inspiring—the worst sides of Skiddaw and Blencathra, and the swelling whale-back moor of Knott—but at least in one respect is is unique. It faces down the Glenderaterra beck, the deep cleavage between the breasts of Skiddaw and Blencathra, which is the northern beginnings of a remarkable series of faults running south through the Vale of St John, Thirlmere, Grasmere and the Rothay valley, to Windermere. From Great Calva the eye sweeps down the fault and you can see at a glance how the land was fashioned all those thousands of years ago. On a fine day, such as the one we had, detail after detail could be identified with amazing clarity—we could even see the sun glinting off the road on Dunmail Raise. It really is a remarkable demonstration of a large-scale fault line, and well worth the attention of any field geography group which comes to study Lakeland.

We had hoped to eat our sandwiches on the summit of Great Calva, but fate had another nasty surprise in store for us. The moment we sat down we were plagued by a swarm of flying ants, which materialized from nowhere. A sharp and violent conflict ensued in which ants died by the score, but it quickly became apparent that they were winning this war of attrition, so we retreated in haste and without dignity down the shallow slopes towards the col at the head of Wiley beck, sandwiches in hand. From time to time throughout the afternoon—whenever we stopped in fact—these ants would suddenly appear, like demons of the fells, specially there to torment walkers.

Knott is the highest of the fells at the 'back o' Skidda''—2,329 feet—but apart from that it is totally undistinguished. It is a great swelling of moor, easy underfoot for a change, and the point from which many of the strange bare-sided gills, ruddy-earthed and pebble-dashed, which are a feature of the Caldbeck Fells, begin. It is these gills—Roughton Gill and Grainsgill are amongst the best known—which provide the sites for most of the famous Caldbeck Mines.

Mining for minerals once was common on many Lake District fells, as we have seen in previous chapters and evidence of Old Man, as the ancient miners are known, can be seen in every part of the district, from Newlands to Coniston, from Borrowdale to Helvellyn, but none were more prosperous or more continuously worked than the mines of Caldbeck. The reason for this lies in the nature of the fells in this part, for it is the geological junction between the Borrowdale Volcanics and the Skiddaw Slates—the same reason, in fact, that the walking hereabouts is so different from the walking on, say, Gable or Scafell Pike. An incredible variety of minerals have been discovered, ranging from the common barytes to the rare (for Britain) wolfram. This is not the place to go into the intricate history of these fascinating mines or to speculate on the unbounded optimism of mining prospectors (for the uncertainty of riches beneath the ground breeds its own special gamblers, and over the centuries the mines have opened and closed with monotonous regularity) but it is sufficient to say that the mines at Caldbeck, like those in the Pennines, are a continuing story of hard endeavour, hope, riches—and bankruptcy.

Knott was about the half-way point on our walk from Skiddaw to Carrock Fell, and the way ahead looked most discouraging. 'Miller Moss', the map says, and when the One Inch Ordnance Survey goes to the trouble of actually naming a bog, you can guarantee it is a real one.

"Only one more peak to go," I said jovially to my truculent companion, carefully avoiding to mention that it was four or five bog-soaked miles away.

"Looks better *that* way," he replied, pointing like a well-trained setter with unerring accuracy towards Comb Heights and the direct line to the Caldew Valley.

Ignoring this treachery I led off down the slopes of Knott into the Miller Moss.

It was a dry day in the middle of a dry season. What Miller Moss is like on a wet day in the middle of a wet season, I shudder to think. Heather and bog combined to make the trip arduous and unpleasant, and detours to avoid the worst of it did little to improve matters. It was with relief that we finally fetched up at the small bothy below Great Ling Hill.

I do not know who maintains this bothy, which is equipped with a table and *matratzen lager* after the style of some very small and old-fashioned alpine hut, but judging from the 'hut book' it has proved a blessing to more than one party caught out in bad weather on these fells. There have been nights, apparently, when the place was crowded.

From the bothy we could look down Grainsgill back into the

Caldew valley and the site of the Carrock Mine. A dozen cars belonging to mineral hunters, clustered round the old workings like flies round a jampot. Carrock Mine (often referred to as Brandy Gill Mine, from a minor beck which flows into the valley at this point) is certainly the geological high spot of all the old workings hereabouts, for no fewer than twenty-seven different minerals have been identified in its locality. Every fine day throughout summer will find specimen hunters combing over the old bing heaps and the surrounding fells, and though one would imagine that anything worth collecting had been unearthed long ago, under such intensive searchings, such is not the case. Only a year or so ago, an acquaintance of mine showed me some fine specimens he had picked up in Brandy Gill.

Of course, one must know what to look for, and where to look. It is also worth repeating that the underground workings of all these old mines are highly dangerous, and should not be entered.

More heather. The long curving ascent of Carrock Fell, though negligible in angle is punishing in execution, and the heather continues almost to the top of the fell, only held back from the summit by a ring of gabbro boulders—all that remains of the ancient hill-fort which crowns it. After all those miles of bog and heather it was good to feel rock again, even though it was of a disjointed kind.

Carrock Fell is the very edge and extremity of the Lake District. It is the last summit of reasonable height—2,174 feet—and the last to have any rock-climbing on it, though in truth the little crags which overlook Stone Ends farm are hardly worth bothering with. From the summit the view extends east over the undulating plains towards the Pennines, and north towards Carlisle. To the south-east lie the swellings which fringe Ullswater, with Great Mell Fell, that curious conical mound, standing out in all prominence.

The Caldew valley lies immediately below the fell, though it cannot be seen because the convex contours are such that Carrock Fell hides its skirts. What is seen, though, and to good effect, is the dark hollow of Bowscale Tarn, immediately across the Caldew valley. Like Low Water at Coniston or Blae Water under High Street, Bowscale is one of those crag-girt high-level tarns

Helvellyn and Thirlmere

that cannot fail to impress by the magnificence of its surroundings.

There is more shape to Carrock Fell than to the other fells at the 'back o' Skidda'', which is as it should be—a suitable finale. It is, of course, ringed round the summit with the tumbled blocks of the ancient fort, though only an expert could make sense out of the debris, and even he would be largely guessing.

Down to Mosedale by heather and steep scree. In the car I asked my son what he thought about the walk.

"If you're stopping at the pub," he said. "I think I'll have a ginger beer."

It is really quite remarkable the way in which the geological bones of a land affect the lives of the people in it. It determines not only what crops are grown, what industries established, but even what sort of houses are built—or at least, it did until the ogre of prefabrication took a grip. The grimy industrial belts of South Lancashire, Durham and South Wales owe their existence to the coalfields there, just as the mellow stone cottages of the Cotswolds owe their existence to the land as well.

In this northern group of fells the geology provides great contrasts perhaps the greatest contrasts in the whole district, and though nobody could claim that it was the best walking country, at the same time nobody can deny that it is full of interest. Consider for a moment the human contrast between Skiddaw and the fells beyond. Skiddaw is massive, easy and perhaps the most popular fell in the Lake District, with hundreds of people making an ascent on every fine day, and yet, scarcely two miles away, the Uldale and Caldbeck fells are deserted. I doubt if Knott or Great Calva has as many ascents in a year as Skiddaw does in a day.

And then, quite different, forming the third part of this trilogy of fells, is Blencathra. Here is no mere lump, no boggy undulating nonentity; Blencathra throws down its ridges at Threlkeld in one of the finest, most spectacular challenges of the district. Its very shape, which gives it the name of Saddleback sometimes, is uniquely distinctive and though it may lack a few feet in height compared with the neighbouring Skiddaw, it is an incomparably finer mountain.

Ah! But at the back, you may say, it is nothing but a boring

12

Ullswater and Patterdale with Dollywagon Pike in the background

soggy moor called Mungrisedale Common, visually amongst the least pleasing sights in the district. True—but there are many mountains which share with Blencathra this undoubted fault, not least of which is Mont Blanc. Seen from Chamonix, Mont Blanc could well be called Mont Blancmange—but see it from the Italian side with its towering ice faces and fantastic granite ridges and your realize why it is unquestionably the finest mountain in the Alps. With Blencathra we are more fortunate: at least it turns its best face to the world at large.

The viewpoint of medium height, as usual, serves us best to see this splendid fell, and none more so than Castlerigg, where the ancient stone circle has formed the foreground for many a photographer's portrait of it. On a clear afternoon the ridges are thrown into sharp relief by their own shadows, but I remember it best with scudding cumulus throwing patches of light and dark, moving and changing constantly, lighting the ridges for an instant then obscuring them as the clouds pass on.

Best of all though, is on a bright winter's day with Blencathra covered in snow. Then it assumes a truly alpine quality with its sparkling white *arêtes* flashing in the sun. Visually at least, Blencathra is for me the supreme winter mountain of the district, because though it is steep, it is not too steep to hold the snow properly as a mountain should. Great End is more savage in appearance, parts of the eastern flanks of the Helvellyn range more imposing in their way, and Causey Pike can look like the Matterhorn on occasions, but as a mountain and a *coup d'œil*, there is nothing to compare with Blencathra.

You could spend the best part of a week climbing this mountain by different routes, and never tire of it, nor complain of monotony —and there are very few peaks in Lakeland about which the same could be said. Each of the superb ridges makes a memorable ascent: Gategill Fell, Hall's Fell, Doddick Fell, Scales Fell and last but by no means least, Sharp Edge. Only the 'ordinary route', up the broad smooth shoulder of Blease Fell, past the Sanatorium, is unworthy of the mountain; climb Blencathra by its great south face or not at all, it deserves no less.

Though the route from Scales, by Scales Fell, is the commonest and easiest way up Blencathra on this side, with some very fine

views of Scales Tarn and Scaley Beck, it is really a flanking movement which avoids direct confrontation with the mountain.
Better by far to attack frontally: to climb by Hall's Fell, for not
only does this ridge lead directly to the summit of Blencathra but
it has an airy final *arête*, known as Narrow Edge, which adds spice
to the climb.

The way leads out of Gategill on to the bracken-covered slopes
of the lower ridge where it plays out into a broad cone shaped
foot. A track, grassy and pleasant, leads through the bracken and
though the ascent is fairly steep it is short and so patently leading
to better things that steepness goes unnoticed. Then comes the
pinnacled ridge which can be followed along its crest or not, as
fancy dictates (and ability too—it is not always simple). There is
usually an escape route, on one side of the crest or the other, but
there is no escaping the tremendous exposure of the steep fellsides plunging down into Gate Gill and Doddick Gill. Narrow
Edge leaves no shadow of doubt that you are at grips with a real
mountain: that you are definitely 'involved' as the current jargon
has it.

And in the end it turns out to be all right, even to nervous souls.
The difficulties are more apparent than real, and all that is required is determination and a steady head. This, I believe, is its
great attraction—where it scores over Striding Edge for example,
for Striding Edge which is rather more difficult a scramble than
Narrow Edge, puts itself on display and lets you know what you
are in for, whereas Narrow Edge is full of little surprises almost to
the very top.

Indeed the summit itself (2,847 feet) comes as a surprise. You
struggle up the last few feet of the ridge, and bingo! There it is.
What could be more perfect?

It is a fine route up a fine mountain, and if it is combined with
a descent of Sharp Edge, you have one of the very best mountain
days that Lakeland affords.

In winter, when the mountain is covered in hard snow, then
this ascent becomes classic in quality, a truly alpine climb and a
superb expedition. Under such conditions, of course, it demands
the proper climbing equipment and a knowledge of how to use
it.

Hall's Fell, with its Narrow Edge, is the perfect way to the summit of Blencathra, but an edge of a somewhat different sort has won for itself the popular glory that goes with steep places. Sharp Edge, aimed like a Stone Age spear-head from the summit ridge down into the wild upper reaches of the Glendermackin Valley is by far the shortest of the ridges, but it is steep, wholly rocky, and with a serrated crest which lives up to its name. It is not a rock-climb in the technical sense of the term, but of all the Lakeland ridges it comes the nearest to being so—much more so than the celebrated Striding Edge of Helvellyn. Except for length, Sharp Edge is more akin to the ridges of Scotland than it is to its counterparts on the neighbouring fells.

It is not really the sort of ridge on which a mountain potterer would be safe—the man who likes to wander up an adjacent fell whenever he parks his car—and it is fortunate that the ridges between Scales Fell and Souther Fell separate the upper Glendermackin from the main Keswick–Penrith road. To reach the Edge means crossing this low ridge, in a mile and a half walk from Scales, which though lovely in itself, is thankfully sufficient to deter the merely curious.

The setting of upper Glendermackin is splendidly wild, especially on the western rim where the precipices of Sharp Edge and Tarn Crag frown in dark grandeur over the tiny Scales Tarn. George and Ashley Abraham, the Keswick brothers who were pioneers of mountain photography, began their careers on these rocks, but the place is so rotten and the holds so dubious that nobody climbs there nowadays. Only Sharp Edge itself receives a constant stream of walkers, lured by the reputation of the airy ridge.

This lure has attracted tourists for almost two centuries. Even in the days when the Jaws of Borrowdale were sufficient to give most visitors the vapours, some hardy souls followed local guides up Sharp Edge. A tourist, writing at the end of the eighteenth century describes it thus:

> Wishing to vary our line in returning to the place we had left [they had descended from the summit of Blencathra by the easier Scales Fell ridge to examine Scales Tarn] we crossed the stream, and commenced a steep ascent at the foot of Sharp Edge. We had not

gone far before we were aware that our journey would be attended
with perils: the passage gradually grew narrower, and the declivity
on each hand awfully precipitous. From walking erect, we were
reduced to the necessity either of bestriding the ridge, or moving on
one of its sides with our hands lying over its top, as a security
against tumbling into the tarn on the left, or into a frightful gully
on the right—both of immense depth. Sometimes we thought it
prudent to return; but that seemed unmanly, and we proceeded;
thinking with Mr. Shakespere that 'dangers retreat when boldly
they're confronted'.

In the context of their times they were obviously game spirits,
and Shakespeare's philosophy carried them through to the summit—though one might add that it is not a philosophy to push to
extremes where mountains are concerned.

Nowadays, we look at Sharp Edge with more experienced
eyes, if we have done much mountain walking at all, and we
sense a glad excitement at its airy challenge. We are even disappointed to find a bit of a track in places, though the awkward
parts cannot be entirely avoided as they can on Striding Edge.

The best view from the Edge is down into the cwm of Scales
Tarn; a real witches' cauldron of a place, its dark waters so hemmed
about by steep crags that it is in almost permanent shadow. The
old locals believed that the tarn was so dark that even at mid-
day one could see the reflections of stars in its surface! Harriet
Matineau tells of one eighteenth-century tourist who was so
intrigued by this that he decided to see for himself. Aided by
guides and taking along a companion he attempted the ascent
but was so terrified that when he reached the edge of the cwm
(where his companion declined to go further) he wished to
have his blood let and make an immediate return to the valley.
However, he was persuaded to continue, though he was
naturally disappointed at not seeing any stars reflected in the
tarn.

In a hard winter the hoar crystals blossom on the Edge like
thick encrustations of quartz, and the upper slabs become trickily
verglassed. It is then the province of the climber, and only he dare
venture into an arctic world where the scale of everything has
been heightened to alpine proportions. What a view then of

Scales Tarn! It is a breathtaking example of savage mountain scenery equal to anything the district has to offer.

What a terrible tragedy that Blencathra has no great rock-climbing crags, or would that be too much to wish for—a gilding of the lily? It is, of course, the chief drawback to all these northern fells, for without great precipices like those of Pillar or Bowfell Buttress, no range of fells is perfect or ever complete. It is the permanent disability of the northern fells that they alone in the entire district should want for rock.

I am certain that this has affected their popularity, and the reason they have received relatively scant attention from writers, because rock has that magnetic quality which draws the tourist as well as the climber. Rock scenery is dramatic and easy to appreciate; much more so than the subtle shifting of cloud patterns on gently swelling grassy fells.

Yet rock is not everything, though there was a time in our youth when we thought it was. Variety can be equally pleasing, and there are few areas more varied than the northern fells. And above all there is Blencathra, one of the finest fells in Lakeland.

8

Helvellyn and Fairfield

MANY years ago, so the story goes, an enthusiastic guide was conducting a party of overseas tourists around the Lake District. As they breasted Dunmail Raise he pointed up at the great swelling fellside ahead. "And that is Helvellyn," he proclaimed with pride, "Queen of Mountains!"

"Gee!" exclaimed a Canadian lady. "I wonder if the Rockies know?"

Well, everything is relative, of course, and the guide was doubtless letting his enthusiasm run away with him, but the story illustrates the extraordinary affection and regard with which Helvellyn is held by Lakeland devotees. Why this should be is not immediately apparent, for when it is seen from the west (as most tourists see it for the first time) it cannot be called a beautiful mountain, by any stretch of imagination. In fact, there are few duller sights in Lakeland, and you need to stand back a considerable distance—by Dale Bottom, for example—to get anything like a balanced picture. Even then, it is hardly exciting.

Most tourists climb it from this side too; but from Thirlspot by the long and easy pony track, or more adventurously from Wythburn Church—but by either route hardly a way calculated to inspire a love of the fells. However, Thirlspot is very accessible, standing as it does on the main Keswick–Ambleside road, and most tourists know that Helvellyn is one of the biggest and most famous of all the fells. It is nearly always climbed for the wrong reasons.

It is certainly climbed very frequently, and by all sorts and conditions of people: Helvellyn, Skiddaw and Coniston Old Man—of the higher fells, these three must surely come 'top of the pops' when it comes to number of ascents, and I suspect that Helvellyn outshines the other two in this respect. This is nothing new, of course, Harriet Martineau was saying the same thing over a century ago.

In her day Patterdale seems to have been the favourite starting point, but the tourist rode by pony as far as Red Tarn where he tethered his beast at some conveniently arranged stakes, before climbing the flanks of Catstycam to Swirrel Edge and the summit of Helvellyn. This is a far superior way of making an ascent than any on the opposite side of the mountain and the Victorians are to be congratulated on their good sense—though to be fair, it should be added that ponies could also be hired at Thirlspot.

The fact of the matter is that Helvellyn is very much an east-ward facing mountain: almost everything of interest is on this one side of the fell. The comment might be extended to Fairfield too, but not to anything like the same extent. Fairfield is a shapely fell, even from the west.

The best views, too, are of the eastern side, where the long ridges and deep valleys contrast sharply with the bald slopes seen on the western flanks. These ridges run right down to Patterdale, each different in height and contour, so that they make a complex mountain for the eye to scan. From Place Fell for example, you can look right into the heart of this ridge system, or from Stony Cove Pike you can look across the ridges, when, in certain lighting conditions, they show a multitude of subtle shades of greys, mauves and blues.

From north to south, that is from Threlkeld to the Kirkstone Pass, the Helvellyn and Fairfield groups form one of the longest mountain chains in the district. From one place to the other is almost thirteen miles, and most of it is continuous ridge, with only three deeply set cols: Sticks Pass, between Stybarrow Dod and Raise; Grisedale Hause, between Seat Sandal and Fairfield; and Scandale Pass between Little Hart Crag and Raven Crag. The first two have long been traditional crossing places over the great range between east and west and continue in favour to this day—especially Grisedale Hause—but Scandale Pass is now little

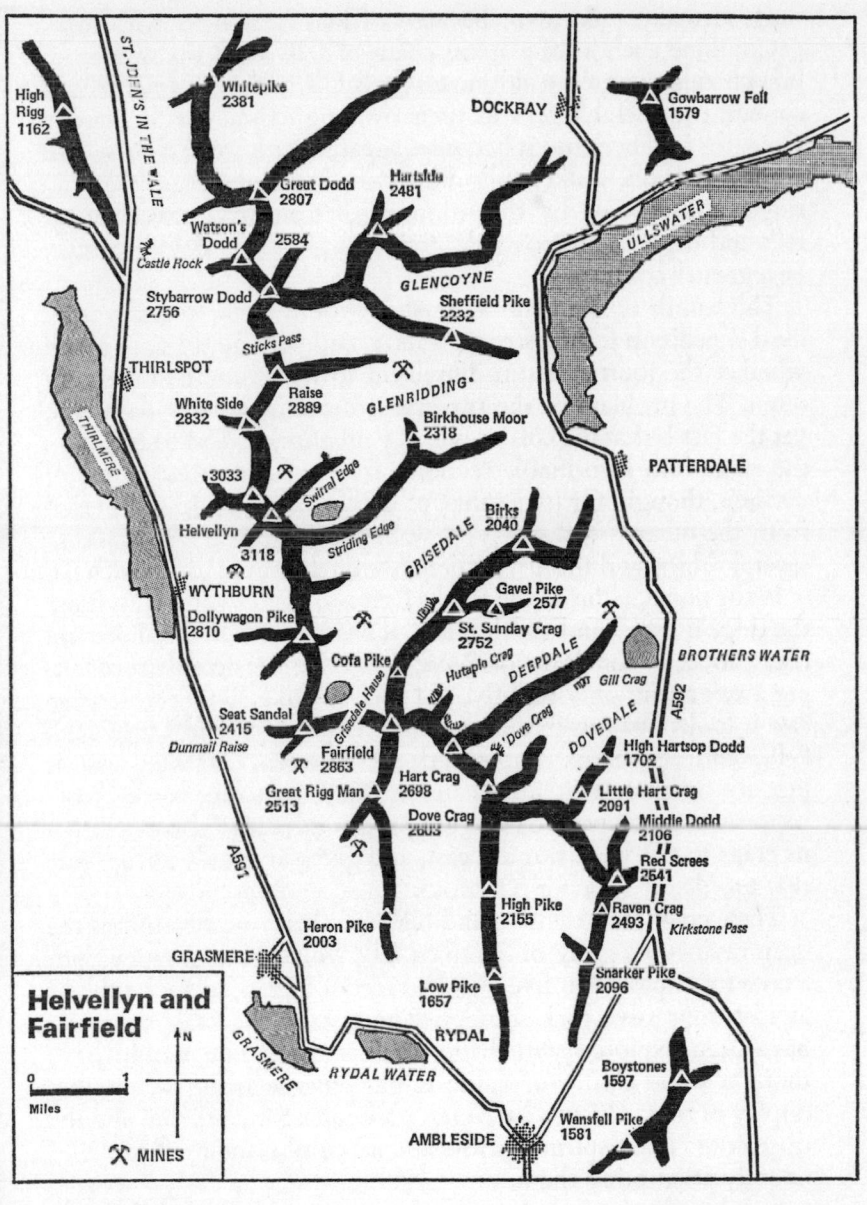

High Rigg 1162

ST. JOHN'S IN THE VALE

Whitepike 2381

DOCKRAY

Gowbarrow Fell 1579

Great Dodd 2807

Hartside 2481

Watson's Dodd 2584

Castle Rock

ULLSWATER

Stybarrow Dodd 2756

GLENCOYNE

Sheffield Pike 2232

THIRLSPOT

Sticks Pass

THIRLMERE

White Side 2832

Raise 2889

GLENRIDDING

Birkhouse Moor 2318

PATTERDALE

3033

Swirral Edge

Helvellyn

Striding Edge

GRISEDALE

Birks 2040

3118

Gavel Pike 2577

WYTHBURN

Dollywagon Pike 2810

St. Sunday Crag 2752

BROTHERS WATER

Cofa Pike

Hutaple Crag

DEEPDALE

Gill Crag

Griesdale House

Dove Crag

DOVEDALE

Seat Sandal 2415

A592

Dunmail Raise

Fairfield 2863

Hart Crag 2698

High Hartsop Dodd 1702

Great Rigg Man 2513

Little Hart Crag 2091

Dove Crag 2603

Middle Dodd 2106

Red Screes 2541

A591

High Pike 2155

Raven Crag 2493

Kirkstone Pass

Heron Pike 2003

GRASMERE

Low Pike 1657

Snarker Pike 2096

Helvellyn and Fairfield

N

RYDAL

0   1

Miles

GRASMERE

RYDAL WATER

Boystones 1597

Wansfell Pike 1581

MINES

AMBLESIDE

used, virtually unknown, because of its nearness to Kirkstone.

Combine such a long main chain of fells with the numerous branch ridges running down towards Ullswater (some of which contain considerable fells in their own rights such as St Sunday Crag, for instance) and it becomes apparent at once that these fells are for the bold walker who likes to swing along from ridge to ridge, unhampered by the minutiae of scenery. Between these fells and those of Borrowdale, for example, there could scarcely be a greater contrast.

The length of the main watershed would seem to make it an ideal expedition for the strong walker, and yet I doubt very much whether the journey from Threlkeld to Kirkstone is done very often. The problem of the traverse is more imaginary than real, yet the fact is that the cols previously mentioned tend to break up the ridge into identifiable sections. It is not simply a matter of division, though, for by a quirk of nature each section is different from the others, so that if you walk the ridge it is like walking several ridges, and this partly destroys the harmony of the whole.

In the north, as far as the Sticks Pass and just beyond it to Raise the ridge is broad and gentle sided. It begins with White Pike and rises at once to the dome of Clough Head (2,381 feet) before falling away again, only slightly, to Calfhow Pike. To the north and east it looks out towards Blencathra, Great Mell and Little Mell Fells, and the barren moorlands in between. To the west it literally overhangs St John's in the Vale, for contrary to what happens in other parts of this range, Clough Head throws down its crags to the west, not the east, and gives St John's in the Vale that profile for which it is famous.

These crags are extensive and big, and their finest feature is the deep ravine-like gully of Sandbed Gill which gives anyone with a taste for exploration five hundred feet of high-grade scrambling amidst impressive rock scenery. The rest of the crag seems to have been explored with little result, though one would have thought some climbs of value might emerge from such a vast display of rock. Given a hard enough winter Sandbed Gill and the crags could make splendid snow and ice climbs, though I know of nobody attempting them.

St John's in the Vale has superb scenery for which it is justly famous—much more so than the great fell overlooking it. Clough Head and its dark crags frown down on one side of the widening vale and the other side is formed by the small ridge of High Rigg (1,163 feet)—a superb viewpoint for Blencathra and the northern fells. In fact, High Rigg is an unjustly neglected fell simply because it lacks height, yet it is a much more worthwhile ascent than many of its immediate, grander neighbours. For one thing it is never dull—the hummocks and craglets see to that, and there are fascinating ways up and down it, especially from Dale Bottom. The fell is literally sprinkled with crags, too, some of which are of reasonable height: an enterprising outdoor activity centre could find plenty to interest pupils and instructors alike here, and relieve the pressure on some of the old favourites like Brown Slabs.

Great Dod (2,809 feet), Watson's Dod (2,584 feet) and Stybarrow Dod (2,756 feet) (the Dods, as they are known for short!) raise the general level of the main ridge and are true forerunners of Helvellyn itself though they still maintain the rounded appearance of the earlier fells. They end at Sticks Pass, the traditional way from Stanah to Glenridding, but the sad fact about all this information is that neither the pass nor the attendant fells inspire the walker. The Dods (and Sticks) are cheerless places, and the subsidiary ridges which fan out to Hart Side (2,481 feet) and Sheffield Pike (2,232 feet) are, if anything, even worse.

It is ironical, to put it mildly, that the Dods, which are amongst the blandest of Lakeland fells should contain on their slopes one of the finest crags in the district. The Castle Rock of Triermain juts out from the lower slopes of Watson's Dod in the manner of its namesake: a veritable rock fortress guarding the entrance to St John's in the Vale. For anyone travelling the main road from Ambleside to Keswick, the sight of this famous crag is one of the highlights of the journey.

Castle Rock is only a few minutes' walk from the roadside. It looks rather small at first sight and it comes as a surprise to learn that some of the climbs which pick their way tenuously up the overhanging North Crag are more than three hundred feet in length. That the climbs are also hard must be obvious to anybody, though only climbers who have tackled them can vouch for the high quality of the routes on this fascinating rock face. Difficulty and quality are not always synonymous in rock-climbing.

The first big route on Castle Rock came on 1st April 1939 when Jim Birkett successfully attacked the most prominent feature of the North Crag—a long sloping ramp, set at a high angle and much more difficult than it appears at first glance. The top of the ramp was guarded by a ferocious overhang, but Birkett found that the overhang was easily avoided and that the crux of the climb was in getting on to the ramp itself. This involved a delicate and sensationally exposed step from the top of a pinnacle on to the almost holdless and smooth ramp: a daring and committing move which would have been hard to reverse if things had not gone well. Fortunately, the climbing became a little easier, and with the overhang cleverly avoided, Birkett led his party to success.

Overhanging Bastion, as the route was called, created something of a sensation at the time of its ascent. It was regarded, probably with some justification, as a breakthrough in Lakeland climbing —not so much for its difficulty (the East Buttress of Scafell was already matching it in that respect) but in its acceptance of steep rock as a challenge anywhere, unfettered by thoughts of mountains—after all, who thinks of Watson's Dod, the parent fell, when climbing on Castle Rock? Ninety per cent of climbers have never even heard of Watson's Dod!

Birkett was an innovator with a superb eye for a climb (Birkett's name on any climb is almost a guarantee that the route is a good one) and with his work on *Overhanging Bastion* and *Zig Zag*, another Castle Rock climb he made shortly afterwards, he laid the foundations which were later to culminate in his fine development of White Ghyll in Langdale.

In the immediate post-war years it was Birkett again who continued the development of the North Crag (though he was not above taking an occasional look at the easier South Crag—witness his delightful little 'severe' called *Chapel Cracks*). His campaign ended in 1949 with *Harlot Face*: his hardest route on the crag and suitably bringing his era of dominance to a fine finish.

New men were coming, attracted by the legendary quality of Castle Rock. Two years after *Harlot Face*, Harold Drasdo arrived and climbed *The Barbican*: fractionally easier than the Birkett routes, so that one wonders how Birkett came to miss it. A year later, having taken his measure as it were, Drasdo teamed up with the young Denis Gray to climb *North Crag Eliminate*, and a year after that the famous Rock and Ice Club, taking time off from their usual Welsh haunts, put up *Triermain Eliminate*, which immediately became the hardest route on the crag. The name of the climbers concerned are legendary in their own lifetime—Don Whillans (who led) and Joe Brown, ably assisted by Dan Cowan.

Through the rest of the '50s and '60s, Castle Rock continued to attract all the leading climbers and the standards there became phenomenal: Ross (of Borrowdale fame), Bonington, Cram—all added their quota to a crag which was now becoming laced with hard routes.

The ultimate result today is that Castle Rock offers the greatest concentration of hard climbs to be found anywhere in the Lake District. Moreover, as I mentioned earlier, they are mostly of high quality, so that the crag remains popular and is likely to do so for a long time to come.

There is nothing on the North Crag for novices or climbers of modest ambitions—all the climbs are 'very severe' or harder. Around the corner however, the South Crag has a number of good routes which are much easier. There is also the tricky little *Direct*, which is 'v.s.', but the style of climbing—the *ambience*, as the French would say—is quite different. Though they might be next to each other physically, the North and South Crags are worlds apart.

It was over the Sticks Pass that the mule trains carrying ore from the Greenside Lead Mine would travel on their way to the smelter at Keswick. It must have been an arduous journey for beasts and men when the weather was bad, though the worst of the winter months were avoided because the mine itself, lodged in its exposed position up the Glenridding beck was closed during this time.

Like the mine at Coniston, the Greenside mine can hardly be missed by anyone exploring the fells round about. As at Coniston, too, where miners once worked hard, Youth Hostellers now take

their ease, closely enfolded in the heart of the fells. These similarities are not coincidental: just as Coniston was the greatest
copper mine in the district during its heyday, so too was Greenside the greatest lead mine. Indeed, north of the extensively rich
King's Field in Derbyshire, it is doubtful whether there ever was
another mine to match that at Greenside.

Now the buildings are ruinous and tend to spoil the landscape
(much more so than those at Coniston) but no doubt time and
weather will work their way on them until they become an
acceptable part of the environment. What must not be forgotten
is that they represent the last remains of an ancient industry which
for sheer guts and enterprise, had no equal.

In terms of mining the Greenside venture is not particularly
old. The lead vein, which runs approximately north–south
through the eastern flanks of Greenside Fell, was thought to have
been discovered about the middle of the seventeenth century
(many Lakeland mines are at least a century older) and was
known to be worked by Dutch miners in 1690. Throughout the
next century the work continued under different auspices until in
1822 the Greenside Mining Company was formed, and continued
in operation until 1934 when the low price of lead temporarily
put a halt to production. A couple of years later another company
took over the mine and by modernization managed to operate it
until all the ore reserves were worked out in 1961. The mine
finally closed in the following year—the last lead mine in the
Lake District and the one with the longest continual record of
production.

Like most mining ventures, Greenside had its share of tragedy:
four men were killed in a disastrous fire in 1952 and another two
died from gas poisoning in 1959, but the best-known disaster, of
which evidence can still be seen, was the great cloudburst of 29th
October 1927 which washed away part of the embankment of
Keppelcove Dam and released a torrent of floodwater on to the
mine and the unsuspecting hamlet of Glenridding. Fortunately
no lives were lost but damage was extensive, and the compensation
for this (paid by the company out of court) almost brought the
mine to ruin. The dam itself was again breached in 1931 and never
used after—the dried-up tarn bed, derelict dam and water leats

are still to be seen though the ravages of time will some day hide
them for ever.

1927 was not the first time Greenside Mine had been affected
by floodwaters. In the 1870s a storm caused the Top Dam to
burst and the sweeping waters carried away a part of the silver
refinery (silver was always an important by-product of lead
smelting) including a plate of silver weighing a thousand ounces,
which was never recovered. Who knows? There may yet be a
treasure trove hidden beneath the storm-tossed boulders of Glenridding beck! Many attempts have been made to find the missing
silver, as you can well imagine, though some people think that it
was found shortly after the flood and hidden away on the principle than finders are keepers!

The nature of the roads on this side of Ullswater, and particularly the good road by Dockray to Troutbeck have probably
been influenced by the economies of the lead mine. The original
miners sent the ore over to Keswick by Sticks Pass, as we have
seen, but in the nineteenth century this was no longer feasible due
to the increased production of the mines. After about 1820 the
ore was carted to the modern smelter built by the London Lead
Company at Alston Moor (another important lead-mining area)
and it is said that the carts were so numerous that the road
authorities directed that every cart in five should have axles of a
wider gauge than usual to level out the ruts made in the road by
the heavy vehicles. The coming of the railway to Penrith meant
a shorter journey for the carts, and the lead was then smelted in
Newcastle, whilst the opening of the Penrith–Keswick line meant
that ore could be taken an even shorter distance by cart to Troutbeck. Thus these major economic roads were kept in good repair.

For a time the lead was smelted at the mine (until it became
uneconomic to run the smelter) but what I find surprising about
the transport of ore and lead from Greenside is that nobody seems
to have considered using barges on Ullswater: especially as the
mine's development coincided with the Canal Age.

Despite transport problems and occasional disasters, the Greenside mine prospered. A share worth £100 in 1827 was worth
£1,000 ten years later, and the mine once paid out 100 per cent
dividend over a three-month period. The total profit has been

estimated at £400,000 from a quarter of a million tons of lead concentrates, but this figure is probably conservative—in today's terms the profits must have been almost ten million pounds.

An interesting relic of the early mine can still be seen on the slopes of Stang. In 1830 a smelter was built at the mine and the chimney erected on Stang, a thousand feet higher (therefore giving the smelter a draught equivalent to that from a thousand-foot chimney). Smelter and chimney were connected by a flue, cut into the rock and arched over with meticulous stonework. Later, this flue served as an aqueduct, but more important than that, the flue was also a crosscut designed to test the southern limits of the Greenside lead veins. One has to admire the way in which those old miners never missed a trick!

Raise (2,889 feet) and White Side (2,832 feet) are harbingers of Helvellyn itself. The nature of the ridge has gradually changed. Raise even has some rocks on it, and crags appear on the Patterdale edge of White Side, making the ridge seem narrow by comparison with what has gone before.

Suddenly the whole lot sweeps up and curves round to Lower Man (3,033 feet), the lesser summit of Helvellyn, then, for half a mile, traverses and rises to Helvellyn proper (3,118 feet).

The summit of Helvellyn is shaly and scarred by a million boots. It is in itself a testament to the popularity of the fell as a tourist ascent, though if further proof were needed there are also two memorial tablets set in the rocks—one of which commemorates of all things, the landing of an aeroplane there in 1926. Why anyone should want to do such a thing is quite beyond comprehension—it ranks with pushing a bedstead up Ben Nevis (which has also been done) as an ultimate indignity to mountains.

The view from Helvellyn is too panoramic for my tastes. Better by far is the downwards glance into the great cirque of Red Tarn, with the two long pinnacled arms of Swirral Edge and Striding Edge enfolding it as a spider might enfold its prey.

These two ridges are, of course, the chief delights of Helvellyn, especially the famous Striding Edge which ranks with Crib Goch on Snowdon as the best-known and most frequented ridge scramble in Britain. Not that Striding Edge and Crib Goch have

The head of Deepdale

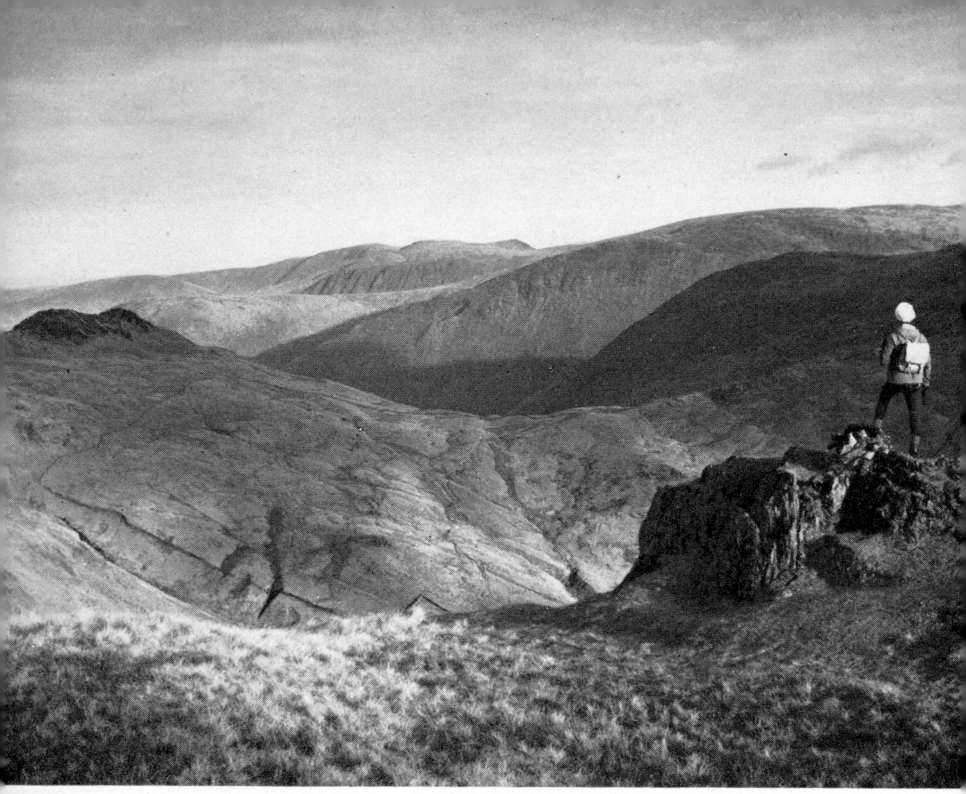

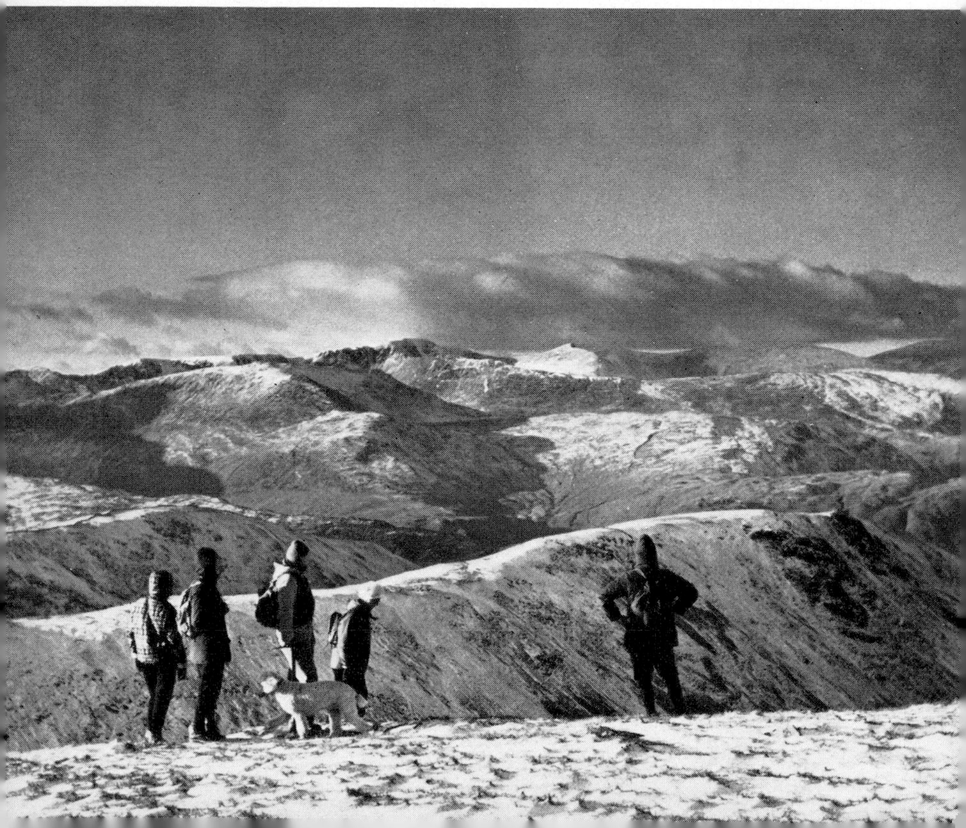

much in common, apart from their popularity—the Welsh ridge is much more of an undertaking than anything Helvellyn can offer.

There is no question that Striding Edge is the most interesting and exciting way to the summit of Helvellyn. The first part of the route out of Patterdale, up Grisedale, is tediously steep and frequently overpopulated but once the ridge is reached, tedium vanishes and the sight of the narrow ridge revives fresh energy in tired legs. Up and down over hummocks and pinnacles goes the route, with sheer fellside on either hand, like some alpine rock arête. At first glance it appears quite fearsome, especially as at the far end it seems to abut directly against the face of the mountain with no means of escape, but the reality is much less frightening—there is a good track all the way and you will only find Striding Edge difficult if you deliberately make it so. It is nothing like as difficult as Jack's Rake, for example, or even, in my opinion, Sharp Edge on Blencathra.

Nevertheless it is airy, and it is the longest and most fascinating ridge of its kind in the district. Where it meets the parent mountain there are steep, tiring slopes up to the summit, though even these turn out to be milder than expected. In winter, with snow and ice everywhere, the route is quite a different proposition: then the final slopes can be quite tricky, and under such conditions Striding Edge should not be attempted by anyone who is not a properly equipped and experienced mountaineer.

Combined with a descent of Swirral Edge, which is a sort of milder little brother, the traverse of Helvellyn by Striding Edge must always be rated as one of the classic ascents of Lakeland. Arguably it is the best ridge traverse in the area, though personally I would always prefer the Hall's Fell–Sharp Edge traverse of Blencathra.

In earlier times Striding Edge was considered a fearful route— "foolhardy", says Harriet Martineau. No doubt this fear was partly inspired by the appearance of the ridge, but it was also boosted by Wordsworth and Scott, both of whom told the story of Charles Gough, who was killed by a fall from the ridge in 1803. His faithful dog watched over his body for two months until it was discovered. The story so intrigued the two poets that they

13

Scandale Pass, with the High Street fells beyond
Westmorland's mountains seen from High Street with Helvellyn in the distance

climbed up to Red Tarn where the body had been found. With them went Sir Humphrey Davy, the inventor of the miner's safety lamp and one of the foremost scientists of his day. It must have been a unique occasion, three men of genius climbing together like that. Some years later Canon Rawnsley, who played a significant part in founding the National Trust, had a memorial stone to Gough erected on the summit of Helvellyn.

From the summit of Helvellyn an interesting route follows the edge of the eastwards facing crags to Nethermost Pike (2,920 feet) and finally Dollywaggon Pike (2,810 feet), which is a most impressive looking fell with fine crags tumbling down towards upper Grisedale. The three principal crags are Eagle Crag (quite low down on a spur of Nethermost Pike), Tarn Crag, and the impressive two-hundred-foot Falcon Crag, looking like a little Pillar Rock and cleft down the middle by a conspicuous chimney. Climbs have been done on all these rocks, mainly because of the nearness of Ruthwaite Lodge, a climbing hut belonging to Sheffield University. Most of the routes are fairly short and good but it is doubtful whether they will ever become popular with anyone other than users of the hut because of the lengthy approach walk.

The most notable features of these crags are the huge gullies which split the face of Tarn Crag. In a hard winter the three principal gullies become ramps of even snow, and I can remember how, some years ago, three of us were descending from Helvellyn when we came across the gullies in perfect condition. Choosing one apiece we held a race to see who could descend the fastest. We must have been quite mad—neither the routes nor the technique have anything to recommend them. We each arrived at the bottom unscathed, panting and laughing—but it was a silly and dangerous game to play, all the same.

Eagle Crag was the site of another lead mine, believed to be of great antiquity. It was nothing like as profitable as the Greenside mine however, and was abandoned in 1877. The vein runs east-west probably through St Sunday Crag to Beckstones where there have been traces of ore found similar to those of Eagle Crag. Towards the end of the last century, two brothers called Watson came across traces of this vein on the surface of St Sunday Crag.

They obtained a sample of ore, then hid the place intending to return later. The sample turned out to be very good and they thought their fortunes were made but they were unable to find the vein again, so well had they hidden it! Watson's Lost Vein still remains a challenge for any curious traveller who wants to explore the fell!

The most conspicuous break in the entire range occurs between Dollywaggon Pike and Fairfield and marks another change in character. In a hollow of the fells lies Grisedale Tarn, the waters of which drain away down the long Grisedale to Ullswater, and at the head of which is Grisedale Hause: a col between Seat Sandal and Fairfield. Beyond the hause a pack-horse track leads steeply down Tongue Gill to the main road about a mile from Grasmere.

Of all the regular ways across these fells, this is the most interesting and pleasant, preferably taken from east to west, that is from Patterdale to Grasmere. If the walk is done in the morning the best of the crags and fells will be in sunlight and the whole journey becomes a photographer's paradise. The aerial view down into the Vale of Grasmere is particularly fine.

At Fairfield the line of the principal watershed, which has been more or less north–south, changes abruptly to north-west–south-east. The lateral ridges become longer, more interesting, and the crags, still principally to be found on the Patterdale side, become increasingly fine.

All sorts of interesting ridge walks can be made in this group, and though the ridges are themselves not difficult to traverse the ways up to them are, almost without exception, steep, or craggy, or long—or all three. This is rough country to explore: in total, perhaps the roughest of all the eastern fell groups, and unless you are to be contented with simple ascents such as Fairfield from Grisedale Hause, you should be prepared for hard days. Perhaps I exaggerate—some might think so—but all the same, the Fairfield massif does demand respect. In mist or bad weather great care is needed because the ridge system is complex and precipitous, crags numerous.

One of the best of the ridges is the seven miles traverse from Rydal to Patterdale over the summit of Fairfield. This can either be begun by the usual way up Tongue Gill to Grisedale Hause and from there by the tourist route, or, better, the long ridge that includes Heron Pike (2,003 feet), Rydal Fell (2,022 feet) and Greatrigg Man (2,513 feet) can be traversed to the top of Fairfield (2,863 feet)—a very long but quite easy walk, ending in the plateau of the principal summit. From here the way to Patterdale looks exciting to say the least. The first obstacle is the unique pinnacle of Cofa Pike, whose terrors are more apparent than real, then down the ridge to Deepdale Hause followed by a climb up the fine ridge-fell that is St Sunday Crag (2,756 feet). From here a short diversion can be made to the pointed top of Gavel Pike (2,577 feet) which gives superb views of the head of Deepdale and the great cirque of crags which bound Fairfield on that side. Finally, the St Sunday Crag ridge leads down almost directly into Patterdale village. This ridge traverse not only combines the two best fells of the group—Fairfield and St Sunday Crag—but it is scenically extremely fine: the great crags of Deepdale, the views across Grisedale to Helvellyn, and perhaps above all, the ever-widening prospect of Patterdale and Ullswater.

The Fairfield Horseshoe, which goes around the head of Rydal Beck, is of about the same length as the walk just described, but has the merit of returning to its starting point, Rydal. It begins, as before, up the long ridge over Greatrigg Man to Fairfield but then follows the principal watershed over Hart Crag (2,698 feet) and Dove Crag (2,603 feet) before descending the long and easy ridge running due south towards Ambleside. In this way it gives glimpses into both Deepdale and Dovedale, both of which contain magnificent crags in profusion, but the glimpses do not show the crags at their best (or indeed the best of the crags) and the walk cannot be compared in scenic quality or interest with the traverse of St Sunday Crag.

What the horseshoe walk does make quite plain though is the importance of the two fine valleys which bite deep into the eastern flanks of the massif. Indeed, from Patterdale these valleys command more interest than the ridges themselves: wild mountain hollows containing some of the most impressive crags in Lakeland.

It is difficult to choose between the two valleys as to which is the more attractive in its variety of wild scenery. Possibly Deepdale may be judged the more startling since it has better shape and the rocks are more concentrated. A long spur ending in magnificent crags runs out from the main ridge and divides Deepdale head into two coves: Sleet Cove beneath Fairfield and Link Cove beneath Hart Crag. In the former the principal rocks are the 500-foot Hutaple Crag and in the latter the smaller but perhaps better Scrubby Crag, unfortunate only in name.

During the '50s and early '60s these two crags, along with Dove Crag in the next valley and an assortment of lesser rocks scattered throughout the area, led to a sudden surge of climbing interest in the Eastern Fells, which until that time had always been considered the poor relations (in climbing values) of the better known Western Fells. Except for the Castle Rock of Triermain, it is doubtful whether the majority of climbers realized that there were any worthwhile crags in the east.

This was changed rapidly. The Drasdo brothers, Jack Soper, Mike James and others, mainly Yorkshire climbers, put up a network of new routes of all lengths and standards in what amounted to an eastern campaign. Seldom has an area been so completely transformed from the point of view of the climber in so short a time. By 1959 the eastern fells had ceased to come under the nondescript "Outlying Crags" section of the Dow Crag guide-book —they demanded a whole book to themselves and Harold Drasdo provided it.

Drasdo's guide-book came as a revelation which in turn provided fresh impetus to exploration of the area, though the original explorers had done such a thorough job that there was little in the way of new crags left to discover.

Drasdo gave his opinion that Deepdale was in many ways the most important centre of the eastern fells and he obviously had in mind the vast buttresses of Hutaple with its climbs of over 400 feet, and the delectable, though somewhat smaller, Scrubby Crag, where routes like *Sennapod* and *Grendel* were becoming popular. But as events turned out, Deepdale fell into something of a backwater, partly because of the reputation for fierceness that became synonymous with Deepdale's next-door neighbour, Dovedale, which drew the hard men like a magnet draws iron.

Dovedale opens out into the fells south-west of Brothers Water. It is not in the least like Deepdale, being wider, shorter, much more diverse in character, and with its screen of trees flanking the entrance, much prettier in the picture postcard sense. Indeed the view across Brothers Water towards Deepdale, with the curiously conical High Hartsop Dod (1,702 feet) standing like a sentinel near the entrance to the valley, is one of the most attractive views in the district.

Though the main course of the little valley twists and narrows up towards Dove Crag a subsidiary beck, Hogget Gill, carves out a secondary valley and the two merge below Gill Crag to form the broad lower reaches of Dovedale. Both the original stream and Hogget Gill end in a complex cirque of impressive crags and rocky knolls.

At the very head of the main valley rises Dove Crag, a fierce, compact bastion of rock, almost three hundred feet in height, whose presence first startles then overawes. It has nothing of the picturesque about it, as Pillar does, for instance, nor yet the all-embracing grandeur of Scafell Crag. Instead, it looks, and is, frighteningly difficult: a sustained overhang on the right, merely vertical on the left. Bold, yes, and brutal with it.

On the left of the crag is South Gully which divides higher up into the so-called Easy Gully and Inaccessible Gully: walkers might like to know that the Easy Gully is not easy and climbers that the Inaccessible Gully is not inaccessible. Between the gully and the main face of the crag a distinct ridge, known as Wing Ridge, comes sharply down—providing the only immediately obvious line of attack for the would-be climber. It was on this ridge, as long ago as 1910, that Harry Westmorland made the first route on the crag: a rather hard 'very difficult' grade climb named after its originator. It was a long time before anyone thought of attacking the main face.

In 1937 attention was directed to the wall of South Gully as being the most amenable rock, and of course, having the obvious challenge of the undercut *Inaccessible Gully*. Birkett climbed *Tarsus* to the right of the gully, and found it severe, then B. G. S. Ward led the gully itself, which required aid because of its curious beginnings, and bordered on the 'very severe'.

Slowly the crag was beginning to yield, and in the summer before the outbreak of war in 1939, J. W. Haggas made a direct attack on the face. The climbing was hard—good 'v.s.', as climbers say—and the rock not too sound, but Haggas and his party produced *Hangover*: the first real harbinger of Dove Crag climbing.

In 1953, a couple of months after they had put up *Triermain Eliminate* on Castle Rock, Whillans, Brown and Cowan arrived at Dove Crag and took a line up the left of the main face near Wing Ridge which had as its climax an overhanging crack about 100 feet high. The route was called *Dovedale Grooves*, and was immediately the hardest on the crag, and one of the hardest in the area. It was not repeated for ten years.

The reputation of Dove Crag began to grow but the crag proved too difficult for most climbers, who turned away to go and put up new routes elsewhere. Only Whillans seemed to be able to make any impression on the crag, though not always at a first attempt. He had tried to do a route between *Hangover* and *Dovedale Groove*, but it was not until 1960 that he met with success.

His companion was Colin Mortlock, who later wrote an account of the climb. This amusing extract gives some idea of the fierceness of the crag:

> It took Don two and a half hours to climb this pitch. It must be the finest piece of rock-climbing I have ever seen. I sang 'rock' to relieve the tension (mine as well as his). Don smoked incessantly in extraordinary resting positions. Two climbers passed the foot of the cliff and the following ensued:
>
> "What route's that?" (looks of disbelief from below Don's overhanging position).
>
> "It ain't—yet," (from above)
>
> "Who are you?" (from below).
>
> "Whillans" (pause as a big grass ledge narrowly misses the amazed ones below—premeditated?).
>
> "Yer must be mad" (parting shot from those below who were not seen again).

The climb was called *Entity*, then the name was changed to *Extol*, which resulted in some confusion until a lesser route was done on the gully wall and named *Entity* to clear up any mistakes.

In the following year—1961—the strong Welsh partnership of Peter Crew and Bas Ingle arrived at Dove Crag and added *Hiraeth* between *Extol* and *Dovedale Groove*, making a trio of routes which have become classics of Lakeland high-grade climbing. Nothing comparable has been done since.

The tide of climbing exploration swept over the Eastern Fells like a huge wave, breaking hard against rocks such as Dove Crag and Scrubby Crag, and lapping more gently against a dozen other smaller crags. In the end it subsided, as waves do, and what remains is the popularity of Castle Rock and Dove Crag—the rest, for all their fine qualities, are conservatively forgotten by most climbers.

Beyond Dove Crag the main ridge traverses easily to Little Hart Crag (2,091 feet), which is an interesting summit and the fell from which the long, easily distinguished spur of High Hartsop Dod (1,702 feet) descends. Beyond that again is the gap of the Scandale Pass, and finally the isolated little group of Red Screes (2,541 feet) which overhangs the Kirkstone Inn.

Like the rest of the Helvellyn range, the Fairfield group have had their share of mining activity. The way up Dovedale passes the old Hartsop Hall mine, the entrance to which is in the woods. It is a very ancient foundation, probably sixteenth century, and it was worked at various times up to 1942, the chief attraction being the high silver content of the lead in the Hartsop vein: about 30 ounces per ton of refined ore. A little way up the valley the remains of an old smelter might be found, the bellows of which were worked by a leat from Hogget Gill. These remnants are probably sixteenth–seventeenth century; the more extensive nineteenth-century buildings were pulled down when the mine temporarily closed in 1860 and the dressed stones were used to build a barn at Hartsop Hall and to extend the Brotherswater Hotel.

On the other side of the range, above Grasmere, where Greenhead Gill cuts into the flanks of Greatrigg Man, are the slight remains of a mine opened by Dutch adventurers between 1569 and 1573. The mine was never reopened and so the remains suffered none of the alterations that most mines underwent in the nineteenth century.

9

High Street and the Kentmere Fells

EAST of the Kirkstone Pass the high fells tumble away in confusion to end in the lonely moors above the Shap road. Though much greater in area than the northern fells, these eastern fells share with them that curious mixture of popularity and unpopularity which is so characteristic of Skiddaw and its satellites. Here, however, there are no extremes: there is no fell to compare in height or tourist attraction with Skiddaw, not yet is there anything to equal the beauty of Blencathra, but on the other hand the fells as a whole are much better known than those at the 'back o' Skidda''.

It is an area of great contrast, and one without any definite form or shape. On the eastern side (the least known) there are valleys as lonely and wild as any in Lakeland, whilst on the southern side there are three valleys of soft beauty: Troutbeck, Kentmere and Long Sleddale, of which Kentmere at least is comparable with the best in the district. It boasts, too, some of the most beautiful tarns—and the ugliest of the great lakes, Haweswater. It also contains the longest single high ridge in the district—from Sour Howes to Arthur's Pike is eleven miles, and virtually a dead straight south-to-north line which only once (at the Garburn Pass) drops below 1,500 feet—and that but briefly. For much of this distance it is quite distinctive, with none of your vague humpy swellings that might or might not be—which is probably why the Romans chose it as the basis for their famous road.

Indeed, High Street and its satellites make ideal ridge walking country. The peaks are more shapely than dramatic, and the going is always good, along ridges which, though broad enough for the most vertiginous walker, nevertheless have flanks of exceeding steepness. This latter, of course, is a further inducement to keep to the crest, and most of the walks end where the ridges end, or perhaps where the one or two acceptable passes cross the ranges. It is not the region for direct frontal assault: such a policy can at best be tiring and in some cases dangerous.

The Ordnance Survey map highlights this steepness of the mountainsides around High Street by adding *hachures* to the closely packed contours. Crags abound, according to the map, and so they do in fact—but they are mostly broken crags of little value to the rock-climber. An explorer considering the climbing potential of the district might well be deluded by the map into thinking that the High Street ridge was one of the best climbing areas of the Lakes, but he would be sadly disappointed. As far as rock-climbing is concerned the district offers two large and well-developed crags in Buckbarrow, near the head of Long Sleddale, and Rainsborrow Crag in Kentmere valley: both dramatic pieces of rock, and indeed, if total height be considered, Rainsborrow must be one of the biggest crags in Lakeland. Yet neither have (as yet anyway) the interest and continuity of the better-known crags elsewhere. They are in a sense the poor relations of the climbing scene, mainly because their geographical location militates against them.

There are, it is true, a few climbs elsewhere in the area—on the high and lonely Raven Crag in the desolate Threshthwaite Cove, for instance, but one cannot walk these ridges without an uncomfortable feeling that there ought to be many more climbs around. There is so much rock—and even if it is mostly broken up, there is still a considerable number of minor buttresses which seem to be totally ignored. But then, climbers always were a conservative bunch, and it takes years before even a major new discovery becomes popular, and anything as remote as these rocks in the eastern fells has no chance whatever. To achieve popularity

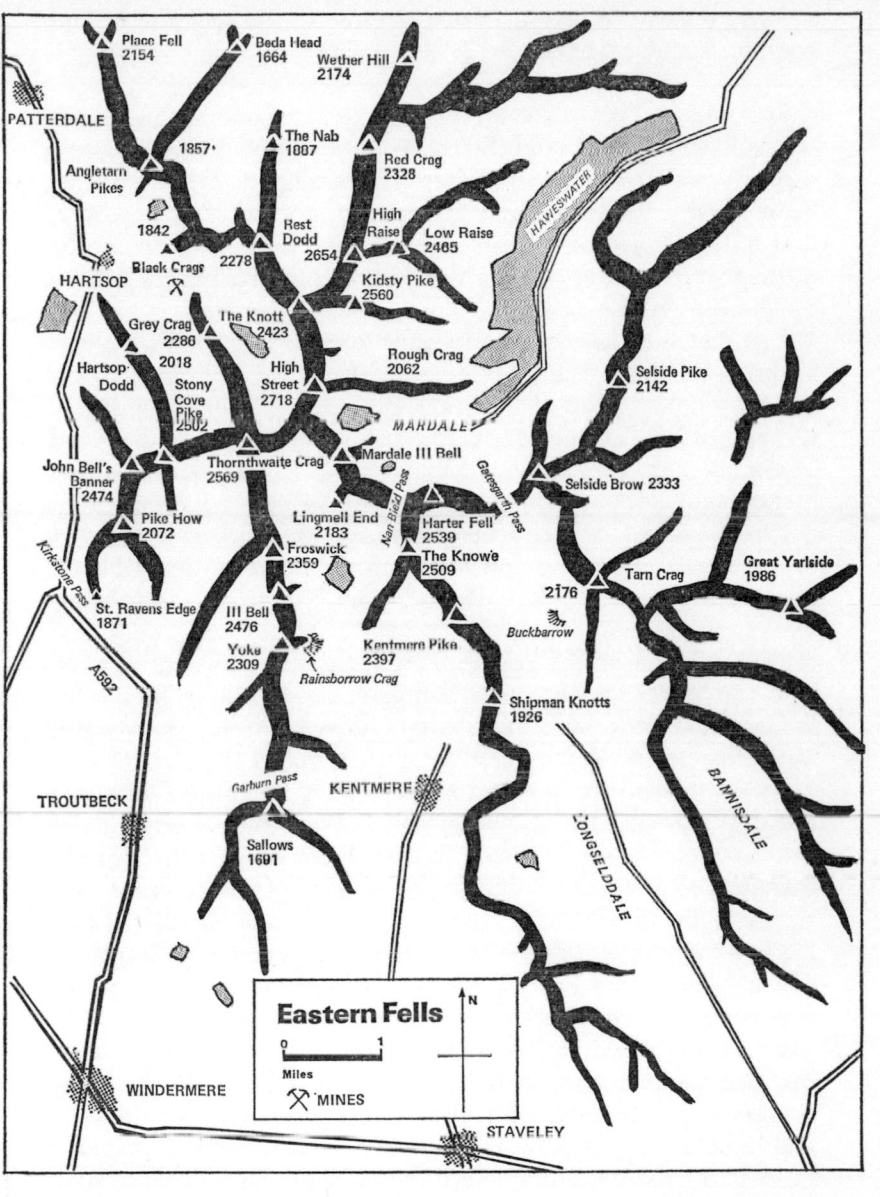

Eastern Fells

a newly discovered crag needs to be close to the valley floor and readily accessible—or on the Welsh coast!

Stony Cove Pike (2,502 feet) is the centre of one of the shorter ridges. It lies west of High Street, roughly parallel with it, and a sort of counterbalance to the Harter Fell ridge on the other side. So seminal is the long High Street ridge to this area, however, that umbilical cords stretch out from it to connect with all the other groups—in this case via the deep and impressive col known as Threshthwaite Mouth.

The Pike itself has been known for years as John Bell's Banner, with is a much more attractive name, though who John Bell was and why he should need a Banner, escapes me. More mundanely it is also called Caudale Moor, but on the principle that the word 'moor' is more evocative of Ilkley or the River Dart, it is best forgotten.

It is something of a cheat to climb, for the Kirkstone Pass lies immediately to the west and it is a simple matter to scramble up St Raven's Edge and follow the ridge with its attendant drystone wall to the summit. The going is easy, if somewhat boring, and the summit, when it is reached, comes as something of a relief. The top is flat and boasts a miniscule tarn, but from sundry vantage points it offers fine views down Troutbeck towards Windermere and down Caudale Beck towards Brothers Water.

As is so often the case, the nearer views are more interesting and dramatic than the wide panorama. From the eastern edge of the summit plateau it is possible to look down into Thresh-thwaite Cove: as wild and austere a hollow as you can find anywhere in the district. The cove is the final corrie of the Pasture Beck which cuts a deep, savage valley between Grey Crags and our mountain, and beyond the cove, the desolate walls of the corrie rise to form the col of Threshthwaite Mouth.

Crags rim the whole valley, though they are not easy to see on this side without actually teetering on their brink. Raven Crag (yet another of that name!) is the boldest piece of rock, and some climbs have been done on it, though it is rather difficult to reach in its particularly inhospitable surroundings. The whole scene is very reminiscent of Gasgale in the Grisedale fells.

From the plateau, the drystone wall which has been a permanent companion all the way from St Raven's Crag, continues in a sweep along the connecting ridge with Hartsop Dod (2,018 feet) which rises in a most attractive fashion, small but elegant. In fact Hartsop Dod is one of the pleasantest little peaks in Lakeland, and the view from its summit is superb. The distant mountains are blue and hazy, but close at hand is the Helvellyn and Fairfield range, and there is a direct view right into the heart of Dovedale with its impressive crags. Then, from the very lip of the mountain (which has extremely steep sides) Patterdale runs away in a copse-sprinkled green carpet to Ullswater. The pleasant greenery of these northern and western views is a startling contrast with the grimness of Grey Crag and High Street, and the desolation of Threshthwaite which press in from the east.

The finest view of all is reserved to the last, for the sides of the fell are so steep that from the summit one cannot see what lies immediately below. Only at the moment of descent do Brothers Water and Hartsop hamlet burst into view, like some idyllic aerial postcard scene. Downward views where one looks upon the roofs of villages are common enough in Alpine valleys, but relatively rare in Lakeland, and seldom impressive. Hartsop is different. Tucked into its little side valley, the cottages clustered together and half-hidden by trees, it lies directly beneath our mountain, and is the perfect Lakeland hamlet.

The long, steep spine of ridge leading down towards the cottages is the best route of descent. The alternative way directly down to Brothers Water is very steep and sprinkled with one or two nasty outcrops—in any case, having seen it from above, nobody could possibly avoid the attraction of Hartsop!

It was a hot day in August as Duncan and I pulled out of Troutbeck up the wide, stony Garburn Road for the start of the famous Kentmere Horseshoe. The Garburn Road is one of those old pack-horseways like the Walna Scar Road and the Borrowdale Toll Road, which serve no modern transport function and have been left to decay in peace. It connects Troutbeck with Kentmere over the Garburn Pass, wide, easy under foot and scenically one of the finest of its kind.

The view really comes into its own at about the level of the copse which hides all traces of the old Garburn Quarry. Across the wide Troutbeck valley is the long, straggling village of Troutbeck, by-passed by the main road to Kirkstone, and thus preserved as one of the most charming villages of the district. Beyond it is the valley head going to Stony Cove Pike and Thornthwaite Crag and it is not too difficult for the eye of faith to pick up the line taken by the old Roman Road as it swept from the valley floor to High Street.

On the right can be seen the ridge which forms the start of our fine walk: the steep-sided, grey-green humps of Yoke, Ill Bell, and Froswick, with the final bulk of Thornthwaite Crag in the background. They look at their worst from this vantage point though, and show nothing of the promise that is theirs.

Scenically then, all would be well were it not for the Leisure Park which sprawls in the bottom of the valley like a piece of the French Riviera; a conglomeration of multi-coloured tents and caravans, alien to the district. What on earth are the planners thinking about to allow developments like this? Surely there is a tradition in the Lakes of *small* camp and caravan sites, in obscure corners, and not these huge developments which can be seen from miles around?

At the Garburn Pass we turned off the road and followed a path which led gently up the slopes to our first summit, Yoke (2,309 feet); a fell which hides its attractions from Troutbeck and Garburn, reserving them all for Kentmere. On the Kentmere side it is splendidly knobbly and has in addition the great crag of Rainsborrow, whose profile is one of the most majestic in Lakeland. The best of the climbing here is of fairly recent development and hard, but the crag, despite its huge size, is unlikely to prove to be another Dow or Pillar. It is, however, a good area for beginners—not only on Rainsborrow itself, but on several good little outcrops scattered on this fellside and all within easy reach of Kentmere village. It is a pity that more novices do not use this valley, and so ease the congestion that sometimes occurs on the Langdale crags.

However, rock-climbing was not our game this day. We were intent on walking the fells around the head of Kentmere, and from the summit of Yoke we could see virtually the whole of our intended route. We could even see in quite clear detail the way we intended to come down into Kentmere, some hours later—rather disconcerting, like peering into the future.

The ridge from Yoke to Thornthwaite Crag is a series of ups and downs at almost regular intervals, which brought to mind the ridiculous notion that it was rather like a large-scale model of the Loch Ness Monster. Down from Yoke and up to Ill Bell (2,476 feet). Down from Ill Bell and up to Froswick (2,359 feet). Down from Froswick and up to Thornthwaite Crag (2,569 feet). But what a marvellous little ridge! Each peak of the trio—Yoke, Ill Bell and Froswick—is one of those steep-sided conical creations that a child will draw if you ask it to draw a mountain.

A track contours the ridge, avoiding the summits, though I cannot imagine why since it converts a happy romp into a tedious level walk. We ignored it and followed what I regret to say is a much less frequented path over the tops themselves. After all, who can resist fells with names like Yoke, Ill Bell and Froswick? And who can resist bagging peaks so easily? There are few high-level walks in Lakeland where one can bag so many good summits at so little cost!

Of this fine trio, Ill Bell is highest and fully justifies in its shape the 'Bell' part of its name, especially when it is seen from Kentmere or looking back at it from the slopes of Thornthwaite Crag. From its summit the whole of the upper part of Kentmere Valley, around the small and not unattractive reservoir, can be seen in detail. Ahead, on the ridge, is Froswick and then the corrie sweeps round in peculiar scree formations by Gavel Crag and Bleathwaite Crag underneath Mardale Ill Bell (a twin in name but not in shape, unfortunately) to the spur of Lingmell End, beyond which is the gash of the Nan Bield Pass and the rocky rise up to Harter Fell. From there to Kentmere Pike the fells assume that moorland quality which persists all the way over east to Shap, though these distant fells are hidden from view. Only the strange landslip gash of Drygroove Gill catches the eye—a curious pale coloured knife-slash down the face of the green fellside.

The scenery has a strange quality which is quite different from that of other fells. It does not have the same exciting ambience

that is such a feature of the western fells, nor yet is it so lost looking as are the fells at the 'back o' Skidda'', but it has its own sort
of beauty, almost desiccated, and quite unique. It is a feature which
becomes increasingly evident when High Street comes into view,
for instance, and yet it is all thrown overboard by the wild
romanticism of Blea Water and Small Water, which would be
equally at home in the Scafell group.

Not that all these features could be seen from Ill Bell, of course,
but the scene at the head of the Kentmere valley does set the tenor
of the district as a whole.

A freshening breeze lightened our steep pull up the last fling
of the ridge to Thornthwaite Crag; a fell that has gained its name
from some rocky knolls on its Troutbeck flanks. The summit
proved to be a small plateau which sweeps away, dish-shaped, to
the heights of High Street.

It is not a distinguished summit by any stretch of the imagination, ranking for a lack of interest with its next-door neighbour,
Stony Cove Pike, and yet it is marked with the most remarkable
'cairn' in the whole of the Lake District. At a corner of drystone
walling, on the eminence of a little rock outcrop, is a beautifully
constructed drystone beacon, round and tapering slightly towards
its top, fourteen feet high. Where now is Helvellyn with its
bric-à-brac of summit memorabilia? Where now Scafell Pike
with its super-cairn? Here on Thornthwaite Crag is the quietus
of summital markings—and incidentally, the epitome of waller's
art.

We ate our sandwiches in the lee of the beacon, and whilst we
were doing this three fell-walkers approached from High Street,
passed the time of day for a few minutes and then continued on
their way to Threshthwaite Mouth and Stony Cove Pike. It was
not until we reached the Nan Bield Pass some time later, that we
met anyone else on our walk, and it is safe to say that despite the
glorious weather we encountered less than a dozen people all day.

The old Roman Road of High Street reaches the ridge at Thornthwaite Crag and sweeps in streamlined fashion across the shoulders of the fell to which it gives its name. Or at least, its modern
equivalent does, for there is nothing left of the stonework with
which the Romans made their road—gone centuries ago, no

Harter Fell and the head of Mardale

doubt, to help construct some local croft or border pele. The Roman roads were of little value to the locals, except as ready-made quarries.

What a strangely desiccated fellside High Street presents on this flank—all streaked and flecked with ochres and reds where the bare bones of the mountain show through the sparse grass covering. It reminds me of the Red Cuillin of Skye: those grotesque hills which point such a contrast with the craggy spires of the Cuillins proper.

This was hands in pockets walking, easy going with splended views down into Hayeswater—another tarn converted into a reservoir, and like Kentmere, hardly the worse for it. The trouble in this part of the walk, was that the going was *too* simple—it was deceptively easy to amble past the mountain altogether, for the top of High Street does not display itself to the world at large.

And we almost did just that. Only some sixth sense made us pause and look at the map, and sure enough we were already level with the summit. Quickly changing course through 90° we walked up a rounded bank to a drystone wall, and there, just over the wall, was the summit cairn (2,663 feet).

I suppose the surveyors were correct in their siting of the cairn, but in truth it could almost have been anywhere on the wide, flat, summit plateau. No wonder the dalesfolk used to hold horse races up here!

But this approach to High Street (what could for once be truthfully called the 'classic' climb!) and its flat, uninviting top, belie the true grandeur of the fell. All its good points are to the east: it is very much a one-sided mountain, just as Blencathra is.

And there are similarities between the two, for like Blencathra, High Street sends down ridges which enfold high and lonely corries, and in Blea Water the fell has a tarn every bit a match for Scales Tarn on Blencathra. Not that the analogy should be over emphasized—Long Stile is the most pronounced ridge, and the best way to climb the mountain, if you happen to be starting from Haweswater, but it is not another Hall's Fell ridge, much less a Sharp Edge.

However, Long Stile was out of our way. Instead, we traversed the knobbly ground that led to Mardale Ill Bell (2,396 feet).

14

The head of Kentmere

What a fine rocky north face this fell has! It comes into view as you descend from High Street, proud and precipitous, shattered and defiant. It is, of course, part of the great cirque of crags surrounding Blea Water, but the tarn itself is not seen at this juncture, so deeply set is it, and indeed it cannot be seen in its entirety unless one descends a considerable way down the north ridge of Mardale Ill Bell, where a little flat promontory amidst the boulders affords an excellent vantage point.

It is certainly worth the detour. A dark tarn, surprisingly large (it is a third of a mile long and a quarter wide) is trapped in a primeval bowl which resembles the mouth of a dead volcano, where one lip has been badly eroded. Steep banks of scree slope up from the water's edge until they meet the even steeper bands of rock where crag piles upon crag to the curving skyline. It is the perfect essay in mountain majesty: the sort of scene that makes mountaineers of us all, if we have a spark of adventure in us.

Is Blea Water the grandest tarn of all? Some say it is: certainly it is comparable with Bowscale, Scales Tarn, or Low Water, which are its nearest rivals in overpowering grandeur of setting.

Though Blea Water is unquestionably the main attraction hereabouts, the mile or so of fellside between Mardale Ill Bell and Harter Fell is full of pleasantness. Small Water, a beautiful little tarn on the Mardale side of the Nan Bield Pass ranks, like its grander neighbour, as one of the finest in the district, but in this case it is the charm of its setting, like a little jewel, that is its attraction. Then too, there is the Pass itself: surely the epitome of what a mountain pass should be—straight up on the one side to a distinctive, even rocky, gap, and straight down on the other, without any of these summital *longueurs* which mar many so-called 'passes'. There is also the black northern crags of Harter Fell to be seen, plunging down into Mardale, and worthy of closer inspection by the climbing fraternity.

Rock and water in perfect combination. That's the secret. That is why this small portion of the eastern fells is so excitingly attractive. There is no competition, and the cynical side of one's mind wonders how it would appear if it were transferred to the craggy fells of the western Lakes. I think it would stand up to the rest rather well.

Below all this incredible beauty lies the head of Haweswater: Manchester's other reservoir. It curves away between the distant fells and only a purist could object to its form when the water is high and the becks are running, so what is all the fuss about? At least they have not hemmed the lake round with conifers as they have their earlier essay at Thirlmere. And this we must grant is an improvement, but at the same time it is not a matter for congratulation. You don't praise a thief who has stolen your wallet because he had the decency not to take your wedding ring as well.

On this fine day, after a dry summer, my son and I looked down on a lake that was obscene. The water was low, and in consequence the whole lake, as far as the eye could travel, was edged with a broad white band of dried-up reservoir, as though a mad artist had gone round it with a paint brush, lining the outlines. It shouted against nature and, contrasted with the immediate beauty of Small Water and Blea Water, which could be glimpsed in the same view, was revolting.

It is the raising and lowering of the water levels which is the principal permanent objection to the creation of large reservoirs in our National Parks. This is the reason why walkers and climbers object so strongly to that newer monstrosity, the pumped storage scheme, in which water from an upper reservoir runs down to a lower one during the day via a hydro-electric plant, and is pumped back up again during the night when the demand for electricity is less. The fluctuating levels mean ugly mudbanks or tidemarks round the reservoirs, visible for miles. These latest horrors have not yet been inflicted on the Lake District, but they have in Wales, and the economic attractiveness of such hydro-electric schemes makes their spread a distinct threat.

Meanwhile, the old scars—Thirlmere and Haweswater—grow no lovelier with advancing age. There are very few people alive today who can remember Thirlmere as it was before the level was raised to make the reservoirs, but there are plenty who can remember Haweswater and the now vanished hamlet of Mardale, for the flooding there took place in 1936. Those who do recall the valley speak of it as though it were some enchanted place—a Lakeland Brigadoon.

They speak nostalgically of the seventeenth-century *Dun Bull* surrounded by rhododendrons, of the old Measand School founded in 1711, of Measand Hall, the ancient church and the scattered farmhouses. It was a remote community which, until 1885, when the last male heir of the Holme family died, had its own 'kings', whose lineage stretched back seven hundred years.

The church at Mardale was in ruins when Harriet Martineau visited the valley, in the middle of the last century. Though built in medieval times it was only a chapel belonging to Shap, and until 1729 the Mardale dead were strapped across horses and taken over the Old Corpse Road on Swindale Common, to Swindale and thence for burial at the mother church. How ironical that the bones of their descendants suffered a similar fate, taken for re-burial at Shap, when the valley was flooded.

No doubt nostalgia paints an over-enthusiastic picture of Mardale as it was, but it must have been a pretty place, for all that. Harriet Martineau describes it thus:

> The inn at Mardale Green is full a mile from the water; and sweet is the passage to it. . . . The path winds through the levels round the bases of the knolls, past the ruins of the old church, and among snug little farms, while, at one end of the dale is the lake, and the other is closed in by the passes to Kentmere and Sleddale; and the great Pikes tower on either hand.

With her journalist's eye for detail Harriet also notes that Mardale was a great dairy producing centre, making 3,000 pounds of butter a week. Ironically, it all went to Manchester!

The climb up from Nan Bield Pass to Harter Fell (2,539 feet) is more reminiscent of walking in the Western Lakes than anything else hereabouts. A rocky ridge (well, by local standards) which rises sharply to the smooth summit. We climbed it rapidly, and barely pausing at the top, turned on the final leg of our journey, towards The Knowe (2,509 feet) and Kentmere Pike (2,397 feet).

The broad crest of this ridge, rounded to the character of moorland, and the easy going, make it one of the simplest walks in the district—at least, when the weather is clear. In mist it can be confusing, like all broad featureless moors, and although there are fences and walls which the knowledgeable can use as sign-posts, it is strictly compass territory. Especially so because these mild-looking fells are not all that innocent of danger! Harter Fell plunges precipitously into Mardale, and the way down to Nan Bield is not at all obvious in a mist. Furthermore, the gentle slopes on the Kentmere side of the Pike tell nothing of the savage confusion of crags which make up its eastern flank. Only a very confident traveller—or a fool—would descend Kentmere Pike to Long Sleddale in bad weather.

But we had none of these problems; the day was fine and the breeze just sufficient to keep down perspiration. We fairly rattled along, over the Pike and then down into the grassy bowl between it and Shipman Knotts, and the hide-and-seek path which leads down to the cottages at Hallow Bank.

As we jogged down, past the outcrops and through the waist-high bracken, a westering sun highlighted the crags and cottages of Kentmere. Rainsborrow held deep shadows but Cawsty Knotts and the innumerable slabs of outcrops which build up the western fellside beckoned their climbing attractions. What matter if we know them to be false gods? They *looked* good, and for the moment that was sufficient.

Grandeur? Kentmere is not aggressive. Long Sleddale head is the place to go for local grandeur; for the harsh realities of mountain landscape. Kentmere is too soft for that: it is the sylvan vale; the dale that has everything a Lakeland valley should have. Were I rash or bold enough, I might be tempted to say that it is the prettiest dale in the Lake District.

Appendix

Walkers' Guidebooks

The standard guidebooks for the area nowadays are the remarkable volumes of A. Wainwright. They are: *The Eastern Fells, The Far Eastern Fells, The Central Fells, The Southern Fells, The Northern Fells, The North Western Fells* and *The Western Fells*.
A useful single-volume pictorial guidebook is: *The Lakeland Peaks* by W. A. Poucher.

Climbers' Guidebooks

The definitive volumes are issued by the Fell and Rock Climbing Club, and are revised periodically. At the moment the series is: *Great Langdale, Scafell Group, Borrowdale, Dow Crag Area, Pillar Group, Great Gable etc., Eastern Crags,* and *Buttermere and Newlands Area*.
Useful selected climbs (up to mild 'v.s.) are contained in the Cicerone Press series, "Climbs in Cumbria": *The Northern Lakes, The Southern Lakes, The Western Lakes*.

Map

The best all-round map is the Ordnance Survey Tourist Edition One-Inch, *The Lake District*. This is essential for any walker or climber.

Rock-climbing courses and guides

Climbing can only be learned in safety under properly qualified instructors. Details of available courses and private guides can be had from the Hon. Secretary, British Mountaineering Council, Room 314, 26 Park Crescent, London W1N 4EE.

Index